# HBase High Performance Cookbook

Exciting projects that will teach you how complex data can be exploited to gain maximum insights

**Ruchir Choudhry**

BIRMINGHAM - MUMBAI

# HBase High Performance Cookbook

First published: January 2017

Production reference: 1250117

Published by Packt Publishing Ltd.
Livery Place
35 Livery Street
Birmingham B3 2PB, UK.

ISBN 978-1-78398-306-3

www.packtpub.com

# Credits

**Author**
Ruchir Choudhry

**Reviewer**
Vinay Kumar Boddula

**Commissioning Editor**
Amarabha Banerjee

**Acquisition Editor**
Larissa Pinto

**Content Development Editor**
Tejas Limkar

**Technical Editor**
Danish Shaikh

**Copy Editor**
Manisha Singh

**Project Coordinator**
Nidhi Joshi

**Proofreader**
Safis Editing

**Indexer**
Mariammal Chettiyar

**Graphics**
Disha Haria

**Production Coordinator**
Arvindkumar Gupta

**Cover Work**
Arvindkumar Gupta

# About the Author

**Ruchir Choudhry** is a principle architect in one of the largest e-commerce companies and specializes in leading, articulating, technology vision, strategizing, and implementing very large-scale software engineering-driven technology changes, with a track record of over 16 years of success.

He was responsible for leading strategy, architecture, engineering, and operations of multi-tenant e-commerce sites and platforms in US, UK, Brazil, and other major markets for Walmart. The sites helped Walmart enter new markets and/or grow its market share. The sites combined service millions of customers and take in orders with annual revenues exceeding $2.0 billion. His personal interest is in performance and scalability. Recently, he has become obsessed with technology as a vehicle to drive and prioritize optimization across organizations and in the world.

He is a core team member in conceptualizing, designing, and reshaping a new platform that will serve the next generation of frontend engineering, based on the cutting edge technology in WalMart.com and NBC/GE/VF Image ware.

He has led some of the most complex and technologically challenging R&D and innovative projects in VF Image Ware, Walmart.com and in GE/NBC (China and Vancouver Olympic websites), Hiper World Cyber Tech Limited (which created the first wireless-based payment gateway of India that worked on non-smart phones, which was presented at Berlin in 1999).

He is the author of more than 8 white papers, which spans from biometric-based single sign on to Java Cards, performance tuning, and JVM tuning, among others. He was a presenter of JVM, performance optimization using Jboss, in Berlin and various other places.

Ruchir Choudhry did his BE at Bapuji Institute of Technology, MBA in information technology at National institute of Engineering and Technology, and his MS Systems at BITS Pilani.

He is currently working and consulting on HBase, Spark, and Cassandra.

He can be reached at ruchirchoudhry@gmail.com

# About the Reviewer

**Vinay Boddula** is pursuing his PhD in computer science focusing on machine learning, big data analytics, and data integration. He is experienced with many open source platforms for data storage, programming, and machine learning, and enjoys applying his research skills in addressing sustainability and smarter planet challenges. His master's degree in embedded system design helps him develop sensor systems for environment monitoring using SoC and microcontrollers.

Vinay has worked and interned as a software developer at companies based in India and United States. His work focuses on developing real-time alert engines using complex event processing on historic and streaming data.

I would like to thank my teacher, colleagues, friends, and family for their patience and unconditional love.

# www.PacktPub.com

## eBooks, discount offers, and more

Did you know that Packt offers eBook versions of every book published, with PDF and ePub files available? You can upgrade to the eBook version at www.PacktPub.com and as a print book customer, you are entitled to a discount on the eBook copy. Get in touch with us at customercare@packtpub.com for more details.

At www.PacktPub.com, you can also read a collection of free technical articles, sign up for a range of free newsletters and receive exclusive discounts and offers on Packt books and eBooks.

https://www.packtpub.com/mapt

Get the most in-demand software skills with Mapt. Mapt gives you full access to all Packt books and video courses, as well as industry-leading tools to help you plan your personal development and advance your career.

## Why Subscribe?

- ▶ Fully searchable across every book published by Packt
- ▶ Copy and paste, print, and bookmark content
- ▶ On demand and accessible via a web browser

# Customer Feedback

Thank you for purchasing this Packt book. We take our commitment to improving our content and products to meet your needs seriously—that's why your feedback is so valuable. Whatever your feelings about your purchase, please consider leaving a review on this book's Amazon page. Not only will this help us, more importantly it will also help others in the community to make an informed decision about the resources that they invest in to learn.

You can also review for us on a regular basis by joining our reviewers' club. **If you're interested in joining, or would like to learn more about the benefits we offer, please contact us**: customerreviews@packtpub.com.

# Table of Contents

Preface                                                          v

**Chapter 1: Configuring HBase**                                 1
  Introduction                                                   1
  Configuring and deploying HBase                                2
  Using the filesystem                                          21
  Administering clusters                                        36
  Managing clusters                                             48

**Chapter 2: Loading Data from Various DBs**                    57
  Introduction                                                  57
  Extracting data from Oracle                                   58
  Loading data using Oracle Big data connector                  67
  Bulk utilities                                                70
  Using Hive with Apache HBase                                  75
  Using Sqoop                                                   77

**Chapter 3: Working with Large Distributed Systems Part I**    83
  Introduction                                                  83
  Scaling elastically or Auto Scaling with built-in fault tolerance   84
  Auto Scaling HBase  using AWS                                 97
  Works on different VM/physical, cloud hardware               104

**Chapter 4: Working with Large Distributed Systems Part II**  111
  Introduction                                                 111
  Read path                                                    115
  Write Path                                                   118
  Snappy                                                       131
  LZO compression                                              132
  LZ4 compressor                                               134
  Replication                                                  135

**Chapter 5: Working with Scalable Structure of tables** | **141**
Introduction | 141
HBase data model part 1 | 142
HBase data model part 2 | 149
How HBase truly scales on key and schema design | 153

**Chapter 6: HBase Clients** | **165**
Introduction | 165
HBase REST and Java Client | 165
Working with Apache Thrift | 180
Working with Apache Avro | 184
Working with Protocol buffer | 196
Working with Pig and using Shell | 201

**Chapter 7: Large-Scale MapReduce** | **205**
Introduction | 205

**Chapter 8: HBase Performance Tuning** | **221**
Introduction | 221
Working with infrastructure/operating systems | 222
Working with Java virtual machines | 230
Changing the configuration of components | 234
Working with HDFS | 237

**Chapter 9: Performing Advanced Tasks on HBase** | **239**
Machine learning using Hbase | 239
Real-time data analysis using Hbase and Mahout | 260
Full text indexing using Hbase | 271

**Chapter 10: Optimizing Hbase for Cloud** | **277**
Introduction | 277
Configuring Hbase for the Cloud | 278
Connecting to an Hbase cluster using the command line | 283
Backing up and restoring Hbase | 284
Terminating an HBase cluster | 286
Accessing HBase data with hive | 286
Viewing the Hbase user interface | 289
Monitoring HBase with CloudWatch | 292
Monitoring Hbase with Ganglia | 295

## Chapter 11: Case Study                                        301
### Introduction                                                 301
### Configuring Lily Platform                                    302
### Integrating elastic search with Hbase                        316
### Configuring                                                  316
## Index                                                         325

# Preface

The objective of this book is to guide the reader through setting up, developing, and integrating different clients. It also shows the internals of read/write operations and how to maintain and scale HBase clusters in production. This book also allows engineers to kick start their project for recommendations, relevancy, and machine learning.

## What this book covers

*Chapter 1*, *Configuring HBase*, provides in-depth knowledge of how to set up, configure, administer, and manage a large and scalable cluster.

*Chapter 2*, *Loading Data*, will deep dive into how we can extract data from various input sources using different process such as bulk load, put, and using MapReduce.

*Chapter 3*, *Working with Large Distributed Systems I*, talks about the internal architecture of HBase, how it connects, and provides a very scalable model.

*Chapter 4*, *Working with Large Distributed Systems II*, gives more details and is an extension of *Chapter 3*.

*Chapter 5*, *Working with the Scalable Structure of Tables*, allows us to understand how data can be modeled and how to design a scalable data model using HBase.

*Chapter 6*, *HBase Client*, allows the users to understand how we can communicate with core HBase using various type of clients.

*Chapter 7*, *Large-Scale MapReduce*, shows how to design a large scale MapReduce job using HBase, how the internals of it work, and how to optimize the HBase framework to do it.

*Chapter 8*, *HBase Performance Tuning*, will walk you through the process of fine-tuning read and write at consistent speeds, agnostic to the scale at which it's running.

*Chapter 9*, *Performing Advance Task*, will discuss some advance topics about machine learning using Mahout libraries and real-time text data analysis.

*Chapter 10, Optimizing HBase for the Cloud*, discusses how to utilize the Amazon cloud HBase framework.

*Chapter 11, Case Study*, integrates HBase with different search engines such as Solr, Elasticsearch, and Lily.

# What you need for this book

This book not only shows you how to set up a large scale HBase cluster using commodity hardware, but also talks about how to use the full potential of a cloud, such as AWS.

It also talks about the internal process of HBase and how it connects in a perfect synchronized way, enabling it to scale without compromising performance.

We tried to simplify things as much as we can with multiple examples and details where needed.

In the end, it talks about machine learning and text analysis using Solr and Elasticsearch.

# Who this book is for

This book will be very useful for the following group of people: students, engineers, infrastructure folk, architects, and for all people who have the fire to learn more.

# Sections

In this book, you will find several headings that appear frequently (Getting ready, How to do it, How it works, There's more, and See also).

To give clear instructions on how to complete a recipe, we use these sections as follows:

## Getting ready

This section tells you what to expect in the recipe, and describes how to set up any software or any preliminary settings required for the recipe.

## How to do it...

This section contains the steps required to follow the recipe.

## How it works...

This section usually consists of a detailed explanation of what happened in the previous section.

## There's more...

This section consists of additional information about the recipe in order to make the reader more knowledgeable about the recipe.

## See also

This section provides helpful links to other useful information for the recipe.

# Conventions

In this book, you will find a number of text styles that distinguish between different kinds of information. Here are some examples of these styles and an explanation of their meaning.

Code words in text, database table names, folder names, filenames, file extensions, pathnames, dummy URLs, user input, and Twitter handles are shown as follows: "The first step will be to create a directory at `user/u/HbaseB` and download the `.tar` file."

A block of code is set as follows:

```
<configuration>
<property>
    <name>fs.default.name</name>
    <value>hdfs://addressofbsdnsofmynamenode-hadoop:9001</value>
 </property>
</configuration>
```

Any command-line input or output is written as follows:

```
ls -ltr will show the below results.
drwxrwxr-x 2 app app  4096 Jun 19 22:22 NameNodeData
drwxrwxr-x 2 app app  4096 Jun 19 22:22 DataNodeData


-bash-4.1$ pwd
```

**New terms** and **important words** are shown in bold. Words that you see on the screen, for example, in menus or dialog boxes, appear in the text like this: "Clicking the **Next** button moves you to the next screen."

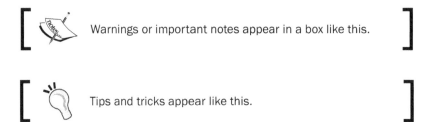

Warnings or important notes appear in a box like this.

Tips and tricks appear like this.

# Reader feedback

Feedback from our readers is always welcome. Let us know what you think about this book—what you liked or disliked. Reader feedback is important for us as it helps us develop titles that you will really get the most out of.

To send us general feedback, simply e-mail feedback@packtpub.com, and mention the book's title in the subject of your message.

If there is a topic that you have expertise in and you are interested in either writing or contributing to a book, see our author guide at www.packtpub.com/authors.

# Customer support

Now that you are the proud owner of a Packt book, we have a number of things to help you to get the most from your purchase.

## Downloading the example code

You can download the example code files for this book from your account at http://www.packtpub.com. If you purchased this book elsewhere, you can visit http://www.packtpub.com/support and register to have the files e-mailed directly to you.

You can download the code files by following these steps:

1. Log in or register to our website using your e-mail address and password.
2. Hover the mouse pointer on the **SUPPORT** tab at the top.
3. Click on **Code Downloads & Errata**.

4. Enter the name of the book in the **Search** box.

5. Select the book for which you're looking to download the code files.

6. Choose from the drop-down menu where you purchased this book from.

7. Click on **Code Download**.

You can also download the code files by clicking on the **Code Files** button on the book's webpage at the Packt Publishing website. This page can be accessed by entering the book's name in the **Search** box. Please note that you need to be logged in to your Packt account.

Once the file is downloaded, please make sure that you unzip or extract the folder using the latest version of:

- ▸ WinRAR / 7-Zip for Windows
- ▸ Zipeg / iZip / UnRarX for Mac
- ▸ 7-Zip / PeaZip for Linux

The code bundle for the book is also hosted on GitHub at `https://github.com/PacktPublishing/HBase-High-Performance-Cookbook`. We also have other code bundles from our rich catalog of books and videos available at `https://github.com/PacktPublishing/`. Check them out!

## Errata

Although we have taken every care to ensure the accuracy of our content, mistakes do happen. If you find a mistake in one of our books—maybe a mistake in the text or the code—we would be grateful if you could report this to us. By doing so, you can save other readers from frustration and help us improve subsequent versions of this book. If you find any errata, please report them by visiting `http://www.packtpub.com/submit-errata`, selecting your book, clicking on the **Errata Submission Form** link, and entering the details of your errata. Once your errata are verified, your submission will be accepted and the errata will be uploaded to our website or added to any list of existing errata under the Errata section of that title.

To view the previously submitted errata, go to `https://www.packtpub.com/books/content/support` and enter the name of the book in the search field. The required information will appear under the **Errata** section.

## Piracy

Piracy of copyrighted material on the Internet is an ongoing problem across all media. At Packt, we take the protection of our copyright and licenses very seriously. If you come across any illegal copies of our works in any form on the Internet, please provide us with the location address or website name immediately so that we can pursue a remedy.

Please contact us at `copyright@packtpub.com` with a link to the suspected pirated material.

We appreciate your help in protecting our authors and our ability to bring you valuable content.

## Questions

If you have a problem with any aspect of this book, you can contact us at `questions@packtpub.com`, and we will do our best to address the problem.

# 1

# Configuring HBase

In this chapter, we will cover the following topics:

- ▸ Configuring and deploying HBase
- ▸ Using the file system
- ▸ Administering clusters
- ▸ Managing clusters

## Introduction

HBase is inspired by the Google big table architecture, and is fundamentally a non-relational, open source, and column-oriented distributed NoSQL. Written in Java, it is designed and developed by many engineers under the framework of Apache Software Foundation. Architecturally it sits on Apache Hadoop and runs by using **Hadoop Distributed File System (HDFS)** as its foundation.

It is a column-oriented database, empowered by a fault-tolerant distributed file structure known as HDFS. In addition to this, it also provides very advanced features, such as auto sharding, load-balancing, in-memory caching, replication, compression, near real-time lookups, strong consistency (using multi-version). It uses the latest concepts of block cache and bloom filter to provide faster response to online/real-time request. It supports multiple clients running on heterogeneous platforms by providing user-friendly APIs.

In this chapter, we will discuss how to effectively set up mid and large size HBase cluster on top of Hadoop/HDFS framework.

This chapter will help you set up HBase on a fully distributed cluster. For cluster setup, we will consider REH (RedHat Enterprise-6.2 Linux 64 bit); for our setup we will be using six nodes.

# Configuring and deploying HBase

Before we start HBase in fully distributed mode, we will be setting up first Hadoop-2.2.0 in a distributed mode, and then on top of Hadoop cluster we will set up HBase because HBase stores data in HDFS.

## Getting ready

The first step will be to create a directory at `user/u/HBase B` and download the TAR file from the location given later. The location can be local, mount points or in cloud environments; it can be block storage:

wget wget –b `http://apache.mirrors.pair.com/hadoop/common/hadoop-2.2.0/` `hadoop-2.2.0.tar.gz`

> This –b option will download the tar file as a background process. The output will be piped to wget-log. You can tail this log file using tail -200f wget-log.

Untar it using the following commands:

```
tar -xzvf hadoop-2.2.0.tar.gz
```

This is used to untar the file in a folder hadoop-2.2.0 in your current directory location.

Once the untar process is done, for clarity it's recommended use two different folders one for `NameNode` and other for `DataNode`.

> I am assuming app is a user and app is a group on a Linux platform which has access to read/write/execute access to the locations, if not please create a user app and group app if you have `sudo su - or root/admin` access, in case you don't have please ask your administrator to create this user and group for you in all the nodes and directorates you will be accessing.

To keep the `NameNodeData` and the `DataNodeData` for clarity let's create two folders by using the following command, inside `/u/HBase B`:

```
Mkdir NameNodeData DataNodeData
```

`NameNodeData` will have the data which is used by the name nodes and `DataNodeData` will have the data which will be used by the data nodes:

```
ls -ltr will show the below results.
drwxrwxr-x 2 app app  4096 Jun 19 22:22 NameNodeData
```

```
drwxrwxr-x 2 app app  4096 Jun 19 22:22 DataNodeData

-bash-4.1$ pwd
/u/HBase B/hadoop-2.2.0
-bash-4.1$ ls -ltr
total 60K
drwxr-xr-x 2 app app 4.0K Mar 31 08:49 bin
drwxrwxr-x 2 app app 4.0K Jun 19 22:22 DataNodeData
drwxr-xr-x 3 app app 4.0K Mar 31 08:49 etc
```

The steps in choosing Hadoop cluster are:

1. Hardware details required for it
2. Software required to do the setup
3. OS required to do the setup
4. Configuration steps

HDFS core architecture is based on master/slave, where an HDFS cluster comprises of solo `NameNode`, which is essentially used as a master node, and owns the accountability for that orchestrating, handling the file system, namespace, and controlling access to files by client. It performs this task by storing all the modifications to the underlying file system and propagates these changes as logs, appends to the native file system files, and edits. `SecondaryNameNode` is designed to merge the `fsimage` and the `edits log` files regularly and controls the size of edit logs to an acceptable limit.

In a true cluster/distributed environment, it runs on a different machine. It works as a checkpoint in HDFS.

We will require the following for the `NameNode`:

| Components | Details | Used for nodes/systems |
| --- | --- | --- |
| Operating System | Redhat-6.2 Linux x86_64 GNU/ Linux, or other standard linux kernel. | All the setup for Hadoop/ HBase and other components used |
| Hardware /CPUS | 16 to 32 CPU cores | NameNode/Secondary NameNode |
| | 2 quad-hex-/octo-core CPU | DataNodes |
| Hardware/RAM | 128 to 256 GB, In special cases 128 GB to 512 GB RAM | NameNode/Secondary NameNodes |
| | 128 GB -512 GB of RAM | DataNodes |

| Components | Details | Used for nodes/systems |
|---|---|---|
| Hardware/storage | It's pivotal to have NameNode server on robust and reliable storage platform as it responsible for many key activities like edit-log journaling. As the importance of these machines are very high and the NameNodes plays a central role in orchestrating everything, thus RAID or any robust storage device is acceptable. | NameNode/Secondary Namenodes |
| | 2 to 4 TB hard disk in a JBOD | DataNodes |

**RAID** is nothing but a random access inexpensive drive or independent disk. There are many levels of RAID drives, but for master or a `NameNode`, **RAID 1** will be enough.

**JBOD** stands for Just a bunch of Disk. The design is to have multiple hard drives stacked over each other with no redundancy. The calling software needs to take care of the failure and redundancy. In essence, it works as a single logical volume:

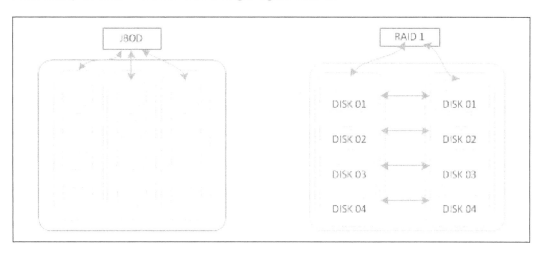

Before we start for the cluster setup, a quick recap of the Hadoop setup is essential with brief descriptions.

## How to do it...

Let's create a directory where you will have all the software components to be downloaded:

1. For the simplicity, let's take it as `/u/HBase B`.

2. Create different users for different purposes.

3. The format will be as follows `user/group`, this is essentially required to differentiate different roles for specific purposes:

   ❑ `Hdfs/hadoop` is for handling Hadoop-related setup

   ❑ `Yarn/hadoop` is for yarn related setup

   ❑ `HBase /hadoop`

   ❑ `Pig/hadoop`

   ❑ `Hive/hadoop`

   ❑ `Zookeeper/hadoop`

   ❑ `Hcat/hadoop`

4. Set up directories for Hadoop cluster. Let's assume `/u` as a shared mount point. We can create specific directories that will be used for specific purposes.

 Please make sure that you have adequate privileges on the folder to add, edit, and execute commands. Also, you must set up password less communication between different machines like from name node to the data node and from HBase master to all the region server nodes.

Once the earlier-mentioned structure is created; we can download the tar files from the following locations:

```
-bash-4.1$ ls -ltr
total 32

drwxr-xr-x  9 app app 4096 hadoop-2.2.0
drwxr-xr-x 10 app app 4096 zookeeper-3.4.6
drwxr-xr-x 15 app app 4096 pig-0.12.1

drwxrwxr-x  7 app app 4096 HBase -0.98.3-hadoop2
drwxrwxr-x  8 app app 4096 apache-hive-0.13.1-bin
drwxrwxr-x  7 app app 4096 Jun 30 01:04 mahout-distribution-0.9
```

5. You can download these tar files from the following location:

```
wget -o https://archive.apache.org/dist/HBase /HBase -0.98.3/HBase
-0.98.3-hadoop1-bin.tar.gz
```

```
wget -o https://www.apache.org/dist/zookeeper/zookeeper-3.4.6/
zookeeper-3.4.6.tar.gz
```

```
wget -o https://archive.apache.org/dist/mahout/0.9/mahout-
distribution-0.9.tar.gz
```

```
wget -o https://archive.apache.org/dist/hive/hive-0.13.1/apache-
hive-0.13.1-bin.tar.gz
```

```
wget -o https://archive.apache.org/dist/pig/pig-0.12.1/pig-
0.12.1.tar.gz
```

Here, we will list the procedure to achieve the end result of the recipe. This section will follow a numbered bullet form. We do not need to give the reason that we are following a procedure. Numbered single sentences would do fine.

Let's assume that there is a /u directory and you have downloaded the entire stack of software from: /u/HBase B/hadoop-2.2.0/etc/hadoop/ and look for the file core-site.xml.

Place the following lines in this configuration file:

```
<configuration>
<property>
    <name>fs.default.name</name>
    <value>hdfs://addressofbsdnsofmynamenode-hadoop:9001</value>
 </property>
</configuration>
```

 You can specify a port that you want to use, and it should not clash with the ports that are already in use by the system for various purposes.

Save the file. This helps us create a master /NameNode.

Now, let's move to set up SecondryNodes, let's edit /u/HBase B/hadoop-2.2.0/etc/hadoop/ and look for the file core-site.xml:

```
<property>
  <name>fs.defaultFS</name>
  <value>hdfs://custome location of your hdfs</value>
</property>
<configuration>
<property>
    <name>fs.checkpoint.dir</name>
```

```
        <value>/u/HBase B/dn001/hadoop/hdf/secdn
            /u/HBase B/dn002/hadoop/hdfs/secdn
    </value>
    </property>
    </configuration>
```

 The separation of the directory structure is for the purpose of a clean separation of the HDFS block separation and to keep the configurations as simple as possible. This also allows us to do a proper maintenance.

Now, let's move towards changing the setup for `hdfs`; the file location will be `/u/HBase B/hadoop-2.2.0/etc/hadoop/hdfs-site.xml`.

Add these properties in `hdfs-site.xml`:

For `NameNode`:

```
    <property>
    <name>dfs.name.dir</name>
    <value>
    /u/HBase B/nn01/hadoop/hdfs/nn,/u/HBase B/nn02/hadoop/hdfs/nn
    </value>
    </property>
```

For `DataNode`:

```
    <property>
    <name>dfs.data.dir</name>
    <value>
    /u/HBase B/dnn01/hadoop/hdfs/dn,/HBase B/u/dnn02/hadoop/hdfs/dn
    </value>
    </property>
```

Now, let's go for `NameNode` for http address or to access using http protocol:

```
    <property>
    <name>dfs.http.address</name>
    <value>yournamenode.full.hostname:50070</value>
    </property>
    <property>
    <name>dfs.secondary.http.address</name>
    <value>
    secondary.yournamenode.full.hostname:50090
    </value>
    </property>
```

We can go for the https setup for the `NameNode` too, but let's keep it optional for now:

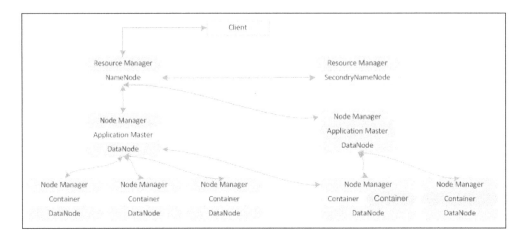

Let's set up the yarn resource manager:

1. Let's look for Yarn setup:

   `/u/HBase B/hadoop-2.2.0/etc/hadoop/ yarn-site.xml`

2. For resource tracker a part of yarn resource manager:

   ```
   <property>
      <name>yarn.yourresourcemanager.resourcetracker.address</name>
   <value>youryarnresourcemanager.full.hostname:8025</value>
   </property>
   ```

3. For resource schedule part of yarn resource scheduler:

   ```
   <property>
   <name>yarn.yourresourcemanager.scheduler.address</name>
   <value>yourresourcemanager.full.hostname:8030</value>
   </property>
   ```

4. For scheduler address:

   ```
   <property>
   <name>yarn.yourresourcemanager.address</name>
   <value>yourresourcemanager.full.hostname:8050</value>
   </property>
   ```

5. For scheduler admin address:

   ```
   <property>
   <name>yarn.yourresourcemanager.admin.address</name>
   <value>yourresourcemanager.full.hostname:8041</value>
   </property>
   ```

6.  To set up a local dir:

```
<property>          <name>yarn.yournodemanager.local-dirs</name>
<value>/u/HBase /dnn01/hadoop/hdfs/yarn,/u/HBase B/dnn02/hadoop/
hdfs/yarn </value>     </property>
```

7.  To set up a log location:

```
<property>
<name>
yarn.yournodemanager.logdirs
</name>
<value>/u/HBase B/var/log/hadoop/yarn</value>
</property>
```

This completes the configuration changes required for Yarn.

Now, let's make the changes for Map reduce:

1.  Let's open the mapred-site.xml:

```
/u/HBase B/hadoop-2.2.0/etc/hadoop/mapred-site.xml
```

2.  Now, let's place this property configuration setup in the `mapred-site.xml` and place it between the following:

```
<configuration >
</configurations >
<property><name>mapreduce.yourjobhistory.address</name>
<value>yourjobhistoryserver.full.hostname:10020</value>
</property>
```

3.  Once we have configured Map reduce job history details, we can move on to configure HBase .

4.  Let's go to this path `/u/HBase B/HBase -0.98.3-hadoop2/conf` and open `HBase -site.xml`.

    You will see a template having the following:

```
<configuration >
</configurations >
```

5.  We need to add the following lines between the starting and ending tags:

```
<property>
<name>HBase .rootdir</name>
<value>hdfs://HBase .yournamenode.full.hostname:8020/apps/HBase /
data
</value>
```

```
        </property>


        <property>
        <name>HBase .yourmaster.info.bindAddress</name>
        <value>$HBase .yourmaster.full.hostname</value>
        </property>
```

6.  This competes the HBase changes.

**ZooKeeper**: Now, let's focus on the setup of ZooKeeper. In distributed `env`, let's go to this location and rename the `zoo_sample.cfg` to `zoo.cfg`:

```
/u/HBase B/zookeeper-3.4.6/conf
```

Open `zoo.cfg` by `vi zoo.cfg` and place the details as follows; this will create two instances of zookeeper on different ports:

```
yourzooKeeperserver.1=zoo1:2888:3888
yourZooKeeperserver.2=zoo2:2888:3888
```

If you want to test this setup locally, please use different port combinations. In a production-like setup as mentioned earlier, `yourzooKeeperserver.1=zoo1:2888:3888` is `server.id=host:port:port`:

```
yourzooKeeperserver.1= server.id
zoo1=host
2888=port
3888=port
```

Atomic broadcasting is an atomic messaging system that keeps all the servers in sync and provides reliable delivery, total order, casual order, and so on.

**Region servers**: Before concluding it, let's go through the region server setup process.

Go to this folder `/u/HBase B/HBase -0.98.3-hadoop2/conf` and edit the `regionserver` file.

Specify the region servers accordingly:

```
RegionServer1
RegionServer2
RegionServer3
RegionServer4
```

RegionServer1 equal to the IP or fully qualified CNAME of 1 Region server. You can have as many region servers (1. N=4 in our case), but its CNAME and mapping in the region server file need to be different.

Copy all the configuration files of HBase and ZooKeeper to the relative host dedicated for HBase and ZooKeeper. As the setup is in a fully distributed cluster mode, we will be using a different host for HBase and its components and a dedicated host for ZooKeeper.

Next, we validate the setup we've worked on by adding the following to the bashrc, this will make sure later we are able to configure the NameNode as expected:

```
etc/profile or etc/bashrc:
export JAVA_HOME=/usr/lib/jvm/jdk1.8.0_05
export HADOOP_HOME=/u/HbaseB/hadoop-2.2.0
export HBASE_HOME=/u/HbaseB/hbase-0.98.5-hadoop2
export HADOOP_MAPRED_HOME=$HADOOP_HOME
export HADOOP_COMMON_HOME=$HADOOP_HOME
export HADOOP_HDFS_HOME=$HADOOP_HOME
export YARN_HOME=$HADOOP_HOME
export HADOOP_CONF_DIR=$HADOOP_HOME/etc/hadoop
export YARN_CONF_DIR=$HADOOP_HOME/etc/hadoop
export HADOOP_LOGS=$HADOOP_HOME/logs
export HADOOP_USER_LOGS=$HADOOP_HOME/logs/userlogs
export HBASE_LOGS=$HBASE_HOME/logs
export SQOOP_HOME=/u/HbaseB/sqoop-1.4.5.bin__hadoop-1.0.0
export PATH=$PATH:$SQOOP_HOME/bin
```

 It preferred to use it in your profile, essentially /etc/profile; this will make sure the shell which is used is only impacted.

Now let's format NameNode:

```
Sudo su $HDFS_USER

/u/HBase B/hadoop-2.2.0/bin/hadoop namenode -format

HDFS is implemented on the existing local file system of your cluster.
When you want to start the Hadoop setup first time you need to start
with a clean slate and hence any existing data needs to be formatted and
erased.
```

Before formatting we need to take care of the following.

Check whether there is a Hadoop cluster running and using the same HDFS; if it's done accidentally all the data will be lost.

```
/u/HBase B/hadoop-2.2.0/sbin/hadoop-daemon.sh --config
$HADOOP_CONF_DIR start namenode
```

Now let's go to the `SecondryNodes`:

```
Sudo su $HDFS_USER
/u/HBase B/hadoop-2.2.0/sbin/hadoop-daemon.sh --config $HADOOP_CONF_DIR
start secondarynamenode
```

Repeating the same procedure in `DataNode`:

```
Sudo su $HDFS_USER
/u/HBase B/hadoop-2.2.0/sbin/hadoop-daemon.sh --config $HADOOP_CONF_DIR
start datanode
Test 01>
```

See if you can reach from your browser `http://namenode.full.hostname:50070`:

```
Test 02> sudo su $HDFS_USER touch /tmp/hello.txt
```

Now, `hello.txt` file will be created in `tmp` location:

```
/u/HBase B/hadoop-2.2.0/bin/hadoop dfs  -mkdir -p /app
/u/HBase B/hadoop-2.2.0/bin/hadoop dfs  -mkdir -p /app/apphduser
```

```
This will create a specific directory for this application user in the
HDFS FileSystem location(/app/apphduser)
/u/HBase B/hadoop-2.2.0/bin/hadoop dfs -copyFromLocal /tmp/hello.txt /
app/apphduser
/u/HBase B/hadoop-2.2.0/bin/hadoop dfs -ls /app/apphduser
```

apphduser is a directory which is created in hdfs for a specific user.

So that the data is separated based on the users, in a true production `env` many users will be using it.

You can also use hdfs dfs -ls / commands if it shows hadoop command as depricated.

You must see `hello.txt` once the command executes:

```
Test 03> Browse http://datanode.full.hostname:50075/browseDirectory.jsp?n
amenodeInfoPort=50070&dir=/&nnaddr=$datanode.full.hostname:8020
```

 It is important to change the data host name and other parameters accordingly.

You should see the details on the `DataNode`. Once you hit the preceding URL you will get the following screenshot:

---

### Contents of directory /app

Goto : /app    go

Go to parent directory

| Name | Type | Size | Replication | Block Size | Modification Time | Permission | Owner | Group |
|------|------|------|-------------|------------|-------------------|------------|-------|-------|
| apphduser | dir | | | | 2016-06-11 00:03 | rwxr-xr-x | hadoop | supergroup |

Go back to DFS home

---

### Local logs

Log directory

---

Hadoop, 2016.

---

On the command line it will be as follows:

```
[hadoop@rchoudhry-linux64 bin]$ ./hdfs dfs -ls /
16/06/11 00:04:22 WARN util.NativeCodeLoader: Unable to load native-hadoop library for your platform... using builtin-java classes where applicable
Found 7 items
drwxr-xr-x   - hadoop supergroup          0 2016-06-11 00:03 /app
drwxrwxrwt   - hadoop supergroup          0 2015-08-16 14:34 /app-logs
drwxr-xr-x   - hadoop supergroup          0 2016-04-16 13:53 /hbase
drwxr-xr-x   - hadoop supergroup          0 2015-08-22 16:39 /mahout-data
-rw-r--r--   2 hadoop supergroup        929 2015-08-22 23:33 /myoutput
drwxrwx---   - hadoop supergroup          0 2014-09-08 16:00 /tmp
drwxr-xr-x   - hadoop supergroup          0 2015-08-22 18:32 /user
```

Validate `Yarn/MapReduce` setup and execute this command from the resource manager:

```
<login as $YARN_USER> /u/HBase B/hadoop-2.2.0/sbin/yarn-daemon.sh
--config $HADOOP_CONF_DIR start resourcemanager
```

Execute the following command from `NodeManager`:

```
<login as $YARN_USER >
/u/HBase B/hadoop-2.2.0/sbin /yarn-daemon.sh --config
$HADOOP_CONF_DIR start nodemanager
```

Executing the following commands will create the directories in the hdfs and apply the respective access rights:

```
Cd u/HBase B/hadoop-2.2.0/bin

hadoop fs -mkdir /app-logs // creates the dir in HDFS

hadoop fs -chown $YARN_USER /app-logs //changes the ownership

hadoop fs -chmod 1777 /app-logs // explained in the note section

Execute MapReduce
```

```
Sudo su  $HDFS_USER
/u/HbaseB/hadoop-2.2.0/sbin/hadoop fs -mkdir -p /mapred/history/done_intermediate
/u/HbaseB/hadoop-2.2.0/sbin/hadoop fs -chmod -R 1777

/mapred/history/done_intermediate
/u/HbaseB/hadoop-2.2.0/sbin/hadoop fs -mkdir -p /mapred/history/done
/u/HbaseB/hadoop-2.2.0/sbin/hadoop fs -chmod -R 1777 /mapred/history/done
/u/HbaseB/hadoop-2.2.0/sbin/hadoop fs -chown -R mapred /mapred

export HADOOP_LIBEXEC_DIR=/u/HbaseB/hadoop-2.2.0/libexec/
export HADOOP_MAPRED_HOME=/u/HbaseB/hadoop-2.2.0/hadoop-mapreduce
export HADOOP_MAPRED_LOG_DIR=/u/HbaseB/hadoop-2.2.0/mapred
```

Start `jobhistory` servers:

```
<login as $MAPRED_USER>

/u/HBase B/hadoop-2.2.0/sbin/mr-jobhistory-daemon.sh start historyserver
--config $HADOOP_CONF_DIR
```

Let's have a few tests to be sure we have configured properly:

Test 01: From the browser or from curl use the link to browse: `http://yourresourcemanager.full.hostname:8088/`.

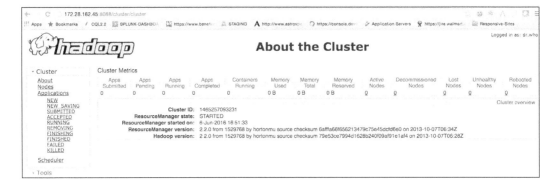

Test 02:

```
Sudo su $HDFS_USER
```

```
/u/HBase B/hadoop-2.2.0/bin/hadoop jar /u/HBase B/hadoop-2.2.0/hadoop-
mapreduce/hadoop-mapreduce-examples-2.0.2.1-alpha.jar teragen 100 /
test/10gsort/input
```

```
/u/HBase B/hadoop-2.2.0/bin/hadoop jar /u/HBase B/hadoop-2.2.0/hadoop-
mapreduce/hadoop-mapreduce-examples-2.0.2.1-alpha.jar
```

Validate the `HBase` setup:

```
Login as $HDFS_USER
```

```
/u/HBase B/hadoop-2.2.0/bin/hadoop fs -mkdir -p /apps/HBase
```

```
/u/HBase B/hadoop-2.2.0/bin/hadoop fs -chown app:app -R  /apps/HBase
```

Now login as `$HBase _USER`:

```
/u/HBase B/HBase -0.98.3-hadoop2/bin/HBase -daemon.sh --config $HBase _
CONF_DIR start master
```

This command will start the master node. Now let's move to HBase Region server nodes:

```
/u/HBase B/HBase -0.98.3-hadoop2/bin/HBase -daemon.sh --config $HBase _
CONF_DIR start regionserver
```

This command will start the `regionservers`:

> For a single machine, direct `sudo  ./HBase` master start can also be used.
> Please check the logs in case of any logs at this location `/opt/HBase B/`
> `HBase -0.98.5-hadoop2/logs`.

You can check the log files and check for any errors:

```
hbase-hadoop-avro-rchoudhry-linux64.log
hbase-hadoop-thrift-rchoudhry-linux64.log
hbase-hadoop-rest-rchoudhry-linux64.log
hbase-hadoop-slave-rchoudhry-linux64.log
hbase-hadoop-regionservers-rchoudhry-linux64.log
hbase-hadoop-slaves-rchoudhry-linux64.log
hbase-hadoop-zookeeper-rchoudhry-linux64.log
hbase-hadoop-master-rchoudhry-linux64.log
```

Now let's login using:

```
Sudo su- $HBase _USER
/u/HBase B/HBase -0.98.3-hadoop2/bin/HBase shell
```

We will connect HBase to the master.

Validate the ZooKeeper setup. If you want to use an external zookeeper, make sure there is no internal HBase based zookeeper running while working with the external zookeeper or existing zookeeper and is not managed by HBase :

For this you have to edit /opt/HBase B/HBase -0.98.5-hadoop2/conf/ HBase -env.sh.

Change the following statement (HBase _MANAGES_ZK=false):

# Tell HBase whether it should manage its own instance of Zookeeper or not.

```
export HBase _MANAGES_ZK=true.
```

Once this is done we can add zoo.cfg to HBase 's CLASSPATH.

HBase looks into zoo.cfg as a default lookup for configurations

```
dataDir=/opt/HBase B/zookeeper-3.4.6/zooData
```

# this is the place where the zooData will be present

```
server.1=172.28.182.45:2888:3888
```

# IP and port for server 01

```
server.2=172.29.75.37:4888:5888
```

# IP and port for server 02

You can edit the log4j.properties file which is located at /opt/HBase B/ zookeeper-3.4.6/conf and point the location where you want to keep the logs.

# Define some default values that can be overridden by system properties:

```
zookeeper.root.logger=INFO, CONSOLE
zookeeper.console.threshold=INFO
zookeeper.log.dir=.
zookeeper.log.file=zookeeper.log
zookeeper.log.threshold=DEBUG
zookeeper.tracelog.dir=. # you can specify the location here
zookeeper.tracelog.file=zookeeper_trace.log
```

Once this is done you start zookeeper with the following command:

```
-bash-4.1$ sudo /u/HBase B/zookeeper-3.4.6/bin/zkServer.sh start
Starting zookeeper ... STARTED
```

You can also pipe the log to the ZooKeeper logs:

```
/u/logs//u/HBase B/zookeeper-3.4.6/zoo.out 2>&1
```

2 : refers to the second file descriptor for the process, that is `stderr`.

```
> : means re-direct
```

```
&1:  means the target of the redirection should be the same location as
the first file descriptor i.e stdout
```

## How it works...

 Sizing of the environment is very critical for the success of any project, and it's a very complex task to optimize it to the needs.

We dissect it into two parts, master and slave setup. We can divide it in the following parts:

```
Master-NameNode
```

```
Master-Secondary NameNode
```

```
Master-Jobtracker
```

```
Master-Yarn Resource Manager
```

```
Master-HBase Master
```

```
Slave-DataNode
```

```
Slave-Map Reduce Tasktracker
```

```
Slave-Yarn Node Manager
```

```
Slave-HBase Region server
```

> ▸ `NameNode`: The architecture of Hadoop provides us a capability to set up a fully fault tolerant/high availability Hadoop/HBase cluster. In doing so, it requires a master and slave setup. In a fully HA setup, nodes are configured in active passive way; one node is always active at any given point of time and the other node remains as passive.
>
> Active node is the one interacting with the clients and works as a coordinator to the clients. The other standby node keeps itself synchronized with the active node and to keep the state intact and live, so that in case of failover it is ready to take the load without any downtime.

Now we have to make sure that when the passive node comes up in the event of a failure, the passive node is in perfect sync with the active node, which is currently taking the traffic. This is done by Journal Nodes(JNs), these Journal Nodes use daemon threads to keep the primary and secondary in perfect sync.

- ▶ `Journal Node`: By design, `JournalNodes` will only have single `NameNode` acting as a active/primary to be a writer at a time. In case of failure of the active/primary, the passive `NameNode` immediately takes the charge and transforms itself as active, this essentially means this newly active node starts writing to Journal Nodes. Thus it totally avoids the other `NameNode` to stay in active state, this also acknowledges that the newly active node work as a fail over node.

- ▶ `JobTracker`: This is an integral part of Hadoop EcoSystem. It works as a service which farms MapReduce task to specific nodes in the cluster.

- ▶ `ResourceManager (RM)`: This responsibility is limited to scheduling, that is, only mediating available resources in the system between different needs for the application like registering new nodes, retiring dead nodes, it dose it by constantly monitoring the heartbeats based on the internal configuration. Due to this core design practice of explicit separation of responsibilities and clear orchestrations of modularity and with the inbuilt and robust scheduler API, This allows the resource manager to scale and support different design needs at one end, and on the other, it allows us to cater to different programming models.

- ▶ `HBase Master`: The Master server is the main orchestrator for all the region servers in the HBase cluster . Usually, it's placed on the `ZooKeeper` nodes. In a real cluster configuration, you will have 5 to 6 nodes of `Zookeeper`.

- ▶ `DataNode`: It's a real workhorse and does most of the heavy lifting; it runs the MapReduce Job and stores the chunks of HDFS data. The core objective of the data node was to be available on the commodity hardware and should be agnostic to the failures.

  It keeps some data of HDFS, and the multiple copy of the same data is sprinkled around the cluster. This makes the DataNode architecture fully fault tolerant. This is the reason a data node can have JBOD01 rather rely on the expensive RAID02.

- ▶ `MapReduce`: Jobs are run on these DataNodes in parallel as a subtask. These subtasks provides the consistent data across the cluster and stays consistent.

We will discuss this in more details in *Chapter 3, Working with Large Distributed Systems Part 1*.

## There's more...

Apache Yarn is a robust, distributed, application management framework that surpasses the traditional Apache Hadoop MapReduce framework to process data in a large Hadoop clusters.

This change was needed because during the map phase of the mapreduce process, the data is chunked into small discrete packets that can be processed, followed by a second phase reduce, which allows this split data to be aggregated and thus produces the desired results. This works well with small, mid-sized and to some extent large clusters, but for the very large cluster (more than 4000 nodes), the unpredictable behavior starts to surface. The core issue was replication of data during the cascading failure.

Thus, it helps us in reliability, scalability, and sharing. Hadoop Yarn essentially works with JobTracker and splits the multiple accountabilities into resource management, job monitoring and scheduling into more granular and distributed by resource manager and application Master.

It works in synchronicity with per-node `NodeManager` and the per-application ApplicationMaster.

`NodeManager` takes a remote invocation from resource manager and manage resources available on a single node.

ApplicationMaster is responsible for negotiating resource with the `resourceManager` and works with the `NodeManager` to start the containers.

HBase provides low-latency random read and writes on top of HDFS, being a large-scale key value store, the main differentiating factor for HBase is that it can scan petabyte of data at a very high speed. It also comes with an inbuilt capability of autosharding by splitting the tables dynamically when the table becomes too large.

This enables HBase to horizontally scale. This is quantified as regions. Regions are a portion of table data, which are stored together and of prime efficiency. This does not make sense. The slave servers in HBase are the region server. It does a fair bit of work and provides true distribution across different regions. It can serve one or more regions based on the needs, each reason is assigned to a region server or start-up.

HBase 0.96 removed the concept of ROOT containing the `META` table location, rather it moved it to `ZooKeeper` as the `META` table cannot split and can be in only single region:

- ▶ `HMaster`: This does administrative operations and coordinated cluster.
- ▶ `HTable`: It allows client `for`, `get`, `put`, `delete`, and other data manipulation options. This interacts directly with the region server. Essentially, it finds the region server, which is responsible for serving the particular row range.
- ▶ `HFile`: This is a physical representation of data in HBase, the read of data in always done using the region servers. It's generated by flush or compactions. There are two versions of HFile V2, and V3.

- ▸ `HFile V2`: The main issues with `HFile V1` were to load all the monolithic indexes and large bloom filter in memory. V2 was introduced to provide efficiency as compared to V1, while sorting large amount of data by using multilevel indexes and a block level bloom filter. It also improves the caching and memory utilization. Index is also moved to block level. This essentially means that each block has its own leaf index, which allows multilevel index. The multilevel index is like b+ tree and uses last key of each block to facilitate intermediate. The detailed explanation is beyond the scope of this book:

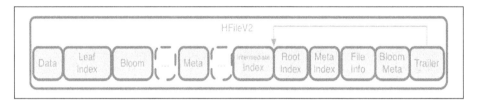

- ▸ `MemStore`: It collects data edits as they're received and buffers them in memory. It helps the system to push the data on the disk at one go, and on the other hand, it keeps the data in memory for subsequent access and avoid the expensive disk seeks. It also helps in keeping the data block size to the HDFS block size specified. It is also needed to mention about the sorting it does before flushing to `Hfile`.

- ▸ `Block cache`: For efficient I/O usage, HBase is programmed to read the entire block at one go and kept in memory (In JVM memory) per region servers. It is initialized during the region server startup and stays the same during the lifetime of the server startup.

- ▸ `LruBlockCache`: The data blocks are cached in-memory (JVM heap). The block is divided into different size, 25% (for single access), 50% (multi access), 25% (in-memory) of total block size, respectively.

- ▸ `SlabCache`: It's a way off-heap memory outside the JVM heap using the DirectByteBuffer.

  SlabCache minimizes the fragmentation but the other part of HBase that is JVM-dependent, still can do fragmentations. The main advantage that we get is, it reduces the frequency of stop the world pause GC cycle, which can lead to the no heartbeats of the region servers and can signal as dead, this can be catastrophic in an actual production system. While reading the data from the slabcache, the data is copied from the disk based on "copy on read approach", which means reading data from the JVM if the data is present. If the data is not copied then the data is copied on the heap from the slab: http://en.wikipedia.org/wiki/XOR_swap_algorithm.

  SlabCache works as an L2 cache, and replaces the FS cache. The on-heap JVM cache works as the L1 cache.

  This approach allows us to use large memory without losing the performance of the system, and it reduces the chances of missed heartbeats because of stop the world GC process.

This is mainly achieved due to the Direct ByteBuffer class available in the java.nio package, which allows us to allocate memory outside the normal Java Heap/JVM very similar to `malloc()` in C programming. The Garbage collection process will not remove the unreferenced objects when the memory is allocated by direct bytebuffer.

▶ `Bucket cache`: It's an implementation of block cache similar to LruBlockCache. It can be also used as a secondary cache to expand the cache space. The blocks of data can be stored in memory or on the file system. It significantly helps the CMS and heap fragments by Java garbage cleaning (GC) process.

▶ `Multilevel caching`: It's a design strategy of effective and large cache management. The first-level cache is an L1 level cache, which is LruBlockCahce. The second level is L2. Both the cache levels interact independently to each other and are checked in case of eviction and retrieve block of data.

## See Also

Refer to the following chapter:

▶ Working with Large Distributed Systems

# Using the filesystem

HBase depends on the **Hadoop Distributed File System** (**HDFS**).

HDFS fundamentally is a distributed file system, which relies on following core principles:

## Getting ready

The following are the benefits of using HDFS:

▶ It's designed to work as a fault-tolerant system and is rack aware.

▶ It works on the low-cost commodity hardware.

▶ HDFS relaxes core system POSIX requirements to facilitate streaming access to the underlying OS access of file system data.

▶ It's designed to write once and read many times. It also supports parallel reading and processing the data (read, write, and append). It doesn't support random writes of data.

▶ It's designed to scale at a very large level, which means file size like petabyte of data.

▸ It works with minimum data motion. The MapReduce processes the data on the machine/node where the data is actually present. This intelligent invocation process, thus avoiding or minimizing the network I/O and keep the expensive I/O operation localized (within the same rack or to the local disk).

▸ HDFS has an excellent checksummed file system at a block level, and if an inconsistency between the checksum and the block contents is observed, This does not make sense!, the communication is sent to the HDFS master, which synchronizes the making of a new replica of the affected block as well, as the removal of the corrupted block immediately.

A lot of work is continuously happening on the core implementations of HDFS; some are as follows:

▸ Much granular file-level permissions and authentication.

▸ Rack awareness was added to optimize the physical location during scheduling task and allocating storage.

▸ For administrative purposes, a new feature was added known as **Safemode**.

▸ In addition to these, for administrators a diagnostics service like fsck was added, this enables is to do an analysis on the missing blocks of a file system.

▸ Rebalancer tool is an internal distribution mechanism which re-distributes the load in the `DataNode`, which becomes unbalanced due to the continuous data between DataNodes.

▸ An upgrade and rollback step was added for administrators, which now allow reverting to the old version of HDFS in case of any unforeseen situations which was caused by the upgrade; this allows us a safe and painless recovery.

▸ The concept of checkpoints by secondary `NameNode` is introduced to make sure size of the file which holds logs of HDFS changes stays within the specified limits at the `NameNode`.

More Information can be obtained at this locations `http://hadoop.apache.org/docs/r0.18.3/hdfs_user_guide.html`.

 We are not considering a local setup of HBase as we are more focused on the HA and larger scale fully distributed setup.

Data in HDFS is not placed homogeneously in the distributed DataNodes. The most obvious reason is addition of new DataNodes is the preexisting cluster. Internally the system (NameNode) performs various checks before is starts sending the data/new blocks to the `DataNode`, which are listed as below:

> ▸ One replica of a blow is kept on the same node which is writing the block.
>
> To make sure the fault tolerant design is compiled, the replicas are kept across the distributed rack within the cluster.

> ▸ To reduce cross-network chattiness, one replica is placed on the same rack of the node writing to the file. This also helps to keep the homogeneousness of HDFS data in a distributed very large DataNode cluster.

> ▸ In some scenario's there can be competing considerations, and this may cause non-uniform data across DataNode.
>
> To overcome this scenario, the new HDFS framework enables administrators with tools which can be use to re-balance, check the data across different DataNodes.

You would need to set up Hadoop 2.2.0 in a fully distributed mode, as discussed in the previous section. Web interface is also used for browsing the file system.

## How to do it...

To use the File system we go as per the following steps:

1. Logging the `NameNode` instance by the following:

   **ssh hadoop@your-namenode**

   **( you can you IP or the fully qualified machine name)**

   **then type cd /u/HBase B/hadoop-2.2.0/bin**

2. Let's run some commands related to `dfs`:

   **Note: this will make sure the setup is proper and we are able to interact with it**

   **/u/HBase B/hadoop-2.2.0/bin/hadoop  dfs -ls /**

   **drwxr-xr-x    - hadoop supergroup   0 2014-08-13 22:48 /nn01**

   **drwxr-xr-x    - hadoop supergroup   0 2014-08-17 23:28 /nn02**

For Putting the file into HDFS:

```
/u/HBase B/hadoop-2.2.0/bin/hadoop dfs  -put hello.txt /nn02/
hello.txt

running /u/HBase B/hadoop-2.2.0/bin/hadoop dfs  -du /nn01/  /nn02

0   /nn02/hello.txt

0   /nn01/hello.txt
```

For the recursive version:

```
/u/HBase B/hadoop-2.2.0/bin/hadoop dfs  -ltr /

drwxr-xr-x   - hadoop supergroup  0 2014-08-13 22:48 /nn01

-rw-r--r--   3 hadoop supergroup  0 2014-08-13 22:48 /nn01/hello.
txt

drwxr-xr-x   - hadoop supergroup  0 2014-08-17 23:39 /nn02

-rw-r--r--   3 hadoop supergroup  0 2014-08-17 23:39 /nn02/hello.
txt
```

Similarly you can use the following commands:

```
touchz, text,tail, stat, setrep, rmr, rm, put, mv, movefromLocal,
mkdir, lsr, ls, getmerge, get, dus, expunge, du, copyToLocal,
chown, chmod, chgrp, cat.
```

3.  Let us take a look at `fsck` commands:

    ```
    hdfs fsck [GENERIC_OPTIONS] <path> [-move | -delete |
    -openforwrite] [-files [-blocks [-locations | -racks]]]
    ```

    ❑   `-move`: This moves the corrupted files to /lost +found

    ❑   `-delete`: This deletes the corrupted files

    ❑   `-openforwrite`: This prints out the files opened for write

    ❑   `-files`: This prints out the files being checked

    ❑   `-blocks`: This prints the block report

    ❑   `-locaitons`: This prints location of every block

    ❑   `-rackes`: This prints network topology for the data-node location

4. Let's take a look on some `NameNode`:

```
hadoop namenode [-format] | [-upgrade] | [-rollback] | [-finalize]
| [-importCheckpoint]

hadoop namenode -format  Formats the namenode.

Hafoop namenode -upgrade ,first it upgraded the namenode and then
distributes and starts the new namenode

Hadop namnode -rollback as the name suggests the Rollsback
namenode to the previous version. This should be used only after
stopping the cluster and distributing the old hadoop version.

hadoop namenode -finalize Resent upgrade will become permanent.

hadoop namnode -importCheckpoint Load image from a checkpoint
directory and save it into the current one.
```

5. Let's consider `seconderynamenode`:

```
hadoop secondarynamenode [-checkpoint [force]] | [-geteditsize]

hadoop secondarynamenode -geteditsize  Prints the Edit Log size

hadoop secondarynamenode -checkpoint [force] checkpoints the
secondary namenode if EditLog size >= fs.checkpoint.size. If -
force is used, checkpoint irrespective of EditLog size.
```

6. We have discussed `DataNode` and its functions:

```
hadoop datanode [-rollback]

It rollsback the datanode to the previous version. This should be
only used after stopping the all the datanode and distributing the
old hadoop version.
```

7. Considering Jobtracker runs the MapReduce job tracker node:

```
hadoop jobtracker
```

## The HBase setup

Configuring HBase in a fully distributed environment:

- ▸ Prerequisites: The `hadoop/hdfs` cluster is healthy
- ▸ It has `namenode`, `data` node, secondary `namenode` setup done as discussed earlier
- ▸ Passwordless access is there between the `namenode, datanode, secondary namenocde`
- ▸ The directory structure is having appropriate access levels
- ▸ Hope paths are set as described earlier

Just for recap you can run this command, and it must show the following details:

```
haddoop@rchoudhry-linux64 hbase-0.98.5-hadoop2]$ vi ~/.bashrc
export JAVA_HOME=/usr/lib/jvm/jdk1.8.0_05
export HADOOP_HOME=/u/HbaseB/hadoop-2.2.0
export HBASE_HOME=/u/HbaseB/hbase-0.98.5-hadoop2
export HADOOP_MAPRED_HOME=$HADOOP_HOME
export HADOOP_COMMON_HOME=$HADOOP_HOME
export HADOOP_HDFS_HOME=$HADOOP_HOME
export YARN_HOME=$HADOOP_HOME
export HADOOP_CONF_DIR=$HADOOP_HOME/etc/hadoop
export YARN_CONF_DIR=$HADOOP_HOME/etc/hadoop
export HADOOP_LOGS=$HADOOP_HOME/logs
export HADOOP_USER_LOGS=$HADOOP_HOME/logs/userlogs
export HBASE_LOGS=$HBASE_HOME/logs
```

[   Please check the compatibility of Hadoop and HBase . ]

In this book, we used hadoop-2.2.0 and HBase 0.98.5-hadoop2.

1.  Let's go to the `NameNode` of Hadoop/HDFS by typing this command:

    **Vi /u/HBase B/hadoop-2.2.0/etc/hadoop/ hdfs-site.xml**

    The setup should be like this:

```xml
<configuration>
<property>
 <name>dfs.namenode.name.dir</name>
 <value>file:///u/HbaseB/hadoop-2.2.0/hdfs/nn</value>
</property>
<property>
 <name>dfs.data.dir</name>
  <value>file:///u/HbaseB/hadoop-2.2.0/hdfs/dn</value>
</property>
<property>
     <name>dfs.replication</name>
          <value>2</value>
             </property>
<property>
 <name>dfs.http.address</name>
 <value>hadoop-namenode:50070</value>
</property>
  <property>
  <name>dfs.secondary.http.address</name>
  <value>hadoop-secondrynamenode:50090</value>
  </property>
  <property>
  <name>dfs.blocksize</name>
   <value>268435456</value>

  </property>
  <property>
  <name>dfs.namenode.handler.count</name>
     <value>16</value>
  </property>
  </configuration>
 Vi /u/HbaseB/hadoop-2.2.0/etc/hadoop/core-site.xml
 The setup should be like this:
<configuration>
<property>
     <name>fs.defaultFS</name>
     <value>hdfs://yourhadoop-namenode:8020</value>
</property>
<property>
     <name>hadoop.tmp.dir</name>
     <value>/u/HbaseB/hadoop-2.2.0/hadoopdatastore</value>
</property>
<property>
     <name>io.file.buffer.size</name>
      <value>131072</value>
</property>
<property>
 <name>fs.checkpoint.dir</name>
 <value>/u/HbaseB/hadoop-2.2.0/hdfs/snn</value>
 </property>
</configuration>
```

These are the data nodes that we will use for regional servers later on. We will use NameNode as an HBase master node.

```
vi  /u/HBase B/hadoop-2.2.0/etc/hadoop/slave

it should have the nodes which will be used as a data node
your-datanode01
your-datenode02
```

The following steps will help you to implement the same:

1. Copy the `hdfs-stie.xml` which is in Hadoop setup to:

   **cd $HBase _HOME/conf**

2. Also, copy it to all the Region servers. Edit the `regionserver` file by:

   **Vi $HBase _HOME/conf/ regionservers on the HMASTER server**

3. Place the IP or the fully qualified name of the region servers.

   **Vi HBase -env.sh and change the export HBase _MANAGES_ZK=true**

4. This will allow HBase to manage the zookeeper internally on port 2181.

## Starting the cluster

For starting the HBase cluster, we will go to:

```
cd $HBase _HOME/bin start-HBase .sh
```

This will start the entire cluster and its region servers.

Please check the logs in the log folder just to make sure the cluster starts properly:

```
cd $HBase _LOGS/
ls -ltr
-rw-rw-r--. 1 hadoop hadoop       0 Aug 29 19:22
SecurityAuth.audit
-rw-rw-r--. 1 hadoop hadoop  92590 Aug 30 15:04 HBase
-hadoop-zookeeper-your-HBase -master.log
-rw-rw-r--. 1 hadoop hadoop 484092 Aug 30 16:31 HBase
-hadoop-master-rchoudhry-your-HBase -master.log

tail -200 HBase -hadoop-zookeeper-your-HBase -master.
log
```

There you will see no binding errors or exceptions.

```
tail -200 hadoop hadoop 484092 Aug 30 16:31 HBase -hadoop-master-
rchoudhry-your-HBase -master.log
```

There should be no errors or exceptions.

## Validating the cluster

Let's validate all of the setup of HBase ; on the master node run jps, it will show the following:

```
[hadoop@rchoudhry-linux64 logs]$ jps
960 SecondaryNameNode  // secondary name node is up
8467 NameNode // Name node is up
11892 HQuorumPeer // zookeeper is running in Quorum mode
25318 Jps // pls neglect this
12008 HMaster // HBase Master is running successfully
8699 ResourceManager // Resource manager is running
12171 HRegionServer  // HBase Region server is running
8974 JobHistoryServer // JobHistory Server is running
```

This will ensure that all the system on the master is working perfectly. We are having a region server on the master node; hence, we are seeing `HRegionServer` listed as earlier.

On the region server (your region server running on different node), use the same command and you will see the following:

```
13026 NodeManager
12425 Jps
12778 DataNode
13567 HRegionServer
```

We will make sure that all the region servers are working. Basic operations on the cluster:

On the HBase Master:

```
cd $HBase _HOME/bin
[hadoop@rchoudhry-linux64 bin]$ HBase shell -d
HBase (main):001:0>
```

This is the command line for `HBase` shell. We are using the `-d` option to manage it in a debug mode. In production, it should be avoided and we should see the logs file to make sure that the `logs` is not having connection errors to any of the components:

```
HBase (main):001:0> list
City_Table
MyClickStream
t1
3 row(s) in 1.1270 seconds


["City_Table", "MyClickStream", "t1"]
HBase (main):002:0>  status
HBase (main):002:0> status 'simple'
HBase (main):002:0> status 'summary'
HBase (main):002:0> status 'detailed'
HBase (main):002:0> describe 'MyClickStream'
HBase (main):002:0> scan 'yourtablename'
HBase (main):002:0> create 'yourtablename','cf01',cf'02'
```

There are many such commands that we can run from the `HBase` shell command line, which we will discuss as we go through different chapters as we go ahead.

The preceding tables are created in the following section. It's just for reference.

The following is the Snapshot process:

- We will consider from Hadoop and then from an HBase prospective; once the directory is marked as ready to snapshot, which essentially means it's not getting any operations of read/write at this particular time, at this time a snapshot can be taken.

- It can be taken on any dir within the Hadoop/HBase data ecosystem. A snapshottable directory has a limit of 65,536 concurrent snapshots. There is no limit on the snapshottable directories (however file descriptor or other OS limitations can come into the picture). It's a good practice for administrators to set any directory to be snapshottable.

 If a snapshottable directory has snapshots, it won't allow deletes or renames before all the snapshots residing are deleted.

- There is a system limitation that doesn't allow nested snapshottable directories.

Create a directory as a snapshot:

```
hdfs dfs -mkdir /snapshot
using this command we can make it enable for snapshots.
hdfs dfsadmin -allowSnapshot /snapshot
hdfs dfs -createSnapshot /snapshot [<snapshotName>]
```

Deleting a snapshot:

Delete a snapshot from a snapshottable directory.

This can be only done using the owners  privilege of the snapshottable directory:

```
  hdfs dfs -deleteSnapshot <path> <snapshotName>
```

Snapshots in HBase :

To reduce the impact on the Region Servers, HBase snapshots by design give flexibility to clone a table without making data copies. In addition to this, we can export the table to another cluster, this will also avoid any impact on the region server.

Configuring HBase Snapshot:

```
    <property>
        <name>HBase .snapshot.enabled</name>
        <value>true</value>
    </property>
```

We are assuming that a table `MyClickStream` is created in HBase . We can also create the table if it's not present:

```
./bin/HBase shell
HBase > create 'MyClickStream' ,'cf01', 'cf2'


cf01-> is represented as a column family  01
cf02-> is represented as a column family 02


./bin/HBase shell -d
HBase > disable 'MyClickStream'
HBase > snapshot 'MyClickStream' ,'MyClickStreamSnapshot-08302014'
```

Listing a Snapshot: List all the snapshots taken:

```
./bin/HBase shell
```

```
HBase > list_snapshots
```

> **Deleting a Snapshot**: We can remove the unwanted Snapshots by running the following command:
>
> ```
> ./bin/HBase / shell
> ```
>
> ```
> HBase > delete_snapshot ''MyClickStreamSnapshot-08212014'
> ```

> **Clone a table from Snapshot**: Cloning allows us to create a new table with the same dataset when the snapshot was taken. Changes to the clone table are isolated to itself, and the changes in the original table are not going to impact the snapshot:
>
> ```
> ./bin/HBase shell
> ```
>
> ```
> HBase > clone_snapshot 'MyClickStreamSnapshot-08212014',
> 'MyClickStreamSnapshot01-08212014'
> ```

> **Restoring Snapshots**: This can be only performed when the table is disabled. The effectiveness of this process is that the table comes up with the same state as before, when we took the snapshot:
>
> ```
> ./bin/HBase / shell
> ```
>
> ```
> HBase > disable 'MyClickSteam' --- the name of the table
> ```

This will disable the table for active use and no operation like read/write it does at this point:

```
HBase > restore_snapshot ''MyClickStreamSnapshot-08212014'
```

Internally there are differences in which replication and snapshot works.

Replication is performed at log level wherein snapshots are always at file system . Thus its essential to sync the states from the master as once the restore operation is done the replica will be different then the master. In case of we performed restore operation, it's pivotal to stop the replication process first and perform the bootstrapping operation again.

In the scenario of limited data loss due to any client, it's recommended to clone the table using the existing snapshot and run a MapReduce job which essentially copies the data from cloned to the main, this way we don't have to go for a full restore which predecessor process is to disable the tables :

Specify the HBase .rootdir of the other cluster:

```
./bin/HBase
```

```
HBase org.apache.hadoop.HBase .snapshot.ExportSnapshot -snapshot
'MyClickStreamSnapshot-08212014 -copy-to hdfs:///mynamendoe
server02:8082/HBase mapper -8
```

In case of a highly used production environment, it's advisable to restrict bandwidth consumption while exporting a snapshot.

This can be achieved by invoking the preceding command with bandwidth parameter, as shown next; the unit of measure is megabyte per second and the value is an integer:

```
./bin/HBase
```

```
HBase org.apache.hadoop.HBase .snapshot.ExportSnapshot -snapshot
'MyClickStreamSnapshot-08212014 -copy-to hdfs:///mynamendoe
server02:8082/HBase mapper -8 -bandwidth 200
```

## How it works...

To better understand the concepts, I have broken down the parameter into:

- **WebInterface**: This shows the details of NameNode and DataNode and display basic information about the cluster. The URL will be `http://your -namenode-name:50070/`. Alternatively you can use the same interface for navigating the filesystem within the NameNode.

- **Snapshots**: Snapshots in HDFS are always read-only and represent the status of the file at the time snapshot was taken. You can restrict Inconsistency throughout chapter of snapshot versus Snapshot to a limited scope of a filesystem or Snapshot can or it can span to the entire file system.

- **HBase Snapshots**: A snapshot is an array of metadata information used by administrators to restore the previous state of the tables on which it was taken. In technical meaning it's not a copy of table but it's a set of operation which calibrates metadata (which is nothing but table and regions) and the actual data (HFiles, me store, WALs).

- **Offline Snapshots**: The standard scenario is to take the snapshot when the table is disabled, This makes sure that all the data is flushed on disk, and no writes or reads are accepted on this dataset. Which means, taking a snapshot is just a matter of working through the table metadata and the HFiles which reside on the disk and keeping a reference to them. The master invokes this operation, and the time required to do this operation is governed by the time taken by the HDFS NameNode to calibrate and provide the list of the files.

- **Online Snapshots**: This type of snapshot works differently; in it, tables are enabled and the regions are getting read and write, or in the other words it's getting put and get by the live traffic, when master receives the request for snapshot, master coordinates it by asking all the region server to take a snapshot of their region. This works on simple-flush and does not provide casual consistency. This type of snapshot has minimal performance overhead.

DFS Administration commands:

- `bin/hadoop dfsadmin -help`: provide you all the commands.
- `bin/hadoop dfsadmin -reports`: provides statistics and file information.
- `bin/hadoop dfsadmin -safemode enter | leave | get | wait -`.
- `Safe mode`: Immediately blocks changes to the name space and converts it to read only. It also blocks replication and any delete operations on the data block.

 An important point to note about the safe mode, is that during the startup process, safe mode is turned on automatically but is switched to normal once the process detects the minimum condition is fulfilled. You can also manual trigger safe mode but in this case you have to switch-off manual mode too.

- `bin/hadoop dfsadmin -saveNamespace`: This command requires su permission and saves the current namespace and resets the edit logs.
- `bin/hadoop dfsadmin -rollEdits`: This rolls the edit logs. Note that this requires super user permission.
- `bin/hadoop dfsadmin -restoreFailedStorage`: This comes with three parameters (Set/Unset/Check) it attempts to restore failed storage replicas only if they become available.

 This can be only done by su option.

- `bin/hadoop dfsadmin -refreshNodes`: This commend updated the NameNode by allowing the `DataNode` to connect to the `NameNode`.
- `bin/hadoop dfsadmin - finalizeUpgrade`: This concludes the upgrade of HDFS. This invokes an internal process and instructs the DataNodes to delete their previous version working directories, and then invoking the Namenode to do the same. This finishes the upgrade process.
- `bin/hadoop dfsadmin -deleteBlockPool`: Arguments are datanodehost:port, blockpool id and an optional argument `force`. If force is passed, block pool directory for the given blockpool Inconsistency between id and ID on the given `DataNode` is deleted along with its contents; otherwise, the directory is deleted only if it is empty. The command will fail if `DataNode` is still serving the block pool. Refer to refresh NameNodes to shut down a block pool service on a `DataNode`:
- `bin/hadoop dfsadmin -help`.

Let's discuss other important components:

- ▸ SecondaryNameNode: NameNode stores changes to the native file system file (edits). During the startup process, the HDFS state is read from the image file commonly known as fsimage. These changes are applied to the edit log files. The latest state of the HDFS is pushed to the fsimage, then the normal process is invoked by generating a blank edit log file. In essence, NameNode combines these two(fsimage and log) files during the startup. This merge process makes the next restart faster.

- ▸ Rebalancer: The HDFS cluster gets easily imbalanced due to the following reasons:

  When a new DataNode joins the cluster, any map task assigned to the machine most likely does not access local data, thus consuming more network bandwidth. When the DataNodes becomes full new, atablocks are placed on full data nodes, thus reducing the read parallelism.

- ▸ Rack Awareness: As NameNode design is for HA/Fault tolerant thus the system attempts to cascade the replicas of block on the multiple racks. Using the variable dfs.network.script, the administrator can govern these settings.

- ▸ Safemode: Makes the HDFS block read-only.

- ▸ fsck: It's designed to report problems with missing blocks, under-replicated blocks; fsck ignores open files. Depending on the needs it can be run on a subsection of files or can be run on the entire file system which is under NameNode.

- ▸ Snapshotting: We will consider from Hadoop and then from the HBase perspective.

  Snapshots process is very flexible and robust and it allows snapshots at directory level, cascaded directory level. Total of 65,536 simultaneous snapshots can be accommodated. In essence there is no limit on snapshottable directories.

 Nested snapshottable directories are currently not possible.

Exporting to another cluster tool helps us duplicate the data between clusters. The data copied is hfiles, logs, and snapshot metadata. This works at a file system (HDFS) level, thus it's necessary to have an HBase cluster fully online also. This is the reason it does not impact the RegionServer workload.

In the preceding section, we discussed the core file system, which is the foundation of HBase . We discussed HDFS and how it's related to Hadoop ecosystem and then how HBase relies on the Hadoop/HBase foundation to work. In doing so, we discussed the internal structure of the HDFS, HBase integration points. In step 1 to 9, we discussed the HDFS/Hadoop commands in a fully distributed mode. This is needed to make sure that HBase runs in the fully distributed environment. We cannot run HBase if we don't have the Hadoop setup; however for development purposes we can run HBase using standalone mode installation; the other way will be to run it in Pseudo-Distributed.

## There is more...

The entire process helps us set up the Hadoop/HDFS file system, and later on HBase can sit on get the benefits of the HDFS distributed architecture.

## See also

Refer to the following chapter:

▶ Working with Large Distributed Systems.

# Administering clusters

It's pivotal at this time to know more about the HBase administrative process, as it stores petabyte of data in distributed locations and requires the system to work smoothly agnostic to the location of the data in a multithreaded, easy-to-manage environment in addition to the hardware, OS, JDK and other hardware and software components.

HbBase and administrative GUI provide the current state of the cluster and and plenty of command-line tools, which can really give us an in-depth knowledge about what is going on in the cluster.

## Getting ready

We must have a HDFS/Hadoop setup in a cluster or fully distributed mode as the first step, which we did it in the earlier section. The second step is to have an HBase setup in a fully distributed mode.

 It's assumed that we have a setup of password-less communication between the master and the region servers on the HBase side. If you are using the same nodes for Hadoop/Hdfs setup, we need to have the Hadoop user also to have a password-less setup from Namenode to Secondary NameNode, DataNodes, and so on.

We must have a full HBase cluster running on top of hadoop/HDFS cluster.

## How to do it...

HBase provides multiple ways to do administration work on the fully distributed clustered environment:

- ▸ WebUI-based environment
- ▸ Command line-based environment
- ▸ HBase Admin UI

The Master run on `60010` ports as default, the web interface is looked up on this port only. This needs to be started on the HMaster node.

The master UI gives a dashboard of what's going on in the HBase cluster.

The UI contains the following details:

- ▸ HBase home
- ▸ Table details
- ▸ Local logs
- ▸ Log levels
- ▸ Debug dump
- ▸ Metric dump
- ▸ HBase configuration

We will go through it in the following sections.

- ▸ **HBase Home**: It contains the dashboard that gives a holistic picture of the HBase cluster.
  - ❑ The region server
  - ❑ The backup master
  - ❑ Tables
  - ❑ A task
  - ❑ Software attributes

▶ **Region Server**: The image shows the region server and also provided a tab view of various metrics like (basic stats, Memory, Request, Storefiles, Compactions):

A Detailed discussion is out of scope at this point. For more details, see later sections. For our purpose, we will avoid to go for backup master:

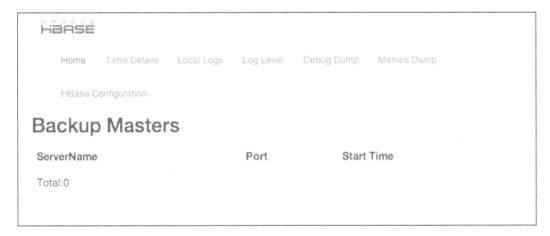

Let's list all the user-created tables using Tables. It provides the details about User Tables (tables that are created by the users/actors), Catalog Tables (this contains `HBase  :meta` and `HBase  :namespaces`), which is seen in the following figure:

Clicking any table, as listed earlier, other important details are shown such as table attributes, table regions, and region-by-region server details. Actions as compaction and split can be taken using admin UI.

Task provides the details of talk, which is happening. We can see Monitored task, RPC Tasks, RPC Handler task, Active RPC Calls, Client Operations, and a JSON response:

The following **Software Attributes** page provides the details of the software used in the HBase cluster:

**HBASE**

Home    Table Details    Local Logs    Log Level    Debug Dump    Metrics Dump

HBase Configuration

## Software Attributes

| Attribute Name | Value | Description |
| --- | --- | --- |
| HBase Version | 0.98.5-hadoop2, rUnknown | HBase version and revision |
| HBase Compiled | Mon Aug 4 23:58:06 PDT 2014, apurtell | When HBase version was compiled and by whom |
| Hadoop Version | 2.2.0, r1529768 | Hadoop version and revision |
| Hadoop Compiled | 2013-10-07T06:28Z, hortonmu | When Hadoop version was compiled and by whom |
| Zookeeper Quorum | 172.29.75.37:2181 | Addresses of all registered ZK servers. For more, see zk dump. |
| HBase Root Directory | hdfs://172.29.75.37:8020/hbase | Location of HBase home directory |
| HMaster Start Time | Fri Aug 29 19:31:22 PDT 2014 | Date stamp of when this HMaster was started |
| HMaster Active Time | Fri Aug 29 19:31:22 PDT 2014 | Date stamp of when this HMaster became active |
| HBase Cluster ID | a05e31b5-6830-4476-bc5d-ae56e389489e | Unique identifier generated for each HBase cluster |
| Load average | 5.00 | Average number of regions per regionserver. Naive computation. |
| Coprocessors | [] | Coprocessors currently loaded by the master |

After clicking on `zk_dump`, it provides further details about the zookeeper Quorum stats as follows:

```
Quorum Server Statistics:
 172.29.75.37:2181
  Zookeeper version: 3.4.6-1569965, built on 02/20/2014 09:09 GMT
  Clients:
   /172.29.75.37:52614[1](queued=0,recved=2845,sent=2890)
   /172.29.75.41:10895[1](queued=0,recved=168,sent=168)
   /172.29.75.37:52625[1](queued=0,recved=170,sent=170)
   /172.29.75.37:52626[1](queued=0,recved=170,sent=170)
   /172.29.75.37:52619[1](queued=0,recved=485,sent=485)
   /172.29.75.37:52620[1](queued=0,recved=1079,sent=1079)
   /172.29.75.37:52621[1](queued=0,recved=297,sent=314)
   /172.29.75.37:52622[1](queued=0,recved=177,sent=177)
   /172.29.75.37:52314[0](queued=0,recved=1,sent=0)
   /172.29.75.37:47050[1](queued=0,recved=24,sent=24)
   /172.29.75.41:10896[1](queued=0,recved=174,sent=178)
   /172.29.75.37:47051[1](queued=0,recved=14,sent=14)

  Latency min/avg/max: 0/0/218
  Received: 5683
  Sent: 5748
  Connections: 12
  Outstanding: 0
  Zxid: 0x6db
  Mode: standalone
  Node count: 38
```

HBase provides various command-line tools for administrating, debugging, and doing an analysis on the HBase cluster.

The first tool is the `HBase` shell, and the details are as follows:

`bin/HBase`

`Usage: HBase [<options>] <command> [<args>]`

```
shell           Run the HBase shell
hbck            Run the hbase 'fsck' tool
hlog            Write-ahead-log analyzer
hfile           Store file analyzer
zkcli           Run the ZooKeeper shell
upgrade         Upgrade hbase
master          Run an HBase HMaster node
regionserver    Run an HBase HRegionServer node
zookeeper       Run a Zookeeper server
rest            Run an HBase REST server
thrift          Run the HBase Thrift server
thrift2         Run the HBase Thrift2 server
clean           Run the HBase clean up script
classpath       Dump hbase CLASSPATH
mapredcp        Dump CLASSPATH entries required by mapreduce
pe              Run PerformanceEvaluation
ltt             Run LoadTestTool
version         Print the version
CLASSNAME       Run the class named CLASSNAME
```

Identify inconsistencies with hbck; this tool provides consistencies, checks for corruption of data, and it runs against the cluster.

`bin/HBase  hbck`

This runs against the cluster and provides the details of inconsistencies between the regions and masters.

`bin/HBase  hbck -details`

The `-details` provides the insight of splits which happens in all the tables.

`  bin/HBase hbck MyClickStream`

The preceding line enables us to `vView` the `HFile` content in a text format.

`  bin/HBase org.apache.hadoop.HBase .io.hfile.HFile`

Use `FSFLogs` for manual splitting and dumping:

`HBase org.apache.hadoop.HBase .regionserver.wal.FSHLog --dump`

`HBase org.apache.hadoop.HBase .regionserver.wal.FSHLog -split`

Enable compressor tool:

```
HBase org.apache.hadoop.HBase .util.CompressionTest hdfs://host/path/to/
HBase snappy
```

Enable compressor tool on the Column Family or while creating a tables:

```
HBase > disable 'MyClickStream'

HBase > alter 'MyClickStream', {NAME => 'cf', COMPRESSION => 'GZ'}

HBase > enable 'MyClickStream'

HBase > create MyClickStream', {NAME =>'cf2', COMPRESSION => 'SNAPPY'}
```

Load Test too Usage below are some of the commands which can be used to do a quick load test on your compression performance:

```
bin/HBase org.apache.hadoop.HBase .util.LoadTestTool -h
```

usage: `bin/HBase org.apache.hadoop.HBase .util.LoadTestTool  <options>.`

Options: includes –batchupdate

-compression: <arg> Compression type , arguments can be LZq,GZ,NONE and SNAPPY

We will limit ourselves with the above commands.

A good example will be as follows:

```
HBase org.apache.hadoop.HBase .util.LoadTestTool -write 2:20:20 -num_keys
500000 -read 60:30 -num_tables 1 -data_block_encoding NONE -tn load_test_
tool_NONE
-write (here we are passing 2 as ->avg_cols_per_key)
20 is the ->avg_data_size>:
20 is number of parallel threads to be used.
-num_key has an integer arguments as 500000, this is the number of keys
to read and write.
```

Now let's look at a read:

-read 60 is the verify percent

30 is the  number of  threads

```
-num_tables a positve interger is passed which is the number of tables to
be loaded in parallel
-data_block_encoding there are various encoding algorithms which can be
passed as an argument, this allow the data block to be encoded based on
the need. Some of them  are [NONE,PREFIX,DIFF,FAST_DIFF,PREFIX_TREE].
```

-tn is a table name prefix which exports the content and data to HDFS in a sequence file using this:

**HBase org.apache.hadoop.HBase .mapreduce.Export <tablename> <outputdir> [<versions> [<starttime> [<endtime>]]]**

 You can configure HBase .client.scanner.caching in the job configuration; this is for all the scans.

Importing: This tool will load data that has been exported back into HBase :

This can be done by the following command:

**HBase org.apache.hadoop.HBase .mapreduce.Import <tablename> <inputdir>**

-tablename: Is the name of the table to be imported by the tool.

-inputdir: Is the input dir which will be used.

Utility to Replay WAL files into HBase :

**HBase org.apache.hadoop.HBase .mapreduce.WALPlayer [options] <wal inputdir> <tables> [<tableMappings>] >**

**HBase org.apache.hadoop.HBase .mapreduce.WALPlayer /backuplogdir MyClickStream newMyClickStream**

**walinputdi:   /backuplogdir**

**tables:   MyClickStream**

**tableMappings→ newMyClickStream**

HBase clean: is dangerous and should be avoided in production setup.

**HBase clean**

Options: as parameters

  **--cleanZk   cleans HBase related data from zookeeper.**
  **--cleanHdfs cleans HBase related data from hdfs.**
  **--cleanAll  cleans HBase related data from both zookeeper and hdfs.**

HBase pe: This is a shortcut to run the performance evaluations tools

HBase ltt: This command is a shortcut provided to run the rg.apache.hadoop.HBase .util.LoadTestTool utility. It was introduced in 0.98 version.

View the details of the table as shown here:

Go to the log tab on the HBase Admin UI home page, and you will see the following details. Alternatively, you can log in to the directory using the Linux shell to tail the logs.

Directory: `/logs/`:

```
SecurityAuth.audit 0 bytes  Aug 29, 2014 7:22:00 PM

HBase -hadoop-master-rchoudhry-linux64.com.log 691391 bytes   Sep 2, 2014
11:01:34 AM

HBase -hadoop-master-rchoudhry-linux64.com.out 419 bytes    Aug 29, 2014
7:31:21 PM

HBase -hadoop-regionserver-rchoudhry-linux64.com.log 1048281 bytes    Sep
2, 2014 11:01:23 AM

HBase -hadoop-regionserver-rchoudhry-linux64com.out 419 bytes    Aug 29,
2014 7:31:23 PM

HBase -hadoop-zookeeper-rchoudhry-linux64.log 149832 bytes    Aug 31, 2014
12:51:42 AM

HBase -hadoop-zookeeper-rchoudhry-linux64.com.out 419 bytes    Aug 29,
2014 7:31:19 PM

HBase -hadoop-zookeeper-rchoudhry-linux64.com.out.1 1146 bytes    Aug 29,
2014 7:26:29 PM
```

Get and set the log levels as required at runtime:

# Log Level

### Get / Set

Log:                  Get Log Level

Log:           Level:          Set Log Level

Hadoop, 2014.

## Log dump

Have a look at what is going in the cluster with Log dump:

```
Master status for HBase -hadoop-master-rchoudhry-linux64.
com,60000,1409365881345 as of Tue Sep 02 11:17:33 PDT 2014
Version Info:
===============================================================
HBase 0.98.5-hadoop2
Subversion file:///var/tmp/0.98.5RC0/HBase -0.98.5 -r Unknown
Compiled by apurtell on Mon Aug  4 23:58:06 PDT 2014
Hadoop 2.2.0
Subversion https://svn.apache.org/repos/asf/hadoop/common -r 1529768
Compiled by hortonmu on 2013-10-07T06:28Z


Tasks:
============================================================
Task: RpcServer.reader=1,port=60000
Status: WAITING:Waiting for a call
Running for 315970s

Task: RpcServer.reader=2,port=60000
Status: WAITING:Waiting for a call
Running for 315969s
```

## Metrics dump

Exposes the JMX details for the following components in a JSON format using Matrix dump:

- ► Start-up progress
- ► Balancer
- ► Assignment Manager
- ► Java Management extension details
- ► Java Runtime Implementation System Properties

 These are various system properties; the discussion of it is beyond the scope of this book.

## How it works...

When the browser points to the http address `http://your-HBase -master:60010/ master-status`, the web interface of HBase admin is loaded.

Internally, it connects to the `Zookeeper` and can collect the details from the `zookeeper` interface, where in zookeeper tracks the Region server as per the region server configuration in the `region server` file. These are the values set in the `HBase -site.xml`. The data for `hadoo/hdfs`, region servers, zookeeper quorum details are continuously looked by the RPC calls, which the master makes via zookeeper.

In the above HBase `-site.xml`, the user/ sets the Master, Backup master, various other software attributes, the refresh time, memory allocations, storefiles, compactions,request, zk dumps etc

Node or Cluster view: In this, the user chooses either monitoring Hmaster or Region server data view. The HMaster view contains data and graphics about the node status. The Region server view is the main and the most important one because it allows monitoring of all the region server aspects.

You can point the http address to `http:// your-HBase -master:60030/rs-status`. It loads the admin UI for the region servers.

The matrix that is captured here is as follows:

- ► Region server Metrics (Base stats, Memory, request, Hlog, Storefiles, Queues) Tasks happening in Region servers (Monitored, RPC, RPC handler, active RPC .JSON, client operations)
- ► Block Cache provides different options for on-heap and off-heap: LurBlockCache and Bucket are off-heap.

Backup master is a design/architecture choice, which needs careful considerations before enabling it. HBase by design is a fault-tolerant distributed system with assumes hardware failure in the network topology.

However, HBase does provide various options to for it such as:

- Data center-level failure
- Accidental deletion of records/data
- For audit purpose

## See also

Refer to the following chapter:

- Working with Large Distributed Systems.

# Managing clusters

In HBase ecosystem, it's must to monitor the cluster to control and improve their performance and states as it grows. As HBase sits on top of Hadoop ecosystem and serves real-time user traffic, it's essential to see the performance of the cluster at any given point of time, this allows us to detect the problem well in advance and take corrective actions before it happens.

## Getting ready

It is important to know some of the details of Ganglia and its distributed components before we get into the details of managing clusters

### gmond

This is an acronym for a low footprint service known as Ganglia Monitoring Daemon. This service needs to be installed at each node from where we want to pull the matrix. This daemon is the actual workhorse and collects the data of each host by listen/announce protocol. It also helps collect some of the core metrics such as disk, active process, network, memory, and CPU/VCPUs.

### gmetad

This is an acronym for Ganglia meta daemon. It is a service that collects data from other gmetad and gmond and mushes it together into a single meta-cluster image. The format used to store the data is RRD and XML. This enables the client application browsing.

## gweb

It's a web interface or a view to the data that is collected by the earlier two services. It's a PHP-based web interface. It requires the following:

- Apache web server
- PHP 5.2 or later
- The PHP json extension

## How to do it...

We will divide our how to do it into two sections. In the first section, we will talk about installing Ganglia on all the nodes.

Once it's done, we will do the integration with HBase so that the relevant metrics are available.

### Ganglia setup

To install Ganglia it is best to use prebuild binary package that is available from the vendor distributions. This will help in dealing with the pre-requisites libraries. Alternatively, it can be downloaded from the Ganglia website, `http://sourceforge.net/projects/ganglia/files/latest/download?source=files`.

If you are using browser from command prompt, you can do it by using following command:

```
wget -o http://downloads.sourceforge.net/project/ganglia/\ganglia%20
monitoring%20core/3.0.7%20%28Fossett%29/ganglia-3.0.7.tar.gz
```

When doing wget, use it as a single line on your shell. Use sudo in case you don't have privilege for the current directory or download it in /tmp and later on copy to the respective location.

1. `tar -xzvf ganglia-3.0.7.tar.gz -c /opt/HBase B`
2. `rm -rf ganglia-3.0.7.tar.gz` // it will delete the tar file which is not needed now.
3. Now let's Install the dependencies

   ```
   sudo apt-get -y install build-essential libapr1-dev libconfuse-dev
   libexpat1-dev python-dev
   ```

   The `-y` options means that apt-get won't wait for users confirmation. It will assume `yes` when question for confirmation would appear.

4. Building and installing the downloaded and exploded binary:

```
cd /opt/HBase B/ganglia-3.0.7
./configure --- is a configuration command on linux env
make
sudo make install
```

5. Once the preceding step is completed, you can generate a default configuration file by:

```
gmond --default_config > /etc/gmond.conf        --use "sudo su - "
in case there is a privilege issue
sudo su - will make you a root user and will allow the system
library to be accessed by the gmond.conf
```

6. `vi /etc/gmond.conf` and change the following:

```
globals
{
user=HBase gangila in place of above.
}
```

 In case you are using a specific user to perform ganglia task then change the above and add this user as shown above.

7. The recommendation will be to create this user by the following commands:

```
sudo adduser --disabled-login --no-create-home ganglia
cluster {
name =HBase B --- name of your cluster will be used
owner ="HBase B Company"
url =http://yourHBase bMaster.ganglia-monitor.com/
--- url of the main monitor or the CNAME
}
```

8. The UDP setup, which is the default setup, if good for fewer than 120 nodes. For more than 120 nodes, we have to switch to unicast.

   The setup is as follows:

```
Change in /etc/gmond.conf
Udp_send_channel
{
#mcast_join=--your IP address to join in
host = yourHBase bMaster.ganglia-monitor.com
```

```
post=8649
# ttl=1
}
udp_recv_channel
{
#mcast_join=--your IP address to join in
port =8649
# bind =--your IP address to join in
}
```

9.  Start the monitoring daemon with:

    **sudo gmond**

    We can test it by `nc <hostname> 8649` or telnet hostname 8649

 You have to kill the daemon thread to stop it using `ps -ef | grep gmond`. This will provide the process ID with the following process:

Execute `sudo kill -9 <PID>`

10. Now we have to install Ganglia meta daemon. It is good to have one if the cluster is less than 100 nodes. This is the workhorse and it will require powerful machine with decent compute power, as these are responsible for creating graphs.

11. Let's move ahead:

    **cd   /u/HBase B/ganglia-3.0.7**

    **./configure --with-gmetad**

    **make**

    **sudo make install**

    **sudo cp /u/HBase B/gangli-3.0.7/gmetad/gmetad.conf /etc/gmetad.conf**

12. Open using `sudo vi /etc/gmrtad.conf` change the code:

    ```
    setuid_username "ganglia"
    data_source "HBase B"  yourHBase bMaster.ganglia-monitor.com
    gridename "<our grid name say HBase B Grid>"
    ```

13. Now we need to create directories, which will store data in a **round-robin database (rrds)**:

    **mkdir -p /var/lib/ganglia/rrds**

    Now let's change the ownership to ganglia users, so that it can read and write as needed.

    **chown -R ganglia:ganglia /var/lib/ganglia/**

14. Let's start the daemon:

    ```
    gmetad
    ```

 You have to kill the daemon thread to stop it using `ps -ef | grep gmetad`. This will provide the process ID with the process. Execute `sudo kill -9 <PID>`

15. Now, let's focus on Ganglia web.

    ```
    sudo apt-get -y install rrdtool apache2 php5-mysql libapache2-mod-php5 php5-gd
    ```

 Note that this will install `rrdtool` (round robin database tool), Apache/httpd, php5 connector (apache to mysql), Php5-mysql drivers, and so on.

16. Copy the PHP-based file to the following locations:

    ```
    cp -r /u/HBase B/ganglia-3.0.7/web  /var/www/ganglia
    ```

    ```
    sudo /etc/init.d/apache2 restart ( others which can be used are,
    status, stop )
    ```

17. Point http:// HBase bMaster.ganglia-monitor.com/ganglia, you should start seeing the basic graphs as the HBase setup is still not done.

18. Integrate HBase and Ganglia:

    ```
    vi  /u/HBase B/HBase -0.98.5-hadoop2/conf /hadoop-metrics2-HBase
    .properties
    ```

19. Change the below parameter for getting different status on the ganglia:

    ```
    HBase .extendedperiod = 3600

    HBase .class= org.apache.hadoop.metrics2.sink.FileSink

    HBase .period=5

    HBase .servers=master2:8649

    # jvm context will provide memory used , thread count in JVM etc.

    jvm.class= org.apache.hadoop.metrics2.sink.FileSink

    jvm.period=5

    # enable rpc context to see the metrics on each HBase rpc method
    invocation.


    jvm.servers=master2:8649
    ```

```
rpc.class= org.apache.hadoop.metrics2.sink.FileSink
rpc.period=5
rpc.servers=master2:8649
```

20. Copy the `/u/HBase B/HBase B/HBase -0.98.5-hadoop2/conf/ hadoop-metrics2-HBase .properties` to all the `nodes` and restart `HMaster` and all the region servers:

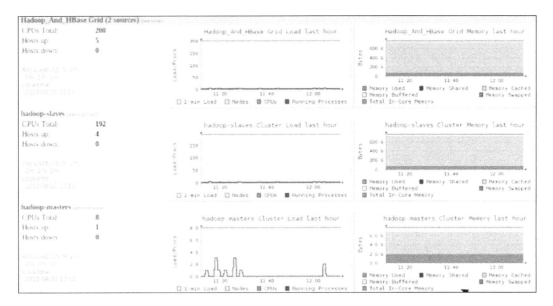

## How it works...

As the system grows from a few nodes to the tens or hundreds or becomes a very large cluster having more than hundreds of nodes it's pivotal to have a holistic view, drill down view, historical view of the logs at any given point of time in a graphical representation. In a large or very large installation, administrators are more concerned about redundancy, which avoids single point of failure. HBase and underlying HDFS are designed to handle the node failures gracefully, but it's equally important to monitor these failure as this can lead to pull down the cluster if a corrective action is not taken in time. HBase exposes various matrix to JMX and Ganglia like HMaster, region servers statistics, JMV (Java virtual machines), RPC (Remote procedure calls), Hadoop/HDFS, MapReduce details. Taking into consideration all these points and various other salient and powerful features, we considered Ganglia.

Ganglia provides the following advantages:

1. It provides near-real-time monitoring for all the vital information of a very large cluster.
2. It runs on commodity hardware and can be suited for most of the popular OS.
3. Its open sourced and relatively easy to install.
4. It integrates easily with traditional monitoring systems
5. It provides an overall view of all nodes in a grid and all nodes in the cluster.
6. The monitored data is available in both textual and graphic format.
7. Works on multicast listen/announce protocol.
8. Works with open standards.
   - JSON
   - XML
   - XDR
   - RRDTool
   - APR – Apache portable runtime
   - Apache HTTPD server
   - PHP-based web interface

HBase works with only 3.0.X and higher version of Ganglia, hence we used 3.0.7 version.

In step 4, we installed the dependencies of libraries, which will be required for the ganglia to compile.

In step 5, we compiled ganglia and installed it by running the configure command, then we used make and then make install command.

In step 6, we created a file gmond.conf, and later on in step 7, we changed the setting to point to HBase master node. We also configured the port to `8649` with a user ganglia who can read from the cluster. By commenting the multicast address and the TTL (time to live), we also changed the UDP-based multicasting to which is a default one to unicasting, which enables us to expand the cluster to above 120 nodes. We also added a master Gmond node in this config file.

In step 8 we started the gmond and got some core monitoring such as CPU, disk, network, memory, and load average of the nodes.

In step 9, we went back to the `/u/HBase B/ganglia-3.0.7/` and reran the configuration, but this time, we added configure `-with-gmetad`, so that it complies with gmetad.

In step 11, we copied the `gmetad.conf` from.

`sudo /u/HBase B/gangli-3.0.7/gmetad/gmetad.conf  to /etc/gmetad.conf.`

In step 12, we added ganglia user and Master details in the `data_source HBase B HBase bMaster.ganglia-monitor.com`.

In step 13/14, we create the `rrds` directory that will hold the data in round-robin databases; later on, we stated the gmetad daemon on the master nodes.

In step 15, we installed all the dependency, which is required to run the web interface.

In step 16, we copied the web .php file from the existing location.

> ▸ (/u/HBase B/`ganglia-3.0.7/web`) to ( `/var/www/ganglia`)

In step 17, we restarted the apache instance and saw all the basic graphs, which provides the details of the nodes and the host but not HBase details. We also copied it to all the nodes so that we have a similar configuration and the Ganglia master is getting the data from the child nodes.

In step 18, we changed the setting in `hadoop-metrics2-HBase .properties` so that it starts collecting the metrics and starts sending it to the ganglia servers on port `8649`. The main class that is responsible for providing these details is `org.apache.hadoop. metrics2.sink.FileSink` and it properties.

Now we point at the URL of master, and once the page is rendered, it starts showing the graphs as described by the image `HBase -Ganglia-MasterAndRegion01-01.png`. It starts showing the following graphs:

- ▸ Memory and CPU usage
- ▸ JVM details (GC cycle, memory consumed by JVM, threads used, heap consumed, and so on)
- ▸ HBase Master details
- ▸ HBase Region compaction queue details
- ▸ Region server flush queue utilizations
- ▸ Region servers IO

## There is more...

Ganglia is used for monitoring very large cluster, and in the word of Hadoop/HBase , it can be very useful as it provides the following:

- ▸ JVM
- ▸ HDFS
- ▸ Map reduce
- ▸ Region compaction time
- ▸ Region store files
- ▸ Region block cache hit ratio
- ▸ Master spilt size
- ▸ Master split number of operations
- ▸ Region block free
- ▸ Name Node activities
- ▸ Secondary name node details
- ▸ Disk status

## See also

You could refer to the following sites for more information:

- ▸ `http://ganglia.wikimedia.org/latest/?r=4hr&cs=&ce=&tab=v&vn=hadoop&hide-hf=false&hreg%5B%5D=.`
- ▸ `http://ganglia.info/.`

# 2
# Loading Data from Various DBs

In this chapter, we will cover the following:

- ▸ Extracting data from Oracle
- ▸ Loading data using Oracle Big Data Connector
- ▸ Bulk utilities
- ▸ Using Hive and Apache Flume Streaming Data in Apache HBase
- ▸ Using Sqoop

This will allow the actor to import data from different RDBMS/flat files.

## Introduction

As we know, HBase is very effective in enabling real-time platforms to access read/write data randomly from the disk with commodity hardware, and there are many ways to do that, such as the following:

- ▸ Put APIs
- ▸ BulkLoad Tool
- ▸ MapReduce jobs

**Put APIs** are the most straightforward way to place data into the HBase system, but they are only good for small sets of data and can be used for site-facing applications or for more real-time scenarios/use cases.

**BulkLoad Tool** runs the MapReduce job behind the scenes and loads data into HBase tables. These tools internally generate the HBase internal file format (HFile), which allows us to import the data into a live HBase cluster.

> In case of huge data or a very high write-intensive job, it's advisable to use the ImportTsv tool. Using MapReduce jobs in conjunction with HFileOutputFormat is acceptable; but as the data grows, it loses its performance, scalability, and maintainability, which are necessary for any software to be successful. To circumvent this, we will go with the HBase BulkLoad Tool, which allows the data to be inserted much faster and with ease by providing good performance, scalability, and maintainability. This is achieved by avoiding the write path.

Essentially, there is no trace in the **write-ahead log** (WAL) files. It is similar to the edit that uses `Put.setWriteToWAL`(true). BulkLoad uses less CPU as compared to **Put**. It is also very important to know when to consider bulk loading and when to use conventional methods such as HBase normal `PUT` APIs and MapReduce. ImportTsv (Tsv stands for tab-separated values) is also used to upload data to HBase in the following cases:

- If we are bypassing the write-ahead logs on a regular basis, then GC tuning is required on a regular basis
- MemStore tuning is required frequently
- Performa of write is not up to the mark
- Compaction and flush queries are in the hundreds

# Extracting data from Oracle

HBase doesn't allow direct interaction or a pipeline for data import from Oracle and MySQL to HBase. The basic concept remains the same: to first extract the data into flat / text files (ImportTsv format), transform the data into HFiles, and then load them into HBase by telling the region server where to find them.

## Getting ready

Let's start with getting public data from the following URL:

`http://databank.worldbank.org/data/download/WDI_csv.zip`

This will have the following files:

- `WDI_Data.csv`
- `WDI_Country.csv` (this is the file we will use)
- `WDI_Series.csv`

- ▸ `WDI_CS_Notes.csv`
- ▸ `WDI_ST_Notes.csv`
- ▸ `WDI_Footnotes.csv`
- ▸ `WDI_Description.csv`

We will be using this as data and nothing else; this is freely available on the aforementioned World Bank site.

We will then create a table in Oracle Schema on your SQL prompt:

The names of the column used have an exact match with `WDI_Country.csv`:

```
CREATE TABLE WDI_COUNTRY

(
"COUNTRY_CODE" VARCHAR2(100 BYTE),

"SHORT_NAME" VARCHAR2(100 BYTE),

"TABLE_NAME" VARCHAR2(100 BYTE),

"LONG_NAME" VARCHAR2(500 BYTE),

"ALPHA_CODE" VARCHAR2(2 BYTE),

"CURRENCY_UNIT" VARCHAR2(100 BYTE),

"SPECIAL_NOTES" VARCHAR2(2000 BYTE),

"REGION" VARCHAR2(100 BYTE),

"INCOME_GROUP" VARCHAR2(100 BYTE),

"INTERNATIONAL_MEMBERSHIPS" VARCHAR2(100 BYTE),

"WB_2_CODE" VARCHAR2(2 BYTE),

"NATIONAL_ACCOUNTS_BASE_YEAR" VARCHAR2(100 BYTE),

"NATIONAL_ACCOUNTS_REF_YEAR" VARCHAR2(100 BYTE),

"SNA_PRICE_VALUATION" VARCHAR2(100 BYTE),
```

```
    "LENDING_CATEGORY" VARCHAR2(10 BYTE),

    "OTHER_GROUPS" VARCHAR2(10 BYTE),

    "SYSTEM_OF_NATIONAL_ACCOUNTS" VARCHAR2(500 BYTE),

    "ALTERNATIVE_CONVERSION_FACTOR" VARCHAR2(100 BYTE),

    "PPP_SURVEY_YEAR_BALANCE" VARCHAR2(20 BYTE),

    "EXTERNAL_DEBT_REPORT_STATUS" VARCHAR2(100 BYTE),

    "SYSTEM_OF_TRADE" VARCHAR2(100 BYTE),

    "GOVERNMENT_ACCT_CONCEPT" VARCHAR2(100 BYTE),

    "IMF_DATA_DISSEMINATION_STD" VARCHAR2(100 BYTE),

    "LATEST_POPULATION_CENSUS" VARCHAR2(1000 BYTE),

    "LATEST_HOUSEHOLD_SURVEY" VARCHAR2(1000 BYTE),

    "SOURCE_OF_MOST_RECENT_INCOME" VARCHAR2(100 BYTE),

    "VITAL_REGISTRATION_COMPLETE" VARCHAR2(10 BYTE),

    "LATEST_AGRICULTURAL_CENSUS" VARCHAR2(20 BYTE),

    "LATEST_INDUSTRIAL_DATA" VARCHAR2(20 BYTE),

    "LATEST_TRADE_DATA" VARCHAR2(20 BYTE),

    "LATEST_WATER_WITHDRAWAL_DATA" VARCHAR2(20 BYTE)

    )
```

Check the limits of columns and other Oracle limitations.

For simplicity, we are using `varchar2()` as a standard. In a live environment, it needs to be changed accordingly.

Now, we insert the data into the preceding table using the following Java code.

The list of JAR files needed to execute the code is as follows:

`Opencsv-2.0.jar` at location:

http://www.java2s.com/Code/JarDownload/opencsv/opencsv-2.3.jar.zip

`Ojdbc6.jar` at location:

http://download.oracle.com/otn/utilities_drivers/jdbc/11204/ojdbc6.jar

For the oracle driver, you may have to create an Oracle user account; if you have it already, you can use that and download it.

You have to add these jars into your eclipse classpath as shown, in the following image or Linux classpath if you are using the console:

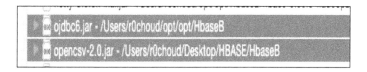

The following is the code to achieve the previously described results:

```java
import java.io.FileReader;
import java.sql.Connection;
import java.sql.DriverManager;
import java.sql.PreparedStatement;
import java.sql.SQLException;

import au.com.bytecode.opencsv.CSVReader;
// importing the class which will be used to read the CSV file

public class HbaseCSVtoOracle {

  public HbaseCSVtoOracle() {
    // TODO Auto-generated constructor stub
  }

  /**
   * @author r0choud
   * @param args
   */
  public static void main(String[] args) {
    Connection conn = null;
```

```
    PreparedStatement sql_statement = null; // Initializing
    try{
    final String inputCSVFile = "/u/HbaseB/WDI_Country.csv"; //getting
the CSV file from the location we have saved.
    Class.forName ("oracle.jdbc.OracleDriver"); // Creating a
connection Object
    conn=DriverManager.getConnection("jdbc:oracle:thin:@//myoracle.
db.com:1521/xe", "scott", "tiger");
    /*
     * using s oracle thin driver connecting to the host "your host"
     * using the port as 1512
     * user scott -> please change accordingly
     * pasword tiget --> please change accordingly
     */

    /* Create the insert statement which will insert the data to the
above created table by
     * getting the data from the CSV file
     * this can be f
     * */
    String jdbc_insert_sql = "INSERT INTO WDI_COUNTRY" +"( "
                    + "(COUNTRY_CODE,SHORT,TABLE_NAME,ALPHA_
CODE,CURRENCY_UNIT,SPECIAL_NOTES,REGION,)"
                    + "(INCOME_GROUP,INTERNATIONAL_MEMBERSHIPS,WB_2_
CODE,NATIONAL_ACCOUNTS_BASE_YEAR,)"
                    + "(NATIONAL_ACCOUNTS_REF_YEAR,SNA_PRICE_
VALUATION,LENDING_CATEGORY,OTHER_GROUPS,)"
                    + "(SYSTEM_OF_NATIONAL_ACCOUNTS,ALTERNATIVE_
CONVERSION_FACTOR,PPP_SURVEY_YEAR_BALANCE,)"
                    + "(EXTERNAL_DEBT_REPORT_STATUS,SYSTEM_OF_
TRADE,GOVERNMENT_ACCT_CONCEPT,IMF_DATA_DISSEMINATION_STD,)"
                    + "(LATEST_POPULATION_CENSUS,LATEST_HOUSEHOLD_
SURVEY,SOURCE_OF_MOST_RECENT_INCOME,VITAL_REGISTRATION_COMPLETE,)"
                    + "(LATEST_AGRICULTURAL_CENSUS,LATEST_INDUSTRIAL_
DATA.LATEST_TRADE_DATA,LATEST_WATER_WITHDRAWAL_DATA,)"+")"
                    + "VALUES"
                    + "(?,?,?,?,?,?,?,?,?,?,?,?,?,?,?,?,?,?,?,?,?,?,?,
?,?,?,?,?,?,?,?)";
    sql_statement = conn.prepareStatement(jdbc_insert_sql);
    /* Read CSV file in OpenCSV */
    @SuppressWarnings("resource")
    CSVReader reader = new CSVReader(new FileReader(inputCSVFile));
    /* Variables to loop through the CSV File */
    String [] nextLine; /* for every line in the file */
    @SuppressWarnings("unused")
```

```
    int lnNum = 0; /* line number */
    while ((nextLine = reader.readNext()) != null) {
            lnNum++;
            /* Bind CSV file input to table columns */
            sql_statement.setString(1, nextLine[0]);
            /* Bind Age as double */
            /* Need to convert string to double here */
            sql_statement.setDouble(2,Double.
parseDouble(nextLine[1]));
            /* execute the insert statement */
            sql_statement.executeUpdate();
    }

    }catch(Exception e)
    {
      e.printStackTrace();
    }finally
    {
      /* Close prepared statement */
      try {
        sql_statement.close();
      } catch (SQLException e) {
        // TODO Auto-generated catch block
        e.printStackTrace();
      }
      /* COMMIT transaction */
      try {
        conn.commit();
      } catch (SQLException e) {
        // TODO Auto-generated catch block
        e.printStackTrace();
      }
      /* Close connection */
      try {
        conn.close();
      } catch (SQLException e) {
        // TODO Auto-generated catch block
        e.printStackTrace();
      }
    }

  }

  }
```

Using the export utility of SQLPlus, you can export the data from the table to a flat file; `HBase_WDI_Country.csv`.

Now we have to convert this file to `HBase_Country_TSV.tsv` using a simple `sed` command:

```
cd /u/HbaseB
 sed 's/,/\t/' WDI_Country.csv > WDI_Country.tsv
```

This also can be used to convert the existing file to tab-separated.

We are assuming that the MapReduce server is already running because the aforementioned process will invoke the MapReduce process.

At this point, we have all that is needed to place this data (`/u/HbaseB/WDI_Country.tsv`) to load it on to the HBase cluster.

## How to do it...

We need to perform the following steps to load the TSV file to HBase using MapReduce:

1.  Create a directory on HDFS. This will be the directory we will use for all our purposes:

    ```
    Hadoop@client01$ $HADOOP_HOME/bin/Hadoop fs -mkdir /user/hbaseb/input
    ```

2.  Let's copy the file to the TSV file in this location:

    ```
    hadoop@client01$ $HADOOP_HOME/bin/Hadoop fs -copyFromLocal  /u/HbaseB/WDI_Country.tsv  /hbaseb/input
    ```

3.  Now we create a table, which we will use for all our purposes:

    ```
    hadoop@client01$ $HBASE_HOME/bin/hbase shell
    ```

    This will prompt you to the HBase shell:

    ```
    Hbase> create 'my_country', {NAME =>'t', VERSION =>5}
    ```

We are assuming that there is no table with this name in HBase.

VERSION 5 essentially means five versions of the data will be stored at a cell level for a column family. If we don't specify, it is set to zero, which disables the feature.

If you are using HBase 0.98.2 and onward, you can specify a global max version for all newly created columns by setting it in `hbase-site.xml`.

In case you are using HBase 0.98.2, this setting can be applied globally by setting it up on `hbase-site.xml`, and it can be propagated to the entire cluster:

1. Now we have to add `hbase-site.xml` to the Hadoop classpath. This will allow communication between the Hadoop system and HBase:

   **`Hadoop@client01$ cp $HBASE_HOME/conf/hbase-site.xml  $HADOOP_HOME/`**
   **`etc/hadoop`**

2. Adding the HBase-related jar to the Hadoop classpath can be done by opening the `hadoop-env.sh` file in a vi editor of any text editor, which is located at `$HADOOP_HOME/etc/hadoop`. Edit this file, and add the following lines:

   **`Export  HADOOP_CLASSPATH=/HbaseB/hbase-0.98.5-hadoop2/lib/`**
   **`zookeeper-3.4.6.jar:HbaseB/hbase-0.98.5-hadoop2/lib/guava-`**
   **`12.0.1.jar`**

3. Run the `importtsv` tool by running the following command:

   **`hadoop@client01$ $HADOOP_HOME/bin/hadoop jar  $HBASE_HOME/ hbase-`**
   **`server-0.98.5-hadoop2.jar import \`**

   **`-Dimporttsv.columns=Hbase_ROW_KEY, t:COUNTRY_CODE,t:SHORT_NAME….`**

   **`t:LATEST_WATER_WITHDRAWAL_DATA \ my_country'\ /Hbaseb /input`**

   The input format is as follows:

   **`importtsv -Dimporttsv.columns=a,b,c <yourtablename>`**
   **`<yourinputdir>`**

The options that may be specified with -D, include the following:

- ▸  `-Dimporttsv.skip.bad.lines=false`: fail if encountering an invalid line
- ▸  `- Dimporttsv.separator=|'`: Separate on pipes instead of tabs-1
- ▸  `- Dimporttsv.timestamp=currentTimeAsLong`: Use the specified timestamp for the import
- ▸  `---Dimporttsv.mapper.class=my.Mapper`: A user-defined Mapper to use instead of `org.apache.hadoop.hbase.mapreduce.TsvImporterMapper`.

If you are planning for a large amount of data that needs to be loaded using the Bulk Loader tool, it's advisable to target the HBase table to pre-split:

1. You can alternatively check the status of this MapReduce process via the MapReduce admin page:

   **`http://masterserver:50030/jobtracker.jsp`**

2. Verify the data that is imported in the target table of HBase by the following command:

```
hbase(main):008:0> scan 'my_country' ,{COLUMNS=>'t:', LIMIT=>10}
row01 column=t:COUNTRY_CODE, timestamp=1409453734860, value=AFG
 row02
column=t:COUNTRY_CODE, timestamp=1409453755971, value=
 row03
column=t:COUNTRY_CODE, timestamp=1409453771036, value=DZA
 row05
column=t:COUNTRY_CODE, timestamp=1409454028718, value=ASM
 row06
column=t:COUNTRY_CODE, timestamp=1409454088675, value=ADO
 row07
column=t:COUNTRY_CODE, timestamp=1409454128366, value=AGO
 row08
column=t:COUNTRY_CODE, timestamp=1409454142524, value=ATG
 row09
column=t:COUNTRY_CODE, timestamp=1409454162831, value=ARB
 row10
column=t:COUNTRY_CODE, timestamp=1409454196520, value=ARG
10 row(s) in 0.0820 seconds
```

## How it works...

In the preceding section, we discussed bulk loading of Oracle data, which is a day-to-day requirement of any **Extract transform Load** (**ETL**) system that uses HBase.

We perform the following steps to do that:

1. Create a temp table in Oracle. By creating a temp table, we are sure that it will be cleaned up/truncated on a daily basis; you can also truncate it manually (using a script) before starting the process.

2. We load the country data to this table. This makes sure the input is streamlined and there are no space characters or binary characters.

3. Then we use the Java code to transform it into the tab-separated format; this step is to prepare the file for the mapreduce2 job.

4. We load the file to HDFS using the command line. This can be incorporated in a shell script to make this process simple and more relevant for day-to-day use.

5. We check by running the scan command and looking at the records in the table.

## There's more...

We can see more details on the effective bulk load process at `http://hbase.apache.org/book/arch.bulk.load.html`

The Data load process depends on the precise design of table schema in HBase; then creating tables, then designing pre-splits , the split points have to be in tandem with the row-key distribution and the number of region servers in the cluster. There can be scenarios where the data can be loaded incrementally; thus, loading it via a batch process makes more sense than going through the entire write path of HBase, which will be intensive and slow.

## See also...

For details on the write path and how the bulk process avoids it to directly reach HDFS and provide scale, refer to Working with large distributed Database sytems.

# Loading data using Oracle Big data connector

If there is a very large volume of data in the system, it is vital to have an extremely efficient data-processing engine between various touch points. Oracle Big Data connector is calibrated to do the following activities. We will only touch upon the loading part of it:

- Connector for HDFS
- Loader for Hadoop
- Data Integrator Adaptor for Hadoop
- R Advanced Analytics for Hadoop
- XQuery for Hadoop

## Getting Ready

Download Oracle connector from the following:

1. Loading data using the Oracle Big data connector:

   `http://www.oracle.com/technetwork/database/database-technologies/bdc/big-data-connectors/downloads/index.html`

2. Download for Linux x86-64
3. Download Cloudera's Distribution (CDH3 or CDH4)

4.  JDK1.6.08 or later

5.  Hive 0.7.0, 0.8.1, or 0.9.0

6.  Oracle DB release 11.2.0.2 or 11.2.0.3, the same version of CDH3,CDH4

## How to do it...

1.  Configure CDH or Apache Hadoop as shown in the preceding section.

 Don't change anything in the HBase setup. Indicate clearly that jars are in HBASE_HOME.

2.  Ensure that the Oracle database has access to HDFS.

SSH to the system where Oracle DB is running.

Open the Hadoop shell and type the following command:

```
Hadoop fs -ls /user
```

You will see the same list of directories that you see in the hadoop fs command in Hadoop cluster NameNode.

Download the ZIP file to the same **directory** that has Oracle Database running.

Unzip it using the following command:

**unzip oraosch-3.1.0.zip:**

bin/hdfs_stream Indicate clearly that jars are in HBASE_HOME:

```
doc/README.txt
examples/sql/mkhive_unionall_view.sql
jlib/ ojdbc6.jar
      ora-hadoop-common.jar
      oraclepki.jar
      orahdfs.jar
      osdt_cert.jar
      osdt_core.jar
```

log/    : It wont have anything as we have not processed any logs until now.

This is a script that has the setting related to PATH.

Point to the right path as per the first chapter:

`/usr/bin` is already in the PATH

```
export PATH=$HADOOP_HOME/bin

# The Java implementation to use. This is required only if JAVA_HOME is
defined as a shell environment variable for running Hadoop.
# set JAVA_HOME to same value used to configure Hadoop
export JAVA_HOME=$JAVA_HOME àAVA_HOME E AVA_HOME  _HOMVM which is in the
classpath.
# Set the OSCH_LOG_DIR to the absolute path of the log directory
# This directory contains the error logging for the pre-processor.
# OSCH_LOG_DIR defaults to ${OSCH_HOME}/log
# Change only if you need a non-default value


OSCH_LOG_DIR=$HADOOP_HOME/logs àlogs _HOME/logs s P_HOME/logs -default
value pre-proc
```

Before running `hdfs_stream`, we need to see the execute permission:

```
Hadoop@client01$ Hadoop@client01$chmod 755 OSCH_HOME/bin/hdfs_stream.
```

This will ensure that a Hadoop user has proper permissions to do their job.

Now we can log in to the Oracle database and create a database directory of `orahdfs-3.1.0/bin`, where `hdfs_stream` resides:

```
SQL >  CREATE OR REPLACE DIRECTORIES osch_bin_path AS '/opt/Hbaseb/
orahdfs-3.1.0/bin'
```

## How it works...

The Oracle connector for HDFS enables the oracle database to access files on HDFS using external tables. External tables allow the data to be queried, which can be on HDFS.

These files can be flat/text files or in the Oracle Data Pump format. This data can be joined with other tables in the database; these files can be read directly by this connector.

At first, the connector executes publish steps.

Generate files that point to URI of the data files on HDFS. After this step, you can query the data in a parallel way.

## There's more...

Oracle Big data connector provides an array of technology options, which can be used on a batch-oriented format or in real time:

- Transform input data

- Loading unstructured data

- Parallel querying and loading

- Flexible and easy use

- Automatic even distribution of load across reducer tasks

- Data can be in HDFS and still queried using SQL in the DB without loading it

- Input data is restricted to text files; other types of data need to be transformed first to the Oracle Data Pump files

## See also...

This tool provides a connector that enables us to load unstructured date to oracle. This is optimized to import very large volumes of data in an optimized way. This connector can be used for various use cases such bulk uploading, loading of unstructured data, and so on.

More data can be found at the following location:

`http://www.oracle.com/technetwork/bdc/hadoop-loader/connectors-hdfs-wp-1674035.pdf`

`http://download.oracle.com/otndocs/products/bdc/hadoop-loader/pdf/oow2013hadoop_bdc.pdf`

# Bulk utilities

The process for loading data using Bulk utilities is very similar:

1. Extracting data from the source.
2. Transforming the data into HFiles.
3. Loading the files into HBase by guiding the region servers as to where to find them.

## Getting ready...

The following points have to be remembered when using Bulk utilities:

▸ HBase/Hadoop cluster with MapReduce/Yarn should be running. You can run jps to check it.

▸ Access rights (user/group) are needed to execute the program.

▸ Table schema needs to be designed to the input structure.

▸ Split points need to be taken into consideration.

▸ The entire stack (compaction, split, block size, max file size, flush size, version compression, mem store size, block cache, garbage collections nproc, and so on) needs to be fine-tuned to make the best of it.

The WAL are not written; thus, data lost during the failure may not be recovered as there is no replication performed by reading the WAL.

## How to do it...

There are multiple ways to do this work, such as writing your own Map reducecII. We will be using the TSV bulk loaded for our use cases.

In the following scenario, we will use a build in the `Tsv` Bulk Loader to do this activity, which is shipped by HBase, called NBA Final 2010 game 1 tip-off time (seconds from epoch). We can download it from the following location:

```
https://dl.dropboxusercontent.com/u/3182023/HBase-BulkLoading/
RowFeeder.csv.zip
```

Extract the ZIP file in the location, say /Hbaseb/input, and unzip it. Open Eclipse and create a Java project (say myHbaseb) and follow the steps listed next:

1. Create a **MyBulkStarter** class

   I have not added import statements. Add it according to the verbose nature of the code.

2. Then we have to create a KeyVaule mapper class. This will essentially map the data into the key-value format, which is an ideal state for bulk processing on an offline system. The name of the class will be **HbaseKeyValueMapper.** This class parses the text messages from the files and outputs if ImmutableByteWritableKey, keyvalue.

   Then this immutable key is used by the TotalOrderPartitioner to map it to the correct HBase region. The key value is the place holder for HBase mutation information.

3. Now let's create another Java class, say `HColumMappingWithText.java`. This class contains the exact mapping of the data structure, which is there in the table in relation to the CSV file.

These Java classes will allow us to convert the input data to the HFile format, which will enable us to read it from the core bulk loading utilities.

The two libraries, `joda-time-2.2.jar` and `opencsv-2.3.jar`, need to be there in the class path as shown in the following image:

```
commons-lang-2.6.jar
commons-configuration-1.6.jar
commons-httpclient-3.1.jar
commons-logging-1.1.1.jar
guava-12.0.1.jar
hadoop-core-1.0.4.jar
hbase-0.94.5.jar
jackson-core-asl-1.8.8.jar
jackson-mapper-asl-1.8.8.jar
log4j-1.2.17.jar
protobuf-java-2.5.0.jar
slf4j-api-1.6.4.jar
slf4j-log4j12-1.6.4.jar
zookeeper-3.4.6.jar
```

▸ Check all the Java files and their compilation errors and export the project as a JAR file, say `myFirst01Bulk.jar`. Once this is done, the `myFirst01Builk.jar` file is created.

▸ Let's make an input directory in HDFS using the following command:

**hadoop@client01$ $HADOOP_HOME/bin/hadoop fs –mkdir myinput/**

**hadoop@client01$ $HADOOP_HOME/bin/hadoop fs –put/Hbaseb/ bulkload/01feed.csv**

▸ In the HBase shell, please create the table `'myFirst01',{NAME=>'mysrv'}, {SPLITS =>['0000','0100','0.200','2100','3600']}`

The five split points will generate five regions; the first row starts with an empty row key. You need to do an analysis to see how the data is distributed. At this point, if you point it to `http://yourHMasterIP:60010/master-status`, you will see a newly created table and its five regions all assigned to regionServer.

Disable 'myFirst01'.

 Before altering a table, it's must to disable table.

▸ Alter 'myFirst01',{METHOD => 'myTable_att', MAX_FILESIZE => '1342177280'}

▸ Enable 'myFirst01'

- ► Lets go to hadoop@client01$ $HADOOP_HOME/bin/hadoop jar /opt/Hbaseb/HBase-BulkImport.jar com.hbaseb.myproject.bulkimport input/ output myFirst01Output/. This runs the MapReduce jobs to generate the HFile.

  The preceding command will create an HFile in Hadoop/Hdfs.

- ► Run the count command on 'myFirst01' in HBase to verify the table data. You can limit the returned rows so that the process is faster in terms of time for response.

## How it works...

- ► When you load the data, it generates HBase data files commonly known as `StoreFiles`. This is internally happening by using a MapReduce process by invoking `HFileOutputFormat`.

- ► This output format writes out data in the HBase internal storage format, which enables the system to effectively load into the cluster by completebulkload.

- ► The `completebulkload` command-line tool is designed to iterate though the prepared files and associate them to a region by invoking region servers, which take the HFile.

- ► The `Completbulkload` tool takes the out path where ImportTsv or a MapReduce job puts its results and the table name to import into. In other words, it imports the data into the running cluster.

- ► Once the data is loaded into the cluster, it can be seen by a scan query on the HBase shell.

## See also...

The write path of HBase is as follows:

The client invokes a PUT or delete to the region server; it can be cached programmatically and can flush in batches.

Changes are written to write-ahead logs, which gives robustness and reliability. In case of system failure, the date updated date is written to WAL before being written to the Memstore.

Data is stored to the Memstore, which is optimized for random writes.

Data is continuously pushed into the Memstore. When it accumulates enough data, the entire stored data in the Memstore is written as a new HFile in HDFS.

For the details and path of execution, please see the following diagram:

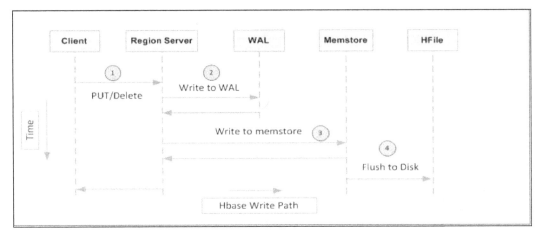

Case 02: The write path of HBase in case of Bulk Load

As per bulkload, it's a three-step process:

1. The first step is to get/create/grab the data into a flat file format.

2. The next step is to transform data into a key-value by mapping the input file and reducing it by using `HFileOutoutFormat.configureIncremantalLoad()`. At this stage, the split of the input file will be done based on the number of regions allocated or configured. The data after the map reduce process will be restructured.

3. The final stage is to `LoadIncrementalHFiles` as detailed in the transformation section of step 3 as follows. Once this process is over, the region server loads the HFiles to the respective regions:

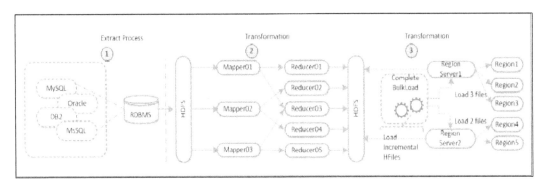

# Using Hive with Apache HBase

Hive is an ETL engine for HBase/Hadoop. It has an SQL-like query language, popularly known as Hive QA for SELECT(read) and INSERT(write). The main objective is to do ad hoc analysis on Petabyte-level data. Hive integration was originally introduced in HIVE-705.

## Getting ready

▸ HBase and Hadoop cluster should be up and running.

Download Hive from `https://archive.apache.org/dist/hive/hive-0.12.0/hive-0.12.0.tar.gz`, or you can use this command:

`wget -o, https://archive.apache.org/dist/hive/hive-0.12.0/hive-0.12.0.tar.gz`

This is if you are using the Linux command line.

▸ Untar it into the location, say `/u/HbaseB`

▸ Hive uses an integration interface as HbaseStorageHandler, which enables Hive to talk to HBase (Hive projects need these optional JAR files to interact with HBase). Extensive discussions are beyond the current scope of this book. For more information, take a look at the see also section.

## How to do it...

The first step is to use HbaseStorageHandler to register the HBase table with the Hive metastore. Edit the `bashrc` using `~/.bashrc` and add the following line:

```
Export  HIVE_SRC=/u/HbaseB/hive-0.12.0/src
```

```
We are targeting this in a cluster mode hence
```

```
$HIVE_SRC/bin/hive --auxpath /u/HbaseB/hive-0.12.0/lib/hive-hbase-
handler-0.12.0.jar,/u/HbaseB/hive-0.12.0/lib/hbase-0.94.6.1.jar,$HIVE_
SRC/u/HbaseB/hive-0.12.0/lib/zookeeper-3.4.3.jar, /u/HbaseB/hive-
0.12.0/lib/guava-11.0.2.jar --hiveconf hbase.zookeeper.quorum=
yourzooKeeperserver.1, yourzooKeeperserver.2
```

Now on the Hive shell, execute the following command:

```
CREATE TABLE myTable01(rowkey int,  a01 String, b01 String)
SORTED BY 'org.aoache.hadoop.hive.hbase.HBasetorageHandler'
WITH SERDPROPERTIES("hbase.columns.mapping"=":key,f:c01,f:c02")
TBLPROPERTIES ("hbase.table.name" = "HiveTestTable",
"hbase.mapred.output.outputtable" = " HiveTestTable ");
```

Note

myTable01 → is within Hive
        HiveTestTable → is in Hbase which will get the inputs from
the mapreduce job and the output will be stored in HiveTestTable as
shown above.

In case of an error, do make sure that the following JAR files are added in the Hive classpath:

```
Export $HIVE_HOME/lib/hbase-0.94.6.1.jar;
Export $HIVE_HOME/lib/hive-hbase-handler-0.12.0.jar;
Export $HIVE_HOME/lib/guava-11.0.2.jar;
Export $HIVE_HOME/lib/zookeeper-3.4.3.jar;
```

You can insert data into this table with the following command:

**INSERT OVERWRITE TABLE  myTable01 SELECT  \* FROM myTable02 WHERE  b01
=200 OR b01=300;**

Now, you can simply write a SELECT statement to get the data in the SQL format:

**SELECT \* FROM  myTable01 on the Hive shell.**

Multiple columns and families:

```
CREATE TABLE myTable03(key int, value1 string, value2 int, value3 int)
STORED BY 'org.apache.hadoop.hive.hbase.HBaseStorageHandler'
WITH SERDEPROPERTIES ("hbase.columns.mapping" = ":key,p:q,p:r,s:t");
INSERT OVERWRITE TABLE myTable01 SELECT my, test01, my+1, my+2 FROM myTable02 WHERE b01=200 or b01=300.
```

## How it works...

When we invoke HbaseStorageHandler, it registers the HBase table in the Hive metastore.

This internally invokes HiveHBaseTableInputFormat and HiveBaseTableOutputFormat.

While registering, we have to specify the column mapping, which interns links/maps between Hive column names to the Hbase row key to column families or columns. This mapping is possible via the hbase.columns.mapping class SerDe properties.

Once the column mapping is defined, we can access the data using the Hive shell.

In addition to the aforementioned, you can also populate data using Hive.

## See also...

```
https://cwiki.apache.org/confluence/display/Hive/HBaseIntegration#HBa
seIntegration-ColumnMapping
```

Internals of the Hive, HBase interaction.

# Using Sqoop

Sqoop provides an excellent way to import data in parallel from existing RDBMs to HDFS. We get an exact set of table structures that are imported. This happens because of parallel processing. These files can have text delimited by ',' '|', and so on. After manipulating imported records by using MapReduce or Hive, the output result set can be exported back to RDBMS. The data imported can be done in real time or in the batch process (using a cron job).

## Getting ready

Prerequisites:

HBase and Hadoop cluster must be up and running.

You can do a wget to `http://mirrors.gigenet.com/apache/sqoop/1.4.6/sqoop-1.4.6.tar.gz`

Untar it to `/u/HbaseB` using `tar -zxvf sqoop-1.4.6.tar.gz`

It will create a **/u/HbaseB/sqoop-1.4.6** folder.

A Sqoop user is created in the target DB, which has read/write access and is not bound strictly with CPU and memory (RAM, Storage) limitation by the DBAs.

## How to do it...

1. Log in to MySQL by executing the following command:

```
Mysql -h yourMySqlHostName -u scoop -p
mysql> create database mySqoop
mysql> use myScoop;
mysql> CREATE TABLE customer (firstname VARCHAR(200), lastname
VARCHAR(200),emailid VARCHAR(200), sex CHAR(1), birth DATE, active
DATE, customerlogin DATE);
mysql> describe customer;
```

```
mysql> describe customer;
+---------------+--------------+------+-----+---------+-------+
| Field         | Type         | Null | Key | Default | Extra |
+---------------+--------------+------+-----+---------+-------+
| firstname     | varchar(200) | YES  |     | NULL    |       |
| lastname      | varchar(200) | YES  |     | NULL    |       |
| emailid       | varchar(200) | YES  |     | NULL    |       |
| sex           | char(1)      | YES  |     | NULL    |       |
| birth         | date         | YES  |     | NULL    |       |
| active        | date         | YES  |     | NULL    |       |
| customerlogin | date         | YES  |     | NULL    |       |
+---------------+--------------+------+-----+---------+-------+
7 rows in set (0.01 sec)
```

```
mysql> INSERT INTO customer VALUES ('JOHN','WAYNE','j@w.com',
'M','1922-03-30','1922-03-30','1922-03-30');
INSERT INTO customer VALUES ('CLEENT','EASTWOOD','C@E.com',
'M','1942-03-30','1942-03-30','1942-03-30');
INSERT INTO customer VALUES ('GEGRY','PECK','g@p.com',
'M','1932-03-30','1932-03-30','1932-03-30');
```

```
mysql> select * FROM customer;
+-----------+----------+----------+-----+------------+------------+---------------+
| firstname | lastname | emailid  | sex | birth      | active     | customerlogin |
+-----------+----------+----------+-----+------------+------------+---------------+
| JOHN      | WAYNE    | j@w.com  | M   | 1922-03-30 | 1922-03-30 | 1922-03-30    |
| CLEENT    | EASTWOOD | C@E.com  | M   | 1942-03-30 | 1942-03-30 | 1942-03-30    |
| GEGRY     | PECK     | g@p.com  | M   | 1932-03-30 | 1932-03-30 | 1932-03-30    |
+-----------+----------+----------+-----+------------+------------+---------------+
3 rows in set (0.00 sec)
```

From the Hive instance, we have to run the following command (we need to be in $SQOOP_HOME/bin):

```
hadoop@client01$ $SQOOP_HOME/bin
sqoop -help , to check if everything is working as expected
sqoop import --connect jdbc:mysql://yourMySqlServer/myScoop --table
customer \
    --columns "firstname,lastname,emailid,sex,
birth,active,customerlogin"
This will import the data from MySql for the specific  column from
table customer
sqoop import --connect jdbc:mysql://yourMySqlServer/myScoop --table
customer \
    --hive-import
this will import customer table data to hive
```

We can extend this to directly import the data to HBase.

Let's first create a table using the HBase shell:

```
hadoop@client01$ $HBASE_HOME/bin
./hbase shell -d( for debugging purpose)
```

Then run the following command:

```
sqoop import --hbase-create-table  --hbase-table customer --column-
family info --hbase-row-key emailid --connect jdbc:mysql://
yourMySqlServer/myScoop --table customer -m 1
Now lets check what we have inserted by running a simple scan command
from hbase shell.
hbase(main):002:0> scan customer
10001    column=firstname:firstname, timestamp=1376772776684, value=1
JOHN
 10002    column=lastname:lastname, timestamp=1376773256317, value=2
WAYNE
```

This setup can be done for any RDBMS supporting JDBC driver's specifications for extracting data to the HDFS format. You can even import the entire schema if all the tables within the schema have primary keys.

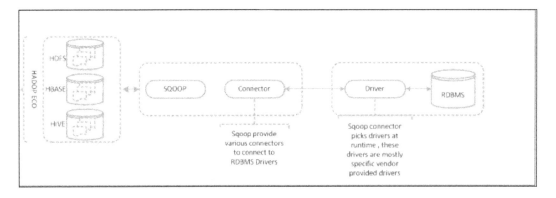

A basic level figure: chap02_hbase_loading_data_from_variousDBs_to_hbase

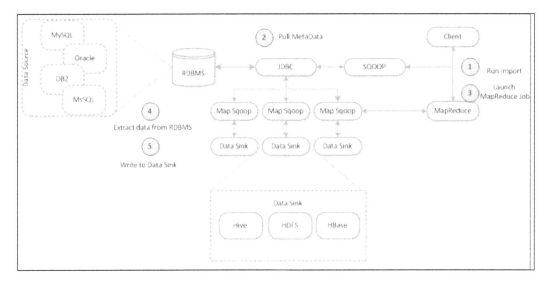

## How it works...

▶ Sqoop will check the URL provided in the command line to see which connector to load at runtime.

▶ When we invoke the command using the Sqoop engine, Sqoop tries to load the best available connectors, which can give the best possible performance.

- ▶ Once the connector is registered, Sqoop invokes the JDBC driver, which is there in the classpath.

- ▶ Internally, it calls the DBInputFormat class, which allows us to read data from the database. This InputFormat class is a Hadoop formalization of a data source; this class provides simple methods to scan entire tables from the database. DBInputFormat uses JDBC to connect to the data source.

- ▶ The setInput() method takes the name of a class that holds the results of on tuple. Internally, a DBWrirtetable adapter interface is called, which allows data to be read and written using the Hadoop serialization format.

- ▶ Once the data is read into, it reads the class fields in the mapper.

- ▶ A DBOutputFormat class allows us to write the data back to RDBMS.

## There's more...

Data compression and parallelism are two important aspects of fast execution.

### Data compression

In addition to the aforementioned, we can use compression while outputting the files. This will enable us to compress the file in various formats as follows:

| --compress | This will compress the file into the .gz format | Using GZip codec |
|---|---|---|
| -cmpress\--compression—codec<br><br>org.apache.hadoop.compress.BZip2Codec | BZip2 compression format is used | |

 Sqoop uses all Hadoop compression codecs that come out of the box, any compression algorithm that is not known to the Hadoop system will throw an exception or will be neglected.

### Parallelism

In case of bigger tables having a large amount of data, it's preferable to provide the number of mappers while executing the import statements, which allows the import process to use parallelism and help us do the job much quicker.

You can use **–num-mappers 11** ß 11 is the count of thread. Usually, it will provide the number of mappers that you have specified, but it is system dependent and not guaranteed. In case the data is small, Sqoop will reduce the number of mappers. For example, if you have only seven tuples/rows in the table, Sqoop will reduce it to seven; this is done to optimize the use of resources.

Importing all tables/Big Import

In some use cases, it's advisable to import all tables at once rather than doing it piece by piece, for example, in case of your pricing schema or your not production schema, where the data is limited for a particular use.

You can use **sqoop import-all-tables \ --connect** ....

In case of the import-all-tables tool, Sqoop does the following:

> ▸ Catalogs queries to retrieve a list of all the tables in your database
>
> ▸ Applies a sequential order, which reduces the stress on the system

You can also use **sqoop import-all-tables \ --connect** … **\exclude-tables, table_01,** and **table_02**.

The support of this tool is restricted, for example, you cannot use target-dir, as Sqoop will create all the tables in same directory, which is not advisable. Instead, you can use the warehouse-dir parameter; --exclude-tables are usually used to skip tables with special needs.

## See also...

http://sqoop.apache.org/docs/1.4.3/SqoopUserGuide.html

http://blog.cloudera.com/blog/2009/06/introducing-sqoop/

# 3

# Working with Large Distributed Systems Part I

In this chapter, we will cover:

- ▸ Large distributed HBase system
- ▸ How each component works independently
- ▸ The entire eco-system and how it fits together

This will allow the actor to walk through the entire technology stack and make informed decision.

## Introduction

With the fast adaptation of Hadoop/HBase ecosystem, various applications, both real-time and batch processing, are built on top of it. It's of utmost importance to plan the entire architecture to have built-in elasticity, regional datacenter adaptation, globally distributed redundancy, and multi-layered globally distributed architecture which ties in with hardware, software, network and growing demands of customers, as the business matures.

In the early years of Hadoop/HBase most of the use cases were driven by batch processing systems, but the trend is converging to make a single platform, which can equally scale if near real-time use cases are used against this eco-system.

It is essential to do a proper planning of the architecture before setting up a very large scale HBase system; this will allow the system to do the following:

- Scale elastically or Auto Scaling with built-in fault tolerance
- Works on different VM/physical and cloud hardware
- Gives near real-time throughput which can be consistently measured
- Its should be secure
- It should provide dependable consistence as per the needs
- It can handle heterogeneous clients
- Work on commodity hardware
- Allow concurrency in read/write
- Allows in-memory cache and off-heap memory management
- Maintainability across distributed regions

> We will touch a few important topics from the preceding list, as detailing each topic is beyond the scope of this book.

# Scaling elastically or Auto Scaling with built-in fault tolerance

Before we go into Auto Scaling we need to give a microscopic view of how HBase accomplishes auto-sharding and how the distributed components within HBase architecture work.

Let's first look at **Region**.

HBase Regions are a subgroup of table's data which is adjoining; these are in a sorted order of range of rows which sit together, and these regions are distributed across the clusters. Region never overlaps with other regions and the job of a single region server is to serve to expose Region details to the region client at any given point of time; this way HBase provides a guarantee a very strong consistency.

The region has many stores.

A stores hosts a MemStore and deals with the store files (commonly known as HFiles). MemStore is an In-Memory state of the data and takes care of the modifications of the key/value pairs. Due to the following reason (as following) when a flush process is initiated the data which is residing in MemStore is captured and written to the disk, which in turn creates a new store file.

MemStore is dependent of the value specified in `HBase .hregion.MemStore.flush.size`.

The use to the region server's MemStore is directly associated with the maximum number of region servers, as each region has its own MemStore. This is a configurable parameter and can be changed in `HBase -site.xml` file. Care needs to be taken in determining it, as a small portion of the memory will be allocated based on `HBase .regionserver.global.MemStore.size` property. In some cases if the usage exceeds this size, HBase may become unresponsive or it can lead to a compaction storm.

The best way to decide will be to use a formula:

*RS=Region Server Memory Size*

*MF=Memory Store Fraction*

*MS=Memory Store Size*

*NF=Number of Column Families*

*{RS x MF}/{MS x NF}*

Let us take an example:

Region server has 8 GB of RAM (8x1024 =8192)

Memstore fraction of 0.4

Memstore with 256 MB RAM

Column family in table is 1

*{8192MB X 0.4}/{256MB x 1}=12.8*, truncating it to next higher number=13 regions

Extra care needs to be taken in case an extensive write operation is performed; we can rather increase the MemStore fraction, but this increase has a negative impact on the block cache.

This can also happen when the global MemStore upper limit is reached for the `HBase .regionserver.global.memestore.uppeLimit` parameter. In this case it is pivotal to reduce the overall usage of MemStore in the Region Servers; to accommodate this the MemStore is flushed to the disk. This process of Flushing the MemStore will continue till the overall usage is following the specified threshold, limit(`HBase .regionserver.global.MemStore.lowerLimit`). The flush order is always the descending order of Region MemStore usage.

In some scenarios WAL count plays a role to trigger flush, when the count reaches the upper limit specified in the `HBase .reagionserver.max.logs` MemStore; once this limit is reached the system triggers flush to bring the count following the specified limit.

**Pre-Splitting**: It is an integral part of designing a very large cluster, while creating a table. We provide the split points during creation of the table. The class used for this is `Regional Splitter`. This in turn uses `SplitAlgorithm`, `HexStringSplit` and `UniformSplit` as predefined algorithms.

- You must use `PreSplitting` as it ensures the distribution of load more effectively; it is a good practice, and it's also handy as it makes you aware of the distribution split beforehand.

In some scenarios in which a region server is extensively used for read/write, it becomes slow. This creates a region hot spot which leads to Zookeeper connection timeout. In case there are multiple timeout which in turn starts assuming no heart beats from the slaves, and hence they the system thinks they are dead, where in they are heavily used. Thus is advisable to create a fixed number of regions and evenly distribute these regions across the region servers.

```
HBase (main):001:0> create 'table_01', 'columnf1', SPLITS=> ['a3',
'b6', 'c9']
```

Three splits will be created based on the number of regions we are using. If we are using 5 regions, the data will be split into 5 regions with four split points.

You can check it using:

```
$ echo -e  "a1\nb1\nc1" >/tmp/splits
HBase (main):001:0> create 'table_01', 'columnf1', SPLITSFILE=>'/tmp/
splits'
```

**Auto Splitting**: HBase  internal housekeeping does the auto-splitting agnostic to the pre-splitting setup. Once the region reaches certain threshold the system fires auto split into regions.

The Internals of HBase  decide to split regions by calculating the split points by using `RegionSplitPolicy` APIs. This is the default split policy which is triggered based on the total size of data in one stores in the regions hits the sealing specified in `HBase .hregion. max.filesize`, which is defaulted to 10 GB (gigabytes); this works seamlessly in case you have setup pre-splitting and are planning to get a lower number of regions per region server.

There are a couple of other predefined split policies like:

- ConstantSizeRegionSplitPolicy
- IncreasingToUpperBondRegionSplitPolicy
- KeyPreFixRegionSplitPolicy

**Force Splitting**: This requires more due diligence as its done by using `HBase` shell as needed or on demand; in this you can slot one region or all the regions by explicitly providing the split points shown as follows:

```
HBase (main):001:0> split 'a07c0034dfe72cb040ae9cf66300a12a', 'ac1'
0 row(s) in 0.1130 seconds
```

 In case you observe uneven load distribution in the HBase cluster and you see some regions are becoming hotspots and some are having little traffic, we can trigger a manual splitting of region; this helps in removing the hotspots by equally distributing the load and improves performance.

Alternatively you can invoke a manual split when you see the previous split is not giving the desired results and the auto split is disabled. This can happen due to any reason, such as the way the data distribution pattern changes as the system grows, or the regions are swapped, or there are unequal distributions of load due to temporary outage in the cluster.

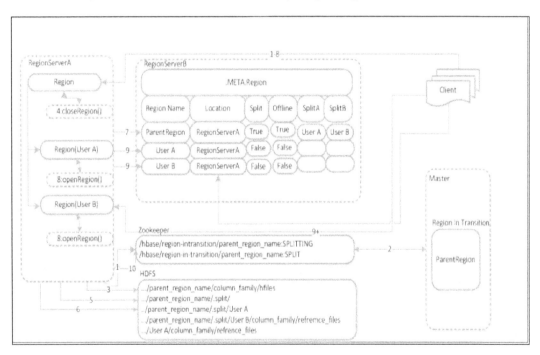

## How to do it...

1. Login to your `HBase` shell by running the following command:

   ```
   ./HBase  shell -d    (-d is for starting HBase  shell in a debug
   mode).
   ```

 It is assumed that you have your `hadoop` and `HBase` cluster intact and `namenode`, `datanode`, `secondary namenode`, `HBase` master, and region server are up and running.

2. You can run the list command to see the table you want to split:

   ```
   HBase (main):001:0> list

   HBase (main):001:0> split  'MyClickStream','2'
   ```

   This will create a split.

3. The other way to split a particular region will be by looking at the table or region in the web Interface. The format is `table_name, start_key, region_id.` as shown in the figure:

4. Once you know the key you can use the following command to split it:

   ```
   HBase  (main):004:0>split  'MyClickStream,2,1418517566751.53fd505f5
   83b22a74044b3f3154e9443.'
   ```

5. You can also split it based on hexadecimal values, as follows:

   ```
   HBase (main):009:0> org.apache.hadoop.HBase .util.RegionSplitter
   'MyClickStream' HexStringSplit -c 2 -f f1
   ```

## How it works...

We will be discussing the sequence of events which will be triggering various events while splitting the data across various regions:

1. Based on the settings or algorithm used, Region server decides locally to split the regions. Before making a split it prepared for the split, in doing so it creates a znode in the zookeeper under /HBase /region-in-transition/region-name in `SPLITTING` state.

2. Immediately master gets an invocation from znode the changes are cascaded to the master for the region in transition.

3. A sub directory split is created in HDFS within the parent region directory.

4. To avoid further changes, parent region servers are closed by the region servers, which in turn imposes a flush of cached in-memory data. During this brief period of time all the client requests coming to the parent region will throw `NotServicingRegionsException`.

5. Region Server creates the region directories under the splits directory, for user Region A and B; with it, it creates the required and data structure. Internally two different reference file per store file is created, these files are created in the parent regions.

6. The job of the region server is referring the individual user separately, which is essentially done by creating separate region directories in HDFS.

7. The region server sends a PUT request to the META table which sets the parent as offline in the META table (please see the note section later). Then the internal process adds information about Users regions. The region is split and observed by the client who is invoking a scan META; this is of no use to the client as the user is still not there META.

8. In case the PUT to META is successful then the parent will see the split. In case there is a failure in Region server and the RPC call invocation is a success then a dirty state is generated. This dirty state of region split is cleaned by Master with work with the next region server. Master always roll-forward the region spits once it get an update of META.

9. The region server is designed for scale and to work in a multithreaded environment and can handle concurrent write request.

10. .META gets a request from Region server to add User A and B, it adds the user, once this is done the clients connecting to these regions will start discovering/interacting with the new regions. The cached data gets an invalidation/eviction request, which is there in the local in-memory of the region server.

11. Region server, Zookeeper and HBase Master communicate instantly and thus changes in the znode for sate SPLIT are communicated immediately. It's the job of the load balancer to assign the users to the region.

12. Once this split is done, there is an internal cleanup process which checks the META and HDFS internal references. This weak reference is removed by this compaction process once the user region rewrites the data file.

META referenced in the HBase landscape/above is system table whose prime responsibility is to keep footprint of regions or mapping of the regions. It contains the region identifier details and the server name.

The region identifier contains a mapping start row-keys to the of table names. This enables the client to get the mapping of start-row-key, the next region start-key with the range of rows which is residing in a region.

A cache copy is always kept at the region location to avoid unwanted lookups to the META table. In case of re-balancing or change in assignment policies in Region Server, due to the Region split or recycle of one region server the client will receive and graceful exception as the cache is evicted and the fresh response and will fetch the updated information from the META table and updated the local cache of META, the subsequent request will always hit the local META.

## There's more...

A lot of complexity is handled by the HBase internal system process which dose a lot of heavy lifting for us like automated sharding through regions, auto cache eviction and management in META and so on. It also provides liberty to the users by providing various tools which can help them to manage the splits process if they are interested in or to configure it based on their needs. Scaling HBase without understanding the deeper part of regions and how the split happened is extremely important.

It's essential to understand the total number of regions and how it is balanced over time. Data plays a crucial role for region split points. You have to monitor the cluster and take manual steps to split.

### Region life cycle

State of the region servers is very important to run a fully scalable cluster. Some of issues that come in the large HBase cluster can be directly contributed to the inconsistent state of Regions. Say a region is assigned to one region server, but the Master thinks it's assigned to a different regions server, or is not aware of the assignment due to any reason, thus it becomes essential to understand what's states a region is in and when.

Following are the states through which the region server goes through:

- ► **OFFLINE**: Region is in an offline state
- ► **PENDING_OPEN**: Sent RPC to a Region Sever to open but has not begun
- ► **OPENING**: Region Sever has begun to open but not begun
- ► **OPEN**: Region Server opened region and updated META
- ► **PENDING_CLOSE**: Sent RPC to Region Server to close but has not begun
- ► **CLOSING**: Region Server closed region and updated META
- ► **SPLITTING**: Region Server started split of a region
- ► **SPLIT**: Region Server completed split of a region:

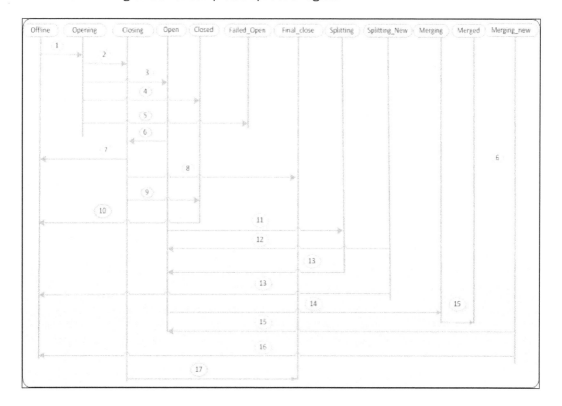

It is very essential to understand the states in which the Regions go through to clearly understand the complexity behind it:

1. Master marks region from an OFFLINE state to OPENING state and then attempts to allot a region to a region server. Throughout this initiation process it's not 100% certain that the region server got open region request. In this scenario master reinitiates open region request to the region server till the RPC call goes through or the max retry condition reached. Region server opens the region once the open region request is received and the internal process of opening the region is processed.

2. In cases where master reaches the max retires, as configured, the master blocks region server to open regions, this is done by marking the region to CLOSING state and invoking the process to close it, this happens even if the region server is starting to open the region.

3. Once region server opens the region, then it tries to reports the master, till the time master changes the region to OPEN state and sends the notification to region server, that its opened.

4. Master is always kept updated, due to any reason if the region server is unable to open the region. The master marks the region to CLOSED state and initiates the process of opening the region on a separate region server using the list of region servers it has.

5. The master server makes numerous retries and if it's still not able to open the region, it marks the region as FAILED_OPEN state, at this point of time it leaves it there. Its advices to manually lookup the logs and see the reasons why the region server is in a dead state.

6. The master moves a region from OPEN to CLOSING state. It not necessary that the region server who has the region might have received the close region request In this case a retry is made from the master for closing the request till the time the RPC call goes through or master exceeds the retry configured.

7. Master contentiously make a lookup on the region server and if its continuously getting NotServingRegionException or in case it's not able to listen to the heart beat, then the master flags the region as OFFLINE and reassigns the live region server.

8. There can be a scenario in which the region server is online but it's not reachable due to any, it will first try to max on reties, then master will initiate a process to marks the region to FAILED_CLOSED state. This state requires a manual lookup and analysis by the administrator and ask for manual intervention by the HBase cluster Administrator using HBase shell. For all practical purpose the region is deemed as dead.

9. In case the region server gets an RPC to call to close a region, it ends the region instantly and gracefully and notifies the master. The master marks the region to CLOSED state. At this point the Master re-directs the next calls to a different region server.

10. A predecessor process is invoked internally before a region assignment is done by master, the internal system which marks the region as OFFLINE state if it observes a status as CLOSED.

11. When a region server is approximately to splitting a region due to any reason, it informs the master, the master initiates as process and moves the region to be split from OPEN to SPLITTINE state, and invoked a spilt which adds the two new regions to region server and keeps the state as SPLITTING_NEW initially.

12. Once the maser is advised to do Split, region server invokes a process to split region, the region server informs master which intern update the META; this ensures the latest information is available in the META. Master waits to notify till the split is successful and then updates the region state. In case a successful split is done, then the region is changed SPLIT state from SPLITTING, thus two new regions are moved from SPLITTING_NEW to OPEN state.

13. In case due to any reason a split fails, the region which are in splitting state is reverted from SPLITTING to OPEN state, and two new regions is marked as OFFLINE from SPLITING_NEW state.

14. There can be a situation where a merging of two regions will be needed, the very first step is to notify the master. As the master get the information it moves the two region to be merged from OPEN to MERGING state and adds the new region; now this regions is having the context of the merged regions to the region server. The new region is in MERGING_NEW state.

15. Once the master gets the information, the region server initiates the process of merge. Once this process in instated a notification is sent to master to make sure the META is updated. But master holds the region state updates till the time it gets a notification, then an initiated merge is fully complete. Once the merge is successful, the state is changed to MERGED state and the new region is changed from MERGING_NEW to OPEN.

16. If merge fails, then two merging regions are progressed from MERGING back to OPEN state, the newly created region, which was holding the context as it was just created, is changed from MERGING_NEW to OFFLINE.

17. Master tries to close regions in FAILED_OPEN or FAILED_CLOSE states. The master tracks the state of region server, and the main class, which is responsible for it, is AssignmentManager. This class has gone through a lot of changes to reach to a stable state some of the major bug fixed are HBSE-6977 (Multithreaded processing Zookeeper assignment events).

The main issues these fixes were trying to address are inconsistent region state. Region state is mainly changing from unassigned to assign and back to unassigned. This is essentially traced in META table, Master server memory and ZooKeeper unassigned znodes. The AssignmentManager responsibility is to maintain these three states synchronized always.

http://people.apache.org/~jmhsieh/HBase /120905-HBase -assignment.pdf

A coprocessor is a structure for malleable basic extensions for distributed computing within server side components in HBase processes. This was introduced in HBase 0.92.0 release. With coprocessor framework the HBase cluster becomes more distributed as the code can now run in parallel across all the Region servers.

These Coprocessors are designed for internal systems processes of HBase thus by design it cannot be used by HBase users, nonetheless this framework allows the developers to embed custom functionality to HBase . The concept of coprocessor stems from BigTable implementation and the talk given by Jeff Dean at LADIS `http://www.scribd.com/doc/21631448/Dean-Keynote-Ladis2009, page 66-67` The core concept is listed as following:

1. Random code can run at each tablet in table server.

2. High-level call interface for clients, the job of a coprocessor client code is to streamline it to the actual location. These calls are addressed for rows or a range of rows.

3. When a call is made for multiple rows, these calls are split into multiple threaded RPC calls which run in parallel. Thus enabling a framework for distributed services like scaling on demand, distributed request routing, auto failovers and so on.

Essentially Coprocessors are categorized in two buckets:

▶ **System Coprocessors**: These coprocessors are internal to the system and all the components (tables, region servers and their internal regions hosted by then) are impacted by this. The administrator has no control on it.

▶ **Table Coprocessors**: If the administrator is specifying which coprocessors can be loaded on all the regions for a table on a per table basis. This framework provides a lot of flexibility, its allows the administrators to handpick the coprocessors which can be loaded per table in a region or can span to all the regions for a table.

This is done by extending the it to observers and endpoints, which will be discussed as follows:

Observers: Are very similar to the triggers in conventional RDBMS. The idea is to give flexibility to the uses to override the core methods implemented by the coprocessors. This allows the HBase internal listeners to fire an event and thus use a callback function. The HBase internal framework morphs the callback process during various HBase activates from the users. This is done by using three different interfaces, `RegionObservers`, `WalObserves` and `MasterObserver`.

▶ `RegionObserver`: Provides ways to influence the data using events like Get, Put, Delete, Scan. `RegionObserver` coprocessor has a granular interface for every table in the region and the boundaries can be defined for that region only and hence allowing all other regions work more independently. We can also customize internal working like flushing the MenStore, Splitting the regions and so on..

- ▶ `WalObserver`: Provides an interface to observe in Write Ahead logs working. This allows you to intercept the reconstruction and writing of the events. There is one such context per region and `WalObserver` in this case always runs in the context of WAL processing.

- ▶ `MasterObserver`: Provides hooks for **Data Definition Languages** (**DDL**) type operations like create, delete, modify. The master observer runs within the context of the HBase master.

The system provides enough flexibility to extend the functionality by allowing loading multiple observers at once in region master or in WAL. These processes are chained processes and are executed in the order of priority. The system is not limiting the implementers to communicate between installed observers. The coprocessors have defined priorities and thus follow a chain of command, the exceptions thrown by the lower priorities will not impact the work done by the higher priority classes.

> These APIs are subject to change as its still evolving.
> These APIs are better stabilized in 0.92 releases.

During the region lifecycle, various methods which are part of his interface are invoked, as the event is triggered. Master splits various responsibilities in the following way:

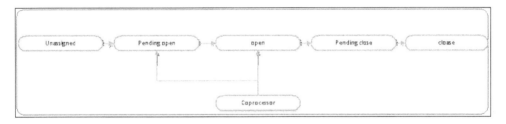

`PendingOpen`: In this scenario a region server is instating a process to bring a region to online state, Coprocessors can attach themselves or fail this process.

`preOpen` and `postOpen`: This is called once before the region is reported to be online and once the region is online.

`Open`: This implies that the region is ready to receive the client request (GET, PUT, SCAN from the client and FLUSH, COMPACT, SPLIT from Admin), which essentially means the region is open on the region server.

Coprocessors can align admin action by:

- ▸ `preFlush` and `postFlush`: As the name suggest, the first action is `preFlush` and this happened just before the MemStore is flushed. And the `postFlush` is called just after the MemStore is flushed in new store file.

- ▸ `preCompact` and `postCompact`: As the compaction process is integral part of the design, a `preCompaction` process is triggered before the actual compaction code is executed. Once compaction is done a post compaction process is triggered.

- ▸ `preSplit` and `postSplit`: Once the Split process is triggered an internal process of presplit is triggered, once all the internal processes of splitting are finished, the regions are called after the region is split.

`PendingClose`: Is triggered once the region server triers to close the region. The region server is closing the region due to following reason:

- ▸ Out of Memory errors
- ▸ Missing heartbeats
- ▸ Mount point, file system corrupted and the `preClose/postClose` has not completed `RegionObserver`

The Objective of `RegionObserver` interface is to observe/arbitrate client actions on the region:

- ▸ `preGet` and `postGet`: Once the client call is intercepted at the region server; this is called before/after the get call is executed in the region

- ▸ `preExists` and `postExists`: This process is called before/after the client tests for existence using a Get

- ▸ `prePut` and `postPut`: Called before/after the client stores a value

- ▸ `preDelete` and `postDelete`: Called before/after client deletes a value

- ▸ `preScannerOpen` and `postScannerOpen`: Called before/after the client opens a new scanner

- ▸ `preScannerNext` and `postScannerNext`: Called before/after the client asks for the next row on a scanner

- ▸ `preScannerClose` and `postScannerClose`: Called before/after the client closes a scanner

- ▸ `preCheckAndPut` and `postCheckAndPut`: Called before/after the client calls `checkAndPut()`

- ▸ `preCheckAndDelete` and `postCheckAndDelete`: Called before/after the client calls `checkAndDelete()`

In case you want to override any of the methods, You extend abstract class `BaseRegionObserverCoprocessor` which has methods which are implemented in `Coprocessor` and `RegionObserver`. It provides you and overridden handle for all the default methods, thus can override specific methods as needed.

`Endpoint` is very similar to a stored procedure; it can be invoked remotely to a target region server at any given point of time to get the resultset back to the client. It's a server side component and it can be invoked with HBase RPC. The client framework of HBase provides methods which can be used to invoke these interfaces. This extension interface provides ability to plugin new functionality to HBase . The process used is simple you need a new protocol interface which extends `CoprocessorProtocol` which interns implements `EndPoint` interface. The region context comes into play as it loads and executes. There are some internal details like class loading which is morphed in-purpose. HBase provides two new client side APIs which is executed on a single Region which works as a proxy.

```
HTableInterface.coprocessorProxy(Class<T> protocol, byte[] row)
```

This is internally executed on various regions:

```
HTableInterface.coprocessorExec(Class<T> protocol, byte[] startKey,
byte[] endKey, Batch.Call<T,R> callable)
```

## See also

We can see more details on the Region split process by clicking on the following link:

`http://HBase .apache.org/book/regions.arch.html`

# Auto Scaling HBase using AWS

Auto Scaling is a concept which came into existence because of the wide spread use of AWS Amazon Web Service platform. It allows the infrastructure to scale elastically, or words as needed. We can create auto-scaling groups from scratch and use the existing production instance to scale up as needed. Auto scaling gives an extra layer of fault tolerance, high availability and flexibility, at a very effective cost. If we are able to predict or plan the traffic pattern, then we can do predictive scaling on top of auto scaling.

In case of HBase  we can create a Auto Scaling groups of region servers, `namenode`, secondary `namenode`, use Amazons **Elastic Map Reduce** (**EMR**), most of the know tools are already integrated with Amazon EMR, like **Pig**, **Hive**, **Ganglia**, **DistCp** and so on.

## Getting Ready

This is based on the Amazon HBase  EMR details and full credit is given to the Amazon doc.

▸ To run HBase  in AWS env there are guideline which a user needs to adhere to. Amazon Elastic MapReduce, used in the book, is HBase  version 0.94.7. (we have to use specific version specified by the Amazon AWS platform).h The first thing which we need is a command line interface (CLI ) which is based on Amazon EMR framework. CLI version 2012-06-12 and later.

▸ Its advisable to use single node for HBase  for resting or evaluation. But for production setup it's better to go with one Master on one EC2 node and Zookeeper on other. You can have slave node running along with HBase region servers. If you want high speed or availability you can use separate nodes for slave and separate region servers.

▸ All the data in HBase  is persisted and Persistent cluster—HBase  only runs on persistent clusters. When we activate the HBase  cluster the alive flag is set automatically.

▸ HBase uses secure shell which allows the master to connecting to different regions via Amazon EC2 key, when we created the Amazon EC2 key pair set (Recommended).

▸ You can choose the instance type. The support instance type on AWS/EC2 is: **m1.large**, **m1.xlarge**, **c1.xlarge**, **m2.2xlarge**, **m2.4xlarge**, **cc1.4xlarge**, **cc2.8xlarge**, **hi1.4xlarge**, or **hs1.8xlarge**.

▸ HBase cluster is supported on Hadoop 20.205 or later. The CLI and Amazon EMR console automatically set the correct AMI on HBase  clusters.

▸ Ganglia is an option in case you want to monitor different types of matrix related to performance of the HBase  cluster. There is an option to create it by bootstrapping it while creating a cluster.

▸ Logs is an good way of doing a post-event analysis. It's a good practice to acquire a S3 bucket for logging rather using the HBase  master to maintain all the logs. You can pipe the logs created at HBase  master to a S3 bucket. This can be done while creating the cluster.

## How to do it...

1. First step is to create an Amazon Web Service Account, just in case if you have not setup an Amazon account or Amazon Prime account.

2. Once you click on the AWS account you will be transferred to the main console.

3. Please click Create Cluster, as follows

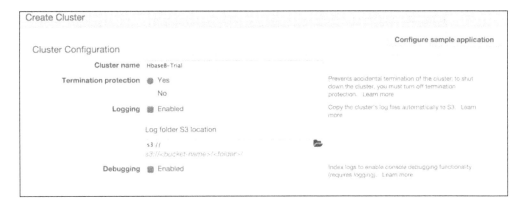

1. **Cluster name**: You can provide, as you want.

2. **Termination protection**: Ensures there is no accidental termination, please mark it as **Yes**.

3. **Logging**: Please enable logging as true as you would like to see the logs, this will push the logs to the S3 locations (`s3://HBase -bucket/hbasb/`).

4. **Debugging**: Please enable it to see the details of the actions in the logs.

4. In the software configuration section, you will be asked to select the Hadoop version, you can select Amazon Hadoop or MapR Hadoop.

5. We have selected AMI version 3.3.1 and Amazon Hadoop 2.4.0.

6. You will see a section Additional Application under which you will select HBase  then click configure and add. You can add the following Ganglia, Hive 0.13.1, Pig 0.12.0, HBase  0.94.18, Impala 1.2.4, Hue, Hunk.

7. Select EC2, from the pull-down, it will ask for a preferred zone, you can either select a zone as per your convenience or leave it as it is.

8. On the EC2 instance type you can select master 1 and core 3, leave the Task section as is.

9. On the security and access section use EC2 key pair and use this link to create a key pair Create an Amazon EC2 Key Pair and PEM File.

10. Review the entire settings once.

11. Once you have reviewed, please go ahead and create cluster.

12. Once the cluster create process starts it takes 20 min to an hr to get a fully functional cluster with all the requested components running.

13. Once the server is started it will show as shown as follow:

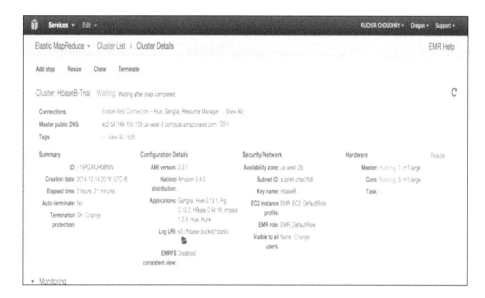

In monitoring section you will see the HBase tab which has the details:

1. Now let's try to `ssh` from your terminal by using this command:

   **`L-SB830T7FFT-M:opt r0choud$ ssh hadoop@ec2-54-149-155-109.us-`**
   **`west-2.compute.amazonaws.com -i ~/opt/opt/HBase B.pem`**

2. `HBase B.pem` file is the same file which is created when you generate key. This this key should never be shared by anyone else then the user associated to the profile:

   In case of such errors:

   ```
   L-SB830T7FFT-M:opt r0choud$ ssh hadoop@ec2-54-149-155-109.us-west-2.compute.amazonaws.com -i ~/opt/opt/HBaseB.pem
   @@@@@@@@@@@@@@@@@@@@@@@@@@@@@@@@@@@@@@@@@@@@@@@@@@@@@@@@@@@@@@@@@
   @        WARNING: UNPROTECTED PRIVATE KEY FILE!              @
   @@@@@@@@@@@@@@@@@@@@@@@@@@@@@@@@@@@@@@@@@@@@@@@@@@@@@@@@@@@@@@@@@
   Permissions 0640 for '/Users/r0choud/opt/opt/HBaseB.pem' are too open.
   It is required that your private key files are NOT accessible by others.
   This private key will be ignored.
   bad permissions: ignore key: /Users/r0choud/opt/opt/HBaseB.pem
   Permission denied (publickey).
   ```

   Please change the permission of the `HBase B.pem` file to 600, and try the same command.

3. Once the command is executed you will see following details on the window:

   ```
   L-SB830T7FFT-M:opt r0choud$ ssh hadoop@ec2-54-149-155-109.us-west-2.compute.amazonaws.com -i ~/opt/opt/HBaseB.pem
   Last login: Mon Dec 15 06:15:21 2014

        __|  __|_  )
        _|  (     /   Amazon Linux AMI
       ___|\___|___|

   https://aws.amazon.com/amazon-linux-ami/2014.09-release-notes/
    package(s) needed for security, out of 58 available
   Run "sudo yum update" to apply all updates.


   --------------------------------------------------------------------
   Welcome to Amazon Elastic MapReduce running Hadoop and Amazon Linux.
   Hadoop is installed in /home/hadoop. Log files are in /mnt/var/log/hadoop. Check
   /mnt/var/log/hadoop/steps for diagnosing step failures.
   The Hadoop UI can be accessed via the following commands:
     ResourceManager    lynx http://ip-172-31-20-148.us-west-2.compute.internal:9026/
     NameNode           lynx http://ip-172-31-20-148.us-west-2.compute.internal:9101/
   --------------------------------------------------------------------
   ```

4. Just to make a final check you can do `ls -ltr` if must show you the following:

```
[hadoop@ip-172-31-20-148 ~]$ ls -ltr
total 20
lrwxrwxrwx 1 hadoop hadoop  33 Nov 13 00:15 pig -> /home/hadoop/.versions/pig-0.12.0
drwxr-xr-x 3 hadoop hadoop 4096 Nov 13 00:16 contrib
lrwxrwxrwx 1 hadoop hadoop  34 Nov 13 00:16 share -> /home/hadoop/.versions/2.4.0/share
lrwxrwxrwx 1 hadoop hadoop  33 Nov 13 00:16 sbin -> /home/hadoop/.versions/2.4.0/sbin
lrwxrwxrwx 1 hadoop hadoop  36 Nov 13 00:16 libexec -> /home/hadoop/.versions/2.4.0/libexec
lrwxrwxrwx 1 hadoop hadoop  32 Nov 13 00:16 etc -> /home/hadoop/.versions/2.4.0/etc
lrwxrwxrwx 1 hadoop hadoop  39 Nov 13 00:16 conf -> /home/hadoop/.versions/2.4.0/etc/hadoop
lrwxrwxrwx 1 hadoop hadoop  32 Nov 13 00:16 bin -> /home/hadoop/.versions/2.4.0/bin
lrwxrwxrwx 1 hadoop hadoop  34 Nov 13 00:16 hive -> /home/hadoop/.versions/hive-0.13.1
lrwxrwxrwx 1 hadoop hadoop  71 Nov 13 00:16 hadoop-examples.jar -> /home/hadoop/share/hadoop/mapreduce/hadoop-mapreduce-examples-2.4.0.jar
lrwxrwxrwx 1 hadoop hadoop  33 Nov 13 00:16 mahout -> /home/hadoop/.versions/mahout-0.9
lrwxrwxrwx 1 hadoop hadoop  40 Nov 13 00:17 cascading -> /home/hadoop/.versions/Cascading-2.5-SDK
lrwxrwxrwx 1 hadoop hadoop  36 Dec 15 04:36 hbase -> /home/hadoop/.versions/hbase-0.94.18
drwxr-xr-x 3 hadoop hadoop 4096 Dec 15 04:36 lib
drwxr-xr-x 2 hadoop hadoop 4096 Dec 15 04:36 impala
-rw-r--r-- 1 hadoop hadoop  484 Dec 15 04:43 Manifest.gz
```

5. This completes the HBase setup on the EC2 cluster.

6. A detailed web UI view will be as follows:

7. On your shell, you can invoke an `HBase  shell` as follows:

```
[hadoop@ip-172-31-20-148 bin]$ hbase shell
```

8. Now you can create a table by using the following command:

```
hbase(main):006:0> create 'mycloudTable','cf01'
```

This will create a table `mycloudTable` with a column family `cf01`. At this time your cluster is fully ready and can scale elastically.

## There's more...

You can resize the cluster till 20 nodes for the core instance, but cannot increase the masters:

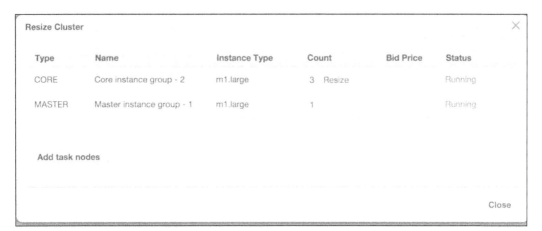

| Type | Name | Instance Type | Count | | Bid Price | Status |
|------|------|---------------|-------|---|-----------|--------|
| CORE | Core instance group - 2 | m1.large | 3 | Resize | | Running |
| MASTER | Master instance group - 1 | m1.large | 1 | | | Running |

Add task nodes

## See also

http://docs.aws.amazon.com/AutoScaling/latest/DeveloperGuide/
AutoScalingGroupLifecycle.html

# Works on different VM/physical, cloud hardware

In case you want to do a scalability based on the VMware architecture, the way to go will be VMware vSphere™ Big Data Extensions:

The benefits to do this are phenomenal, which we can list as follows:

> ▸ **Rapid provisioning**: Virtualization allows very sophisticated facilities like cloning, templates, resource allocation and optimizations, speed of deployment. A large scale distributed Hadoop/HBase cluster which is deployed on multiple nodes and can scale on demand and downscale as needed.

> ▸ **High Availability (HA) and Fault Tolerance**: By design hadoop/HBase ecosystem comes with HA as the underlying layer is HDFS but some of the core components of the system like `namenode`, `HBase master`, secondary `namenode`, `jobtracker` becomes single point of failure. VM Ware provides very advanced underlying technology, which can help us do this by using vSphere and vMotion.

> ▸ **Datacenter efficiency**: It can be achieved by using the infrastructure flexibly or elastically/on demand, by Share the hardware, software and network effectively like Disk RAM, VCPUS, Load balancers, Global traffic monitors, firewalls, proxies and so on and bring efficiency, resiliency in the ecosystem.

> ▸ **Resource utilization**: Distributing the cluster based on the resource needs, grouping different clusters based on needs of the group, like `namenode`, `HBase Masters` on the high capacity group and `datanode` and region servers on the less resourceful machines.

> ▸ **Time sharing**: Allows us take advantage of unused capacity in the virtual environment by running jobs during periods of low hardware usage by spinning up and down virtual machines easily.

> ▸ **Low cost maintenance**: Moving a cluster from one environment to another is very easy as compared to movement on the physical hardware.

> ▸ **Sharing the resource**: VMware optimizes the capacity utilization and switches it on demand.

> ▸ **Hadoop as a service**: VMware vCloud director can be configured to offer hadoop as a service.

> ▸ **Efficient storage**: Virtualization of the Hadoop/HBase ecosystem provides us the technique to use mixed model in which the data which is changed frequently can be kept at local disk and the HDFS can be hosted on a SAN. The capacity which is available at the runtime can be given for the efficiency of the Hadoop/Map reduce jobs.

## Getting ready

**Prerequisite**: Before we install Big Data Extension, we must set up the following:

- ▶ Install vSphere 5.0 or later Enterprise or Enterprise Plus
- ▶ When installing Big Data Extension on vSphere 5.1 or later we must use vCenter single signon to provide user authentication
- ▶ Enable vSphere **Network Time Protocol** (**NTP**) on the ESXi host, this ensures all the time dependent time-dependent processes are in perfect sync
- ▶ For cluster setting:
    - ❑ Enable host monitoring
    - ❑ Enable Admission control and set desired policy. The default policy is to tolerate one host failure
    - ❑ Enable vMotion for fault tolerance
    - ❑ Set monitoring sensitivity to high
- ▶ Post 8080, 8443, used by Big Data extension, must be opened
- ▶ Port 22 is used by `ssh`
- ▶ 8-12 disk drive per host
- ▶ 1 to 1.5 disk drive per processor core
- ▶ 7200 RPM disk serial ATA disk drive
- ▶ Resource pool with at least 27.5GB
- ▶ 50 GB or more disk space is required for HBase /Hadoop template virtual disks

Also important to have the following points in order:

- ▶ The `datastore` free space needs to be adequate
- ▶ HA is available for `namenode`, `HBase   masternodes`, secondary `namenode`
- ▶ 8 GB of memory per processor core and IGB Ethernet Inter interface
- ▶ 45 physical host running a total of 182 VM

## How to do it...

1. Log in to the vSphere GUI.
2. Select Big Data cluster.
3. Click new Big Data cluster in the Big Data cluster list lab.
4. A create new data cluster dialog display.

5. Specify the information for the cluster we would like to create.

6. Options:

   ❏ Description

   ❏ Hadoop cluster name, say `Hadoop-HBase -01`

   ❏ Select a Hadoop Distribution say cloudera, MapR, Hartonworks and so on

7. Customize: The type of cluster you create determines the available node group selections.

 If you select Customize, a dialog box displays that lets you load an existing cluster specification file. You can edit the file in the text field to further refine the cluster specification.

8. The `ComputeMaster` node is a virtual machine that runs the Hadoop `JobTracker` service. This node assigns tasks to Hadoop `TaskTracker` services deployed in the worker node group.

 The Data Master node is a virtual machine that runs the Hadoop `NameNode` service. This node manages HDFS data and assigns tasks to Hadoop `JobTracker` services deployed in the worker node group.

Select a resource template from the drop-down menu, or select Customize to customize a resource template. For the master node, use shared storage so that you protect this virtual machine with VMware HA and FT.

9. Select a resource template from the drop-down menu, or select Customize to customize a resource template.

10. For the master node, use shared storage so that you protect this virtual machine with VMware HA and FT.

11. The `HBase Master` node is a virtual machine that runs the HBase  master service.

12. This node orchestrates a cluster of one or more `RegionServer` slave nodes.

13. Now select a resource template from the drop-down menu, or select Customize to customize a resource template.

 For the master node, use shared storage so that you protect this virtual machine with VMware **HA (High Availability)** and **FT (Fault tolerant)**.

14. Select the number of nodes and the resource template from the drop-down menu, or select Customize to customize a resource template.

 Worker nodes are virtual machines that run the Hadoop DataNodes and TaskTracker service. These nodes store HDFS data and execute tasks.

15. For worker nodes, use local storage.

 A client node is a virtual machine that contains Hadoop client components. From this virtual machine you can access HDFS, submit MapReduce jobs, run Pig scripts, run Hive queries, and HBase commands.

16. Select the number of nodes and a resource template from the drop-down menu, or select Customize to customize a resource template.

 You can add nodes to the client node group by using Scale Out Cluster. You cannot reduce the number of nodes.

17. Select the topology configuration you want the cluster to use:
    - RACK_AS_RACK
    - HOST_AS_RACK
    - HIVE
    - D NONE
    - Network

18. Select the network that you want the cluster to use.

    Say mynetwork.

19. Select one or more resource pools that you want the cluster to use.

 The Serengeti Management Server clones the template virtual machine to create the nodes in the cluster. When each virtual machine starts, the agent on that virtual machine pulls the appropriate Big Data Extensions software components to that node and deploys the software.

## There's more...

**Resource Usage and Elastic**: Scaling allows you to adjust the compute capacity of Hadoop data-compute separated clusters. An elasticity-enabled Hadoop cluster automatically stops and starts nodes to match resource requirements to available resources. You can use manual scaling for more explicit cluster control.

Automatic elasticity is best suited for mixed workload environments where resource requirements and availability fluctuate. Manual scaling is more appropriate for static environments where capacity planning can predict resource availability for workloads.

When automatic elasticity is enabled, Big Data Extensions dedicates some number of nodes for elasticity.( all the configurations as identical to the other nodes) its also sets a list of minimum numbers to keep the traffic alive.

When manual scaling is in effect, Big Data Extensions sets the number of active compute nodes to the configured number of target compute nodes.

vCenter Server does not directly control the number of active nodes. However, vCenter Server does apply the usual reservations, shares, and limits to the cluster's resource pool according to the cluster's vSphere configuration. The vSphere **Dynamic Resource Scheduler** (**DRS**) operates as usual, allocating resources between competing workloads.

Big Data Extensions also lets you adjust cluster nodes' access priority for datastores by using the vSphere Storage I/O Control feature. Clusters configured for HIGH IO shares receive higher priority access than clusters with NORMAL priority. Clusters configured for NORMAL IO shares receive higher priority access than clusters with LOW priority. In general, higher priority provides better disk I/O performance.

Scaling Modes

When you enable and disable elastic scaling, you change the scaling mode:

- ▸ AUTO: Big Data Extensions automatically adjusts the number of active nodes from the configured minimum to the number of available nodes in the cluster.

- ▸ Elastic scaling operates on a per-host basis, at a node-level granularity. That is, the more nodes a Hadoop cluster has on a host, the finer the control that Big Data Extensions elasticity can exercise. The trade-off is that the more nodes you have, the higher the overhead in terms of runtime resource cost, disk footprint, I/O requirements, and so on.

- ▸ When resources are overcommitted, elastic scaling reduces the number of powered on nodes. Conversely, if the cluster receives all the resources it requested from vSphere, and Big Data Extensions determines that the cluster can make use of additional capacity, elastic scaling powers on additional nodes.

Resources can become overcommitted for many reasons, such as:

- The nodes have lower resource entitlements than a competing workload, according to vCenter Server's application of the usual reservations, shares, and limits as configured for the cluster.

- Physical resources are configured to be available, but another workload is consuming those resources.

- MANUAL Big Data Extensions sets the number of active compute nodes to the configured number of target compute nodes.

Default Cluster Elasticity Settings

By default, when you create a cluster, it is not elasticity-enabled:

- The cluster's scaling mode is MANUAL.

- The cluster's minimum number of compute nodes is zero.

- The cluster's target number of nodes is not applicable.

- Interactions Between Scaling and Other Cluster Operations

Some cluster operations cannot be performed while Big Data Extensions is actively scaling a cluster.

If you try to perform the following operations while Big Data Extensions is scaling a cluster, Serengeti warns you that in the cluster's current state, the operation cannot be performed.

Concurrent attempt at manual scaling

Switch to AUTO scaling while MANUAL scaling is in progress

If a cluster is elasticity-enabled when you perform the following cluster operations on it, Big Data Extensions changes the scaling mode to MANUAL and disables elasticity. You can re-enable elasticity after the cluster operation finishes.

1. Delete the cluster

2. Repair the cluster

3. Stop the cluster

If a cluster is elasticity-enabled when you perform the following cluster operations on it, Big Data Extensions temporarily switches the cluster to MANUAL scaling. When the cluster operation finishes, Serengeti returns the elasticity mode to AUTO, which re-enables elasticity. In case there is a need to re-size the cluster based on the capacity needs we have to rebalance the cluster which can be a cumbersome job.

If Big Data Extensions is scaling a cluster when you perform an operation that changes the scaling mode to MANUAL, your requested operation waits until the scaling finishes, and then the operation begins.

## See also

https://cwiki.apache.org/confluence/display/AMBARI/Ambari

# 4

# Working with Large Distributed Systems Part II

In this chapter, we will cover the following topics:

- ▶ Internals of the HBSE system
- ▶ How design decisions allow Hbase to truly scale

This chapter will allow the actor to have a closer look at the design decisions and how these designs allow Hbase to scale without losing its integrity and performance.

## Introduction

As you know Hbase is a database, which essentially takes all the advantage of using the core foundation of HDFS and MapReduce. This allows it to scale in a distributed architecture. Its schemaless design allows us to bring in a unique ability and flexibility to make design decisions based on the way the data needs to be stored at a very large scale. It also allows fast scans, growth at a rate of petabytes and still gives cell level transaction flexibility to the application. As in any efficient database, Hbase I/O is designed to perform at high concurrency and I/O. The internal design incorporates an ordered write log and a log-structured merge-tree algorithm, which allows us to do this. It's very important to understand these fundamental blocks, which will enable us to make the right choice of design for scalability.

We will discuss some of the core concepts by the individual recipes, as follows:

- ▸ Seek versus transfer
- ▸ Storage
- ▸ Write Path
- ▸ Read Path
- ▸ Replication
- ▸ WAL(Write Ahead logs)

**Note:**

We will touch a few important topics from the aforementioned list, as detailing each topic is beyond the scope of this book.

## Seek versus transfer

Before we go into the details of seek versus transfer, we must spend some time understanding the code design on which Hbase is based of which *Log-Structure Merge Tree (LSM-Tree)* (http://en.wikipedia.org/wiki/Log-structured_merge-tree) is a part. The LSM-Tree uses an append-only structure in memory to achieve low write latency; at memory capacity, in-memory data are flushed to other storage media. In LSM, inserts and updates are indistinguishable and are implemented with the same put operator, while in B-tree, insert and update are two separate operators. This implies that in **LSM**, a put does not know whether it is actually an insert or an update. As a consequence, the associated index update needs to incur a read into the data table in order to get the old index value and later remove it, that is, a read operation is added to the path of a write in index maintenance. The LSM-Tree is the basis of lots of modern NoSQLs, such as LevelDB, SQLite4, RockDB, Apache Cassandra, WiredTiger, RockDB, and Hbase.

## The log-structured merge-tree

In a highly scalable transactional system application such as Hbase, the system inserts a row in a history log table in a sequential way. This keeps a trace of events or activity in the WAL. These are later passed to MemStore, where the date they are received is recorded, and they are buffered in memory. BlockCache is where it keeps the data blocks in memory once they are read. WAL is the place where all the edits happen, which is essentially the puts coming from different clients/regions. The writes in the WAL file are sequenced in a way that additions are always made to the end of the file stored on the disk. When WAL files reach a sizes of 95% of the HDFS block size, the system closes the old WAL file and opens a new one. In this process, it flushes the entire data to disk. This process is termed as rolling the WAL file.

In this scenario, the history tables will be growing at a rapid pace; hence we require a fast and effective way to index it. Indexing it using an account ID gives the option to achieve it. This process brings lots of challenges on the disk-based indexing algorithm and also impacts the performance in a negative way, as now we have to take care of the transactions and recalibrate indexing in real time.

The LSM-tree algorithm is designed to handle rapid read and write using a low-cost indexing without causing a degradation in the performance of read and write operations. The core part of the algorithm intelligently batches data changes and pushes it from in-memory to disk. This disk can be a cascade. As this internal process is triggered and done, all the indices are still available for read either from memory or from the disk or disks.

Note that during the locking period, which is very short, this won't be accessible.

## Date Read

In case of a read request, the in-memory store is searched first. Once this is a cache miss, the request goes to the store file on the disk.

## Data Delete

The data is marked for delete (as a logical delete, marked as a tomb stone). The system background housekeeping job merges the store files into a larger one and applies a merge sort which in turn allows us to reduce disk seeks. During this internal optimization, data is permanently deleted.

The LSM-tree is comprised of two or more tree-like data structures. It is an n-level merge-tree that transforms random writes into sequential writes. The best part is that the updates are in memory; thus, it reduces the I/O and gives an additional benefit as compared to B+ tree.

Let's consider the C0 tree, which is totally in memory and C1 tree as a large component, which is on disk. There will be a portion of the C1 tree that will be very frequently looked up and will be always in memory as this is used frequently. C1 can be deemed as a memory resident. Please refer to the following figure:

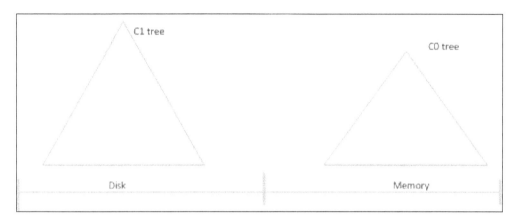

As rows are written sequentially to the WAL, the index entries are inserted into the in memory C0 tree. Once it reaches the limit, the WAL is closed and the entire data is flushed to the disk C1 tree. This data will be first looked up at the C0 tree; on cache miss, it will be looked up at the C1 tree. In case of recovery, the WAL is referred to, and the index is recreated. Now as the process is inserting the index entry in memory, it's C0 in this case, there is o I/O, and hence it becomes very effective and provides a very good performance.

The details and the deep-rooted concepts of the preceding matter can be found on the following websites (these are beyond the scope of this book):

http://www.cs.umb.edu/~poneil/lsmtree.pdf

http://www.inf.ufpr.br/eduardo/ensino/ci763/papers/lsmtree.pdf

http://www.eecs.harvard.edu/~margo/cs165/papers/gp-lsm.pdf

It's courtesy to the above articles.

## Storage

Hbase storage is designed to scale and use distributed and parallel computing to the maximum. This also involves dealing with lots of internal complex issues and smart and intelligent design decisions. In doing so, we have to discuss many internal components of Hbase, and the reason why they are important for storing the data.

We will discuss the following:

- ▸ Read/write path
- ▸ Compression
- ▸ Write-ahead logs
- ▸ HFile (as discussed in Chapter 2)
- ▸ Replication

# Read path

Hadoop design is based on the Sequence file format, which is used to append key/value pairs; this stems from the HDFS append-only capability.

This design is retrofitted by a concept of MapFiles and an extension of SequenceFile.

MapFile is nothing but a bundle of two Sequences Files in a directory. The first file is /data and the second is /index. This allows us to append key/value pairs and every N key; we can configure N as needed. This setup also allows us to store the key and the offset in the index. This gives us the flexibility to do extremely fast lookups as the data and the index have less entries. Once you are aware of the block, data file location can be done at a very fast pace.

MapFile is effective as we can look up keys and the values:

| Row Length short | Row Key Byte[] | Family length byte | Column Family byte[] | Column Qualifier bytes[] | Timestamp long | Key Type byte |
|---|---|---|---|---|---|---|

Hbase key has the preceding structure: row key, column family, column qualifier, timestamp, and type.

To rectify the problem of deleting the key/value pair at runtime and rebalancing the data structure for a clean and optimized design, it's good to use a type field, which is also known as a tombstoning marker. This allows the key to be marked as deleted (logical delete). This allows us to replace the key/value pairs by picking the latest timestamp.

To solve the non-ordered key issue, we set a threshold, and the key values are added to the in-memory till the panned threshold is reached. Once we reach this benchmark, we flush it to MapFile. Let's discuss it in a more granular way.

As a put is executed by the client, table.put is invoked and the key/value is added to the memstore. Essentially, an internal process sorts the memstore using a Java collection class known as ConcurrentSkipListMap. At this point, the pre-memstore threshold that is set by using `hbase.hregion.memstore.flush.size` comes into play and checks whether the RegionServer is using the upper limit of the memory for memstores, which is primarily governed by `hbase.regionserver.global.memstore.upperLimit`. The data residing in this MapFile is flushed to disk, and immediately a new MapFile is created. This implies that for a scan, one or more MapFiles need to be searched, and potentially, it might slow down the process of data retrieval.

To optimize this process, Hbase initiates a process of compaction. The internal system threads constantly measure the maximum value set in `hbase.hstore.compactipon.max`. Once the system threads detect that the maximum is reached, it merges them together and creates a larger file. This decreases the hop between many files and increases the read performance of the scan process.

Hbase performs two type of compactions:

- Minor compaction
- Major compaction

  - **Minor compaction**: This merges two or more files and creates a fresh merged sorted file.

  - **Major compaction**: This does a lot of additional work as compared to minor compaction; it merges all the files in a region, purges all the key values that are marked for tombstone, performs a duplicate check, removes the older version, and keeps the latest so that a fresh, clean compacted file is created, which allows us to boost the performance of the system.

Note that a new Hbase-specific MapFile is introduced. For more details, you can follow this Jira ticket **Hbase-61** (`https://issues.apache.org/jira/browse/HBASE-61`). The version 0.20 still uses the MapFile format.

## How to do it...

1. Let's edit `hbase-env.sh`, which is located at the RegioServer and change the `HBASE_OFFHEAPSIZE`. Let's change it to 8G. The internal slicing will be 4G for our off-heap cache, and the other 4G is utilized for other processes; for example, DFSClient in RegionServer can make use of off-heap memory.

2. Let's connect to the Region Servers:

   **ssh hadoop@your region server CNAME or IP**

   **/HbaseB/hbase-0.98.5-hadoop2/conf**

3. Edit the file by adding the following properties to the `hbase-site.xml`:

```
<property>
  <name>hbase.bucketcache.ioengine</name>
  <value>offheap</value>
</property>
<property>
  <name>hfile.block.cache.size</name>
  <value>0.2</value>
</property>
<property>
  <name>hbase.bucketcache.size</name>
  <value>8192</value>
</property>
```

4. Restart the cluster, check the logs, and see if there are any issues.

We will discuss the read path:

1. Client queries Memstore, which is in-memory data for the target row. If it finds the data Memstore, it returns from there.

2. In case the in-memory does not have the requested data, which means there's an in-memory miss, the process looks for the data in BlockCache.

3. If this process fails to get data, the process will look it up in the HFile and load the target row.

4.  In case we are using multi-level caches, the path followed will be totally different, as shown in the following figure:

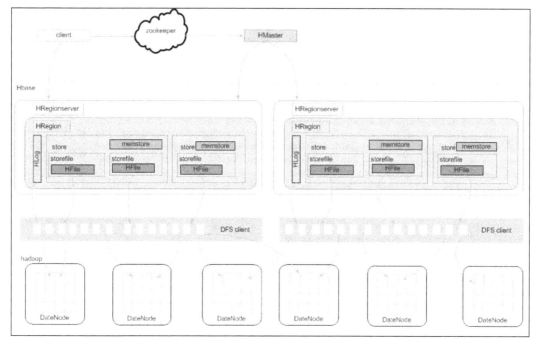

Hbase-01

▶   (http://www.slideshare.net/Hadoop_Summit/hbase-storage-internals?related=4)

▶   (http://www.larsgeorge.com/2009/10/hbase-architecture-101-storage.html)

# Write Path

HBase is designed to optimize writes. This is achieved by splitting the load across all the Region Servers. The design is optimized to handle Region Server failure and data loss. HBase data is orchestrated very similarly to store map, such as sorted key space partitions located in different shards/regions.

HBase tables are managed by a series of servers, as follows:

- One active master server
- Multiple backup master servers (you can use one backup too)
- Many Region Servers

When a Region Server receives a write request, it relays the call to the specific region. Each region stores sets of rows. Row data can be separated into multiple column families (we will discuss this in the chapter about schema design). The data of a particular column family is stored in HStore, which has Memstore and a set of HFiles. Memostore is kept in the Region Server main memory, during which the HFiles are written to HDFS.

 Note that you can plan to flush the changes in the form of batches by switching off auto flush. Now the system will do a flush based on the `hbase.client.write.buffer` parameter or will wait for invocation of flush commit.

The row keys in HBase are kept in a sorted order. Thus, it comes in handy in calibrating which region server administers which key. In HBase, changes are always row specific, and these rows are tied to a specific region server that is serving put or delete.

## How to do it...

1. Assuming HBase is running in Fully-Distributed mode and can be `put()`, `get()`, or `scan()`, the first step is to create a Java project in Eclipse.

2. Once you have created the Java project, you can copy the HBase lib from the following locations by adding it as an external jar:

   `/HbaseB/ hbase-0.98.5-hadoop2/lib/`

   `hbase (hbase-<version>.jar)`

   `log4j (log4j-<version>.jar)`

   `slf4j-api (slf4j-api-<version>.jar)`

   `slf4j-log4j (slf4j-log4j12-<version>.jar)`

   `zookeeper (zookeeper-<version>.jar)`

   The following is the code for the Hadoop lib files:

   `commons-configuration (commons-configuration-<version>.jar)`

   `commons-lang (commons-lang-<version>.jar`

   `commons-logging (commons-logging-<version>.jar)`

   `hadoop-core (hadoop-core-<version>.jar)`

3. To communicate with the cluster, you have to add the zookeeper node details as properties, as shown next:

```
${HBASE_HOME}/conf/hbase-site.xml on both clusters and add the
following:

<property>

<name>hbase.zookeeper.quorum</name>

<value>zookeeper1,zookeeper2,zookeeper3</value>

</property>
```

4. Restart the HBase cluster only if the changes are new; if the configurations are already there, there is no need to restart the cluster.

5. To connect using the client, the Java code needs to have the following:

```
Configuration conf = HBaseConfiguration.create();
conf.set("hbase.zookeeper.quorum", "zookeeper1,zookeeper2,zookeep
er3");
```

6. Now you can write a Java class, as follows:

```java
import java.io.IOException;
import org.apache.hadoop.hbase.client.Put;
import org.apache.hadoop.hbase.client.Result;
import org.apache.hadoop.hbase.client.ResultScanner;
import org.apache.hadoop.hbase.client.Scan;
import org.apache.hadoop.conf.Configuration;
import org.apache.hadoop.hbase.HBaseConfiguration;
import org.apache.hadoop.hbase.client.Get;
import org.apache.hadoop.hbase.client.HTable;
import org.apache.hadoop.hbase.util.Bytes;

public class HBaseWritePathTest throws MasterNotRunningException,
ZooKeeperConnectionException {
    {
        public static void main(String[] args) throws IOException
{
            try {
                HBaseAdmin.checkHBaseAvailable(conf);
            } catch (Exception e) {
                System.err.println("Exception at " + e);
                System.exit(1);
            }
            Configuration conf = HBaseConfiguration.create();
            conf.set("hbase.zookeeper.quorum", "infinity");
            conf.set("hbase.zookeeper.property.clientPort",
"2181");// zookeeprs port on which zookeepr is listening.
```

```
            HTable table = new HTable(conf, "MyWriretestTable");
            Put p = new Put(Bytes.toBytes("myWriteTestRow"));
    p.add(Bytes.toBytes("myWriteTestFamily"), Bytes.toBytes("myWriteTe
    stQualifier"),
    Bytes.toBytes("myWriteTest"));

            HBaseAdmin admin = new HBaseAdmin(conf);
            try {
                HBaseAdmin.checkHBaseAvailable(conf);
                System.out.println("Test for success ! ");
            } catch (Exception error) {
                System.err.println("Error connecting HBase:  " +
    error);System.exit(1);
            }
        }
    }
```

7. You can now run the command, and you will see Test got success in your Eclipse logs.

Note that this code traverses the entire write path of HBase.

You can check by adding a scan method in the preceding code and invoke it once the insert is done.

Alternatively, you can issue a direct command as scan table MyWriretestTable on HBase console:

```
 /**
     * Scan for table, this needs to be passed as a parameter
     */
    public static void getAllRecord (String tableName) {
ResultScanner ss= null;
        try{
            HTable table = new HTable(conf, MyWriretestTable);
            Scan s = new Scan();
            ss = table.getScanner(s);
            for(Result r:ss){
                for(KeyValue kv : r.raw()){
                    System.out.print(new String(kv.getRow()) + "
");
                    System.out.print(new String(kv.getFamily()) +
":");
                    System.out.print(new String(kv.getQualifier())
+ " ");
                    System.out.print(kv.getTimestamp() + " ");
```

```
                              System.out.println(new String(kv.getValue()));
                    }
                }
            } catch (IOException e){
                e.printStackTrace();
            }finally { ss.close();}
        }
    }
```

It will show the all the data in the table that was just created.

## How it works...

1. HBase client locates the address of a region server by presenting the Root region from the Zookeeper quorum.

2. This client invocation allows the system location of the region server to host the Meta regions.

3. From the Meta region server, it locates the actual region server, which serves the requested regions.

4. Immediately, the request is on the correct region server. However, the changed data that we are getting cannot be directly written to the HFiles as the data is random, which, if good for reading and thus for writing the internal in-memory process, does the sorting and is written to a new file.

5. Before being written to the new file, the changes are stored randomly in the in-memory, commonly referred to as memstore; data is stored in the same manner as it's stored in HFile.

6. Once the data reaches the size specified, it's flushed to the HDFS and then to disk; a new HFile is created in HDFS.

## There's more...

There are some challenges with this process that we need to be aware of, so we can use it with a lot of caution. Memstore writes are in memory and are very fast, but all the data are in memory and are volatile; thus, system failure may lead to a loss of this data. To rectify this flaw, HBase saves the data in **write-ahead logs** (**WAL**). This is persisted on disk and can sustain a system, crash so the information that resides in the memstore is recoverable.

Note that this brings an interesting thought about when to use WAL and when not to. By default, WAL writes are on, and the data are always written to, WAL. But if you are sure the data can be rewritten or a small loss won't be impacting the overall outcome of the processing, you disable the write to WAL. WAL provides an easy and definitive recovery. This is the fundamental reason why, by default, it's always enabled. In scenarios where data loss is not expectable, you should leave it in the default settings; otherwise, change it to use memstore. Alternatively, you can plan for a DR (disaster recovery).

As the WAL files are on disk and every write needs to be optimized and recoverable, the organization of data in the WAL file is significantly different from that of the HFile.

Any unit of operation, such as put or delete, comprises the information and the region where it needs to be applied. All the edits are in chronological order for safe persistence; thus, there is never a need to write to random places.

Once the data in the WAL file touches a certain limit (a predefined threshold), they are closed, and a new active WAL file is created, which takes on the write operations. Once the WAL file is closed, it becomes immutable. This process is known as rolling the WAL file.

The internal process/algorithm of HBase rolls the WAL file once it reaches the threshold of 95% of the HDFS block size. There are multiple ways to optimize or change the default process. `hbase.regionserver.logroll.multiplier`, and the block size using parameter: `hbase.regionserver.hlog.blocksize`. The WAL file is also rolled periodically based on the configured interval `hbase.regionserver.logroll.period`, an hour by default; even the WAL file size is smaller than the configured limit.

Forcing a limit on the WAL file allows us to recover very fast. It becomes critical, especially when we are executing a replay and the regions are not available. In this case, all the changes from each WAL file need to be written to the HFile and persisted. Once this process is done, the Log Cleaner process daemon thread can execute the clean up of the archived files.

A WAL file is not generated on all the regions as a single region servers can have many regions. HBase creates a single WAL file per region server and shares it to all its regions.

At a given time, only one WAL file per region server is active even though they may be having many WAL files on the region server disk/shared location.

It's also essential to know how Memstore and other memory management works within the landscape of JVM memory and off-heap memory.

Memory management in HBase is done by two components: one is MemStore and the other is BlockCache, which is an interface that has an implementation of block Cache; it keeps the data blocks in memory after it has been read:

- **MemStore**: This holds the in-memory data and its modification of key/values to the Store. Thus, it is important to access recent edits using MemStore. MemStore maintains a skip list structure, which requires no disk I/O.

- **BlockCache**: Hbase serves random read with millisecond latency using this. It's a placeholder for the data that is pulled from HDFS. Once the data is in the BlockCache, subsequent reads don't have I/O latency. This execution can be organized by three different modes: heap, off-heap, and file. Agnostic to the execution, BucketCache is responsible for an area of memory called "buckets". This is used for holding cached blocks. The specified block side is associated with each bucket. In case of heap implementation, these buckets are created using Java heap.

- **Off-heap**: As the name suggests, the bucket is managed outside the JVM heap by using DirectByteByffers; in this scenario, a file mode process is invoked with the path of the filesystem. This is the place where all these buckets will be created, in-memory or SSDs. Agnostic to the implementation we choose, BucketCache creates 14 buckets of different sizes. This process has a backed-in algorithm, which constantly keeps a tab on the utilization and the pattern in which the block is accessed, analogous to LruBlockCache, and has the same single-access, multi-access, and in-memory breakdown of 25%, 50%, and 25%. Internally, it uses an LRU algorithm to evict the cache similar to the default cache eviction strategy.

- **Multilevel caching**: When we use the multilevel cache, we use SlabCache and **BucketCache**, which essentially means that we are reserving a part of BlockCache as LruBlockCache and the other part as SlabCache. Conceptually, it's known as L1 and L2 cache.

- **SlabCache**: This is designed to capitalize both levels of cache, in-memory Java heap and off-Java heap, which can be an SSD. The thought is to operate individually where getting a block or evicting a block happens agnostic to each other. The approach used is DoubleBlockCache, which also uses multilayered caching architecture.

- **BucketCache**: It has a different approach and focus; L1 cache is used only for bloom and index blocks. L2 is used for data blocks and caching the data. In the event of L1 block eviction, the block is deprecated and moved to L2 SlabCache. This approach is also called CombinedBlockCache.

- **SlabCache**: One major issue with the JVM is addressed by using SlabCache. In the Java world, as the footprint of the increases, it starts impacting the garbage collection process and eventually, after some GC cycle is triggered, stops the world GC, which in turn allows the client to enable threads to pause thereby causing a delay in the request. SlabCache provides an option to manually manage the cache via slab allocation, which provides an option to avoid garbage collection altogether. This came into the picture due to the implementation of HBASE-4027. The SlabCache strategy is to relate a big portion of memory and then within this memory block, do a slab allocation. This is an advanced allocation of caches, which are of the same size or likely the same size. The fragmentation issues are internalized by the cache. This process is a very effective way of space utilization as blocks converge into a single size. This avoids the creation of fragmentation, but other parts of HBase can still have this issue. The good part of this is that it decreases the stop the world pauses. But in certain cases, the JVM can still govern to move the slabs with the in-memory data, which can lead to pauses. To rectify this problem, SlabCache invokes `DirectByteBuffers`. Direct ByteByffers, available in the `java.nio` package, allows you to allocate memory outside the conventional Java heap, which is very similar to the `malloc()` process in C. Now with this way of garbage collection, the max GC time will never come. Reads on SlabCache are different from the read performed using the conventional JVM invocation. In case of SlabCache, the data from SlabCache is copied to the heap of Java, which is known as the copy-on-read approach. In this case, SlabCache works as an L2 cache for HBase, thus allowing the system to store a large amount of data without losing the speed and consistency in performance.

▸ **LruBlockCache**: This is the default implementation and the JVM-based caching solution. In this scenario, cache blocks are split into single-access, multi-access, and in-memory. The portion is divided as 25%, 50%, and 25% of the total BlockCache size. The initial read from HDFS is parked in the single-access area. Subsequent read to the same data moves the data to the multi-access area. The in-memory area is reserved for the data that is loaded from column families marked IN_MEMORY. The eviction policy used to evict the blocks is the Least Recently Used Algorithm:

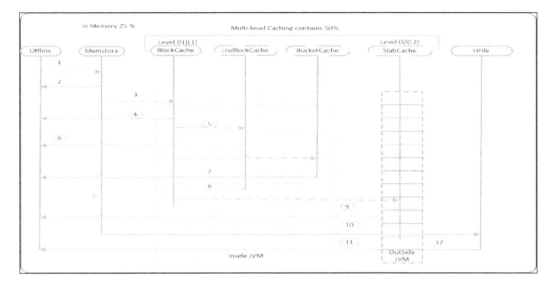

1. MemStore accumulates data edits as they keep coming and buffers them in memory.

2. The data then comes to a memory area called bucket for holding cache blocks. The size of the block is predefined.

3. Internally, it's allocated to the lruBlockCache and then to the off-heap SlabCache (steps 6, 7, 8, 9 in the preceding sequence diagram).

4. Based on the block size, the data is flushed to the HFile and HDFS (steps 11 and 12 in the preceding sequence diagram):

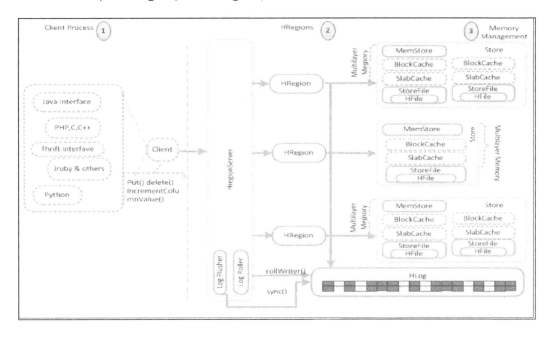

5. Clients initiate an RPC as a key/value object (any client coming from a variety of interfaces can be a batch process or a streaming request). Invoked `put()`, `delete()`, or `incrementColumnValue()` instances are intercepted by the HRegionServer. Then the request is transferred to the respective HRegion that has the row on which the changes need to be made.

6. The data is first written to WAL and then to the MemStore of the corresponding Store that has the record. The size of the MemStore is precisely and constantly monitored by the system's internal process.

7. The multilayer memory split process kicks in and the memory is chunked based on the MemStore, BlockCache, and SlabCache specified in the system.

8. Eventually, once the MemStore size reaches the specified size in the configuration file, it moves the data to the BlockCache and then to the SlabCache. The Slabcache data is eventually pushed to disk by the internal process.

 Note that this process helps the stop-the-world GC process, where the system is adversely impacted.

# Transactions (ACID) and multiversion concurrency control (MVCC)

HBase is not an ACID (Atomicity, Consistency, Isolation, Durability) compliant database as per the general rule of ACID compliance. It achieves it in a different way, as described next:

**Atomicity:**

1. HBase provides ACID semantics on a per-row basis due to performance-related considerations. Any put operations will either fully succeed or fully fail.

2. This scenario is true in the cases where modification spans multiple column families within a row.

3. The checkAndPut API acts like compareAndSet as an automatic process giving HBase the row-level granularity.

4. The mutation is very well organized for each row with no interleaving.

5. Consistency & Isolation is the row returned via scan will be a complete row, which will exist in the table history.

6. It's only possible to move the states forward through the history of edits on it.

7. At this time, if a scan is performed, it will always provide the consistent view.

8. The scanning gets all the data that was written prior to the scan operation.

**Durability:**

1. The visible data is that which is persisted on the disk.

2. If the call returns success, it means that the data is persisted on the disk, and in case of failure/exceptions, it means that the data will not persist.

3. All reasonable exceptions/failure will not affect the guarantee of this document.

HBase uses multiversion concurrency control to solve the performance overhead of locking a particular cell for a specific transaction.

Let's discuss this step by step by following the sequence of events that happen internally, as shown in the following figure:

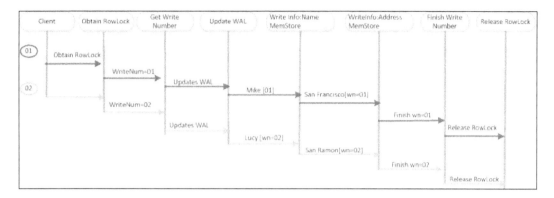

Say the client makes a call to obtain a lock; a new write number is assigned. Once the client gets the write number, it updates the WAL.

In our case, the client with the name Mike is associated with the write number 01, and the address key is also associated with 01, in our case, San Francisco 01.

Then it goes on to finish the write number once the data is persisted; row lock is now released.

Let's say in the meantime, a new write request comes in; it will take a different write number case 02 and follow the same path but with a different write number. Hence, these two calls will have a multiversion.

While the next read after the second call will be picking the name Lucy and the address as San Ramon, this will be the latest version in the system.

Bloom filters is an algorithm used to optimize the usage of in-memory. As the reads are more parallel, the performance increases. This is one of the core designs that this algorithm provides. It resides in the metadata field of the HFile, and hence, no update is needed. It's invoked and loaded into memory whenever an HFile is opened due to the region being deployed to the region server. Bloom filter is fine-tuned to work with HBase as it reduces the size and keeps the false positive rate within the required limit.

Bloom filters were introduced in HBASE-1200. Since HBase 0.96, row-based bloom filters have been enabled by default. (HBASE-). It's not very good for scanning queries.

It's pivotal to monitor and know BlockCacheHitRatio in the RegionServer matrix. This gives a clear pattern of how data is loaded in our cluster. We must enable row and column combinations in case we see an increase in the `BloomFilter` filtering blocks, deeming that they are not needed. This process is very effective when the size of the data is a few kilobytes. In the case of large StoreFiles, the overhead is further reduced as it avoids additional disk I/Os during low-level scans to find a specific row.

Note, however, that delete is a problem in `BloomFilter`. Thus, it's not very effective where a large number of deletes are performed as `BloomFilter` needs to be rebuilt.

**Enabling Bloom Filter**: Bloom filter is enabled at `ColumnFamily`; this can be done by the `setBloomFilterType` method of `HColumnDescriotor`. The valid values are `None`, by default, `ROW`, or `ROWCOL`.

The command to do it is as follows:

```
hbase> create 'address',{NAME => 'colf1', BLOOMFILTER => 'ROWCOL'}
```

**Compression:**

To understand the internals and to make sure the large, distributed cluster of HBase continuously performs, its essential that the right compression is done at the right time with the right compression technique.

HBase is compatible with an array of compression algorithms, which can be done at ColumnFamily.

1.  Compression reduces the size of large bit-rate reduction/byte array in cells, thus reducing the storage space in a significant way.

2.  This enables more cost-effective ways to keep, manage, and support data across various locations and network bandwidth.

3.  As the data is reduced significantly, the read process using the decompression algorithm allows rapid reading, which reduces the CPU cycle.

 Note that by default, HBase does not specify any type of compression on the data that resides in the cell, but it provides multiple alternative options, such as BLOCK and RECORD.

**Block Compressors:**

- Snappy
- LZO
- LZ4
- GZ

# Snappy

Snappy is a library that uses very effective algorithms for compression and decompression of data. However, the goal is not to maximize compression or compatibility with other compression libraries but to focus on speed and reusable compression. HBase supports different compression mechanisms such as Izo, gzip, or snappy. Gzip comes built in with HBase while Izo/snappy compression needs to be configured separately. When creating a table, you can specify the compression/compression library; HFiles are compressed when written to disk if compression is used.

## How to do it...

1.  Let's log in to our HBase setup.

2.  Once you log in, check the file on this location:

    ```
    /opt/HbaseB/ hbase-0.98.5-hadoop2/snappy-1.0.5/libs/snappy-java-
    1.0.4.1.jar → this has a JNL interface to the libsnappy.so.1.x.x
    which is a native linux-amd64-64 bit lib.
    ```

3.  Once you have verified the path and the JAR file, let's do a quick test to make sure the library is performing as expected:

    ```
    $ hbase org.apache.hadoop.hbase.util.CompressionTest hdfs://host/
    path/to/hbase snappy
    ```

4.  Let's create a column family with snappy compression using the HBase shell:

    ```
    $hbase> create 'ct1', {NAME => 'cf1', COMPRESSION =>'SNAPPY'}
    ```

5.  This creates a column family that has a compression enabled for SNAPPY.

6.  On the same HBase shell, run the following code:

    ```
    $hbase > describe 'ct1';
    ```

The output will show the compression as **"COMPRESSION=> 'SNAPPY'"**.

## How it works...

1.  The Snappy library is invoked by calling the column family compressor parameter SNAPPY.

2.  This inter invokes the corresponding native library using the JNL interface, which invokes the `libsnappy.so` file and hence connects to the code native library and applies the relative algorithm.

## There's more...

```
https://code.google.com/p/snappy/
```

# LZO compression

LZO compression can be split; the LZO block format allows us to decompress the block at a random offset of the file. As the compression has many small blocks of compressed data, it allows the MapReduce jobs to be split along the boundaries thus allowing parallel threads to work on it. Hence, we get incredible speed to write and read.

## How to do it...

This is the library that is shipped with most of the Linux distribution. In case you don't have it, you can download it from `http://pkgs.repoforge.org/lzo/` or from `http://www.oberhumer.com/opensource/lzo/`.

Based on the Linux version, you have to download appropriately:

```
> port fetch lzo2 # If for some reason LZO2 is already installed, please
uninstall first before doing this
> port edit lzo2 # A vim editor should open
// Add the following block of text in the file and save the file.
variant x86_64 description "Build the 64-bit." {
    configure.args-delete      --build=x86-apple-darwin ABI=standard
    configure.cflags-delete    -m32
    configure.cxxflags-delete -m32
    configure.args-append      --build=x86_64-apple-darwin ABI=64
    configure.cflags-append    -m64 -arch x86_64
    configure.cxxflags-append -m64 -arch x86_64
}
## END ##
> port install lzo2 +x86_64
```

1.  Then go to this location by typing it:

    ```
    $ file /usr/local/lib/liblzo2.2.0.0.dylib
    /usr/local/lib/liblzo2.2.0.0.dylib: Mach-O 64-bit dynamically
    linked shared library x86_64
    ```

2. Then run the following command:

```
Env JAVA_HOME=/System/Library/Frameworks/JavaVM.framework/
Versions/1.6/Home/ \C_INCLUDE_PATH=/path/to/lzo64/include LIBRARY_
PATH=/path/to/lzo64/lib \CFLAGS="-arch x86_64" ant clean compile-
native test tar
```

>  Note that in case there are permission issues during the install even as root, you can change the permissions so that the build can go through.

3. Once the install is completed, a JAR file and some LIB files have been created in HADOOP_HOME. All these files *must* be copied both into your HADOOP_HOME and HBASE_HOME directories using the following commands:

```
> cp build/hadoop-gpl-compression-0.1.0-dev/hadoop-gpl-
compression-0.1.0-dev.jar $HADOOP_HOME/lib/
```

```
> cp build/hadoop-gpl-compression-0.1.0-dev/hadoop-gpl-
compression-0.1.0-dev.jar $HBASE_HOME/lib/
```

```
> tar -cBf - -C build/hadoop-gpl-compression-0.1.0-dev/lib/native
. | tar -xBvf - -C $HADOOP_HOME/lib/native
```

```
> tar -cBf - -C build/hadoop-gpl-compression-0.1.0-dev/lib/native
. | tar -xBvf - -C $HBASE_HOME/lib/native
```

>  Note that alternatively, you can also build an LZO compression library by compiling it on the Linux 64-bit machine.

4. At this point, you can recycle the HBase cluster and type the following command:

```
create 'tb05', {NAME=>'colfam05:', COMPRESSION=>'lzo'}
```

## How it works...

The invocation path is very similar to the Snappy invocation.

## There's more...

```
https://github.com/toddlipcon/hadoop-lzo-packager
```

# LZ4 compressor

This library provides access to two compression methods, both of which generate a valid LZ4 stream:

1. Fast scan (LZ4):
   - Low memory footprint (~16 KB)
   - Very fast (fast scan with skipping heuristics in case the input looks incompressible)
   - Reasonable compression ratio (depending on the redundancy of the input)

2. High compression (LZ4 HC):
   - Medium memory footprint (~ 256 KB)
   - Rather slow (~10 times slower than LZ4)

A good compression ratio (depending on the size and the redundancy of the input).

The streams produced by these two compression algorithms use the same compression format; they are very fast to decompress and can be decompressed by the same decompressor instance.

## How to do it...

LZ4 comes bundled with Hadoop. Check for the shared object(so) file, libhadoop.so, which has proper read, write, and execute rights while starting HBase. This can be done post setup too by creating a symbolic link from HBase libraries to the Hadoop native libraries.

For example, suppose your platform is Linux-amd64-64:

1. Then from the user HOME directory use the following command:

```
$ cd $HBASE_HOME
$ mkdir lib/native
$ ln -s $HADOOP_HOME/lib/native lib/native/Linux-amd64-64
```

2. Once this is executed, you can test the setting with the following command:

```
hbase(main):004:0> alter 'tb05', {NAME => 'colfam05', COMPRESSION => 'LZ4'}
```

There's more...

https://code.google.com/p/lz4/

**Data block encoding types:**

- ▸ **Fast Diff**: This is much faster than the regular diff process. It also has some changes made to effectively identify and track the changes in the data, which it does by adding a field that stores a single bit to track the changes with the previous row. In case the data is the same, it's not stored again.

- ▸ **Prefix Tree**: This data structure is extremely useful when we want fast and random access at the cost of slower encoding. This works by tagging every string with an object and is sometimes used as a substitute for hash map.

# Replication

As the system grows and becomes more distributed, the need for data replication grows rapidly. It works on the core principle of moving a transactional data from one cluster to another. Usually, the master initiates the push to the slave. These transactions are usually done in an asynchronous manner. This is done to minimize the overhead on the master system. Usually, these transactions are done in a batch mode, and the size of the data packets can be controlled by the configuration size.

The benefits of HBase replication are as follows:

- ▸ Data aggregation

- ▸ Online data ingestion combined with offline data analysis

- ▸ Geographic data distribution across multiple data centres

- ▸ Backup and disaster recovery

## How to do it...

1. Let's edit `hbase-site.xml`:

   ```
   ${HBASE_HOME}/conf/hbase-site.xml on both clusters and add the
   following:
   <property>
   <name>hbase.replication</name>
   <value>true</value>
   </property>
   ```

2. Copy or SCP `hbase-site.xml` to all nodes.

3. Recylce the HBase cluster if it's running.

4. Execute the following command using the master's shell:

```
add_peer
add_peer '<n>', "slave.zookeeper.quorum:zookeeper.
clientport.:zookeeper.znode.parent"
```
In this case `<n>` is nothing but a peer ID

5. The following command can be used to add peers:

```
hbase> add_peer '1', "zk.server.com:2181:/hbase"
```

6. One way to do this is to alter the table and set the scope, as follows:

```
disable 'your_table'
alter 'your_table', {NAME => 'family_name', REPLICATION_SCOPE =>
'1'}
enable 'your_table'
```

Currently, a scope of zero (default) means that the data will not be replicated, and a scope of 1 means that it will. This could change in the future.

To list all the peers:

- ▸ List peers
- ▸ You will see the following
- ▸ Considering 1 rs, with ratio 0.1
- ▸ Getting 1 rs from peer cluster # 0
- ▸ Choosing peer `<IP>:62020`
- ▸ This indicates that one Region Server from the slave cluster was chosen for replication

## Deploying Master-Master or Cyclic Replication

For master-master or cyclic replication, repeat the aforementioned steps on each master cluster: add the `hbase.replication` property and set it to true, push the resulting `hbase-site.xml` to all the nodes of this master cluster, use `add_peer` to add the slave cluster, and enable replication of the column families.

## How it works...

1. The replication works with an internal process that cascades transactions running on master to slave; before this process fully starts, the system internally looks at the WALEdit replay cycle, which is a dependent service.

2. Before WALEdits are pushed from master to slave, they're split into batch sizes. The WAL reader process keeps reading till the EOF. Once this is reached, it pushes the residual WALEdits, which is read in read buffer.

3. The master knows the clusterID (ClusterID is a UUID type, which is autogenerated by HBase). To avoid the loss of clusterID during the recycle or node restart, the clusterID are kept in HDFS, which is the filesystem HBase is using internally. This resides inside the /hbase/hbaseid znode. This ID helps to perform master-master/acyclic replication. WAL knows the number of regions that are served by a region server as one WAL is used per region server. When the replication process kicks in, the code is smart enough to filter out the key-value that are planned for the replication. This is orchestrated by matching the key-values of column family with the WAL edit column family data structure. Usually, when a key value is planned to be replicated, an edit is performed on the cluster ID of the key-value of the HBase clusterID of the slave and hence facilitates replication.

4. ZooKeeper plays the role of a coordinator and manages major replication activities, such as registration of slave cluster, starting/stopping replication, handling region server failovers , enqueuing new WALs. For better reliability, it's advisable to have multiple nodes of Zookeeper (3+ is advisable).

There are three different possibilities to perform replication:

- Master-slave (case 01 in the following figure)
- Master-master (case 02 in the following figure)
- Cyclic replication (case 03 in the following figure)
  - **Master-slave**: In this setup, one cluster acts as the master cluster, and the replication can happen from the master to the slave and not reverse. In essence, the transactions are cascaded from the master to the slave; in this case, the slave cluster is an independent cluster and can have its own setup and traffic patterns.
  - **Master-master**: In this setup, the replication can happen in both the directions, which essentially means that both the clusters are taking a live traffic and work as standby for each other. This process of replication seems to get in call collision and tends to go toward an infinite loop. This scenario is solved by creating a mutation-based clusterID. Thus, both the systems get to know when it actually got changed, and hence it works seamlessly.

❑ **Cyclic replication**: In this scenario, there are multiple HBase clusters (more than two) that are actively involved in the replication process. Now each cluster has different scenarios independently, such as master-master, master-slave, and so on. We discussed it in the preceding scenarios. However, there is one unique scenario that comes into picture when we set up a cycle. To discuss this particular scenario, we bring in case 03. The following figure depicts how exactly this works. Say cluster 01 receives a fresh change M and needs to cascade this replicate to clusters:

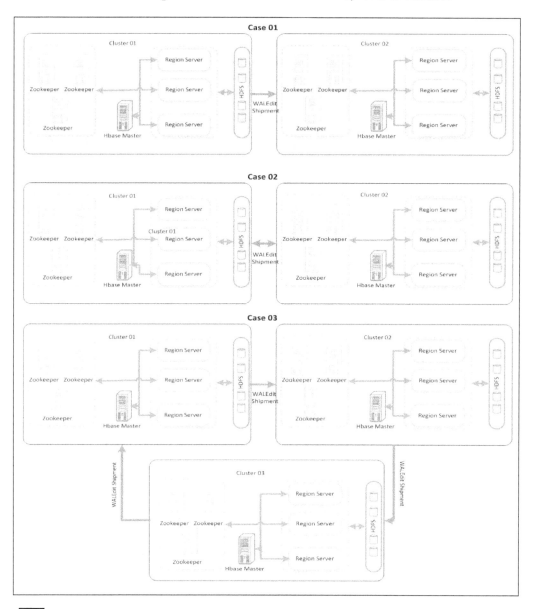

## There's more...

### Disabling Replication at the Peer Level

By running the `disable_peer` on the HBase shell, you can disable the replication for a specific peer. This allows you to stop the replication to the peer without mutating anything in the log; this log can be looked up for future references. Similar to this, if you want to reinstate the replication process, you can run the `enable_peer(<"peerID">)` at HBase shell, and it will start working:

```
Hbase (main):001:0> disable_peer("1")
```

To re-enable peer 1:

```
Hbase (main):001:0> enable_peer("1")
```

Replication can sometimes be risky and may cause issues. In such cases, stop the replication at runtime by the following command:

```
hbase(main):001:0> stop_replication
```

To start replicating again, execute the following command from the HBase shell:

```
Hbase (main):001:0> start_replication
```

This starts the replication process as designed.

# 5

# Working with Scalable Structure of tables

In this chapter we will cover the following topics:

- ▶ HBase data model part 1
- ▶ HBase date model part 2
- ▶ How to truly scale on this key and schema design

This chapter will allow you to have a closer look on the internal key and schema design decisions and how these designs allow **HBase** to scale by providing a true flexible schema and give optimum performance at any scale.

## Introduction

HBase is uniquely designed for scale and provides ability to read and write individual cells, columns, column families, column qualifier, row-keys, versions of data, and timestamps updating data without usage of **MapReduce**. It is totally different from the traditional RDBMS databases. An RDBMS system takes advantage of the following structural concepts such as schema (logical representation of various grouped objects), tables, columns, foreign keys, joins, indexes, store procedures, queries, hints cache, and so on. This works well if the data is structured, but starts getting very complex if the data grows very fast (exponentially); the data structure changes very frequently.

# HBase data model part 1

It is very important to understand the data model of HBase and the core principle on which it stands and provides the foundation to scale. We will go through the following concepts:

- Logical view
- Physical view
- Tables
- Namespace
- Rows
- Columns
- Column families
- Column qualifier
- Cells

**Logical view** of HBase represents distributed, persistent multinational store map, which represents the data in a column and row, key along a timestamp. It also shows a representation of how data is kept to get maximum scalability and performance.

The following screenshot shows data that is represented in an HBase table:

```
hbase(main):014:0> scan 'MyClickStream'
ROW                           COLUMN+CELL
2016-12-29 11:56:52,026 DEBUG [main] client.ClientScanner: Advancing internal scanner to startKey at '2'
 row01                        column=cfWeb:web, timestamp=1409453734860, value=www.google.com
 row02                        column=cfWeb:web, timestamp=1409453755971, value=www.yahoo.com
 row03                        column=cfWeb:web, timestamp=1409453771036, value=www.bing.com
 row05                        column=cfWeb:web, timestamp=1409454028718, value=www.fries.com
 row06                        column=cfWeb:web, timestamp=1409454088675, value=www.ebay.com
 row07                        column=cfWeb:web, timestamp=1409454128366, value=www.walmart.com
 row08                        column=cfWeb:web, timestamp=1409454142524, value=www.amazon.com
```

The logical representation of the preceding table is as follows:

| rowkey | Column family | Column qualifier | timestamp | value |
|--------|---------------|------------------|-----------|-------|
| row01 | cfWeb | web | 1409453734860 | www.google.com |
| row02 | cfWeb | web | 1409453755971 | www.yahoo.com |
| row03 | cfWeb | web | 1409453771036 | www.bing.com |

| rowkey | Column family | Column qualifier | timestamp | value |
|--------|---------------|------------------|-----------|-------|
| row05 | cfWeb | web | 1409454028718 | www.fries.com |
| row06 | cfWeb | web | 1409454088675 | www.ebay.com |
| row07 | cfWeb | web | 1409454128366 | www.walmart.com |
| row08 | cfWeb | web | 1409454142524 | www.amazon.com |

**Tables** in HBase are stored in regions. These tables are present in separate partitions and are fine-tuned as a cohesive logical group of row/columns. The region servers in coordination with HBase master make sure they are synced and the table has the latest data.

The name of the table is a string, and is collection of characters which are used in the filesystem path.

**Namespace** is a reasonable federation of tables comparable to a database in RDBMS. HBase provides a default namespace and the tables, which has no explicit defined namespace automatically falls in the default namespace. Thus any rights granted at these levels is cascaded to all child objects. An HBase admin who has access to make changes to the namespace can perform various activities such as create/drop tables, take a snapshot, and restore from a snapshot, splits or major compactions on tables that are within the boundaries of the namespace.

The following commands are used in the context of namespace in HBase:

- `create_namespace`
- `alter_namespace`
- `describe_namespace`
- `drop_namespace`
- `list_namespace`
- `list_namespace_tables`

For creating a namespace, log in to the HBase shell and run the following commands for creating, listing, and describing the namespaces:

```
hbase(main):001:0> create_namespace 'my_project_ns'
hbase(main):007:0> list_namespace
NAMESPACE

default
hbase
my_project_ns
4 row(s) in 0.3030 seconds

hbase(main):013:0> describe_namespace 'my_project_ns'
DESCRIPTION
{NAME => 'my_project_ns'}
1 row(s) in 0.0660 seconds

hbase(main):017:0> alter_namespace 'my_project_ns',{METHOD =>'set','table_name'=>'my_click_stream'}
0 row(s) in 0.2380 seconds
```

 We added a table to the existing namespace here. We will go into the details of this in the *How to do it...* section.

**Columns family** is a logical and physical group of columns separated by same prefix, such as `cfWeb` is a column family. Column family needs to be declared upfront at schema definition time, whereas column is not mandatory to be defined at schema time. All the rows are tagged to the same column family, but it's not mandatory to store data in all its families. The HBase table design framework allows us to create columns at runtime without hindering to the operations happening on the table. The columns in one family are stored separately from the columns in another family. If you have data that is not often queried, assign that data to a separate column family.

Columns and column families are stored together in an HFile. This is the level the core features like compression.

**Column qualifier** is of 3 or 5 bytes with the first byte as an ID, which denotes the column as a qualifier. It's defined with the data value by which we can accurately and uniquely identify it.

Column qualifier is associated to the data at one side and as a parent reference to column family, thus is not must to be defined while table creation. It can be inconsistent between rows. Column qualifiers is not having any datatype and is always referenced using byte[]. Column qualifier can be unlimited in content length. It is assigned default by the HBase in case you have not defiled it during the create process. It's also variable, which means new data can be added to column families as we progress. These flexibility makes HBase highly flexible and scalable.

 It is advisable to keep the column qualifier short and meaningful as it will be expensive as the storage needs grow and may start impacting performance, for example `CN = City Name`.

Cells store everything that is written to HBase from the logical representation perspective, but physically the data is stored in HDFS with a pointer reference in the cell. Logically speaking cells are the smallest units for the data storage and are identified by a multidimensional key:

```
{row, column, qualifier, timestamp}
```

**Namespace | tables | column families | cell**

 Value in HBase is a byte[] as it does not have any datatype.

## How to do it...

Let us connect to the cluster we created earlier and make sure all the components are working:

1. Let's login to the HBase Master by executing the following command:

```
hbase(main):023:0> create_namespace 'mywebproject'
0 row(s) in 0.0750 seconds
```

This creates a namespace in the Master schema. This way we won't be using the default namespace.

2. Now associate the table with the namespace using the following commands:

```
hbase(main):024:0> create 'mywebproject:myclickstream','web','websitedata','websiteurls','websiteurlsclick'
0 row(s) in 2.4960 seconds
```

3. Check the namespace for its contents, it must contain the namespace which we just created as shown in the following screenshot:

```
hbase(main):025:0> list_namespace 'mywebproject'
NAMESPACE
mywebproject
1 row(s) in 0.0070 seconds
```

4. Let's put some records in the web column family:

```
hbase(main):002:0> put 'mywebproject:myclickstream','row02','web','www.yahoo.com'
0 row(s) in 0.0360 seconds
hbase(main):004:0> put 'mywebproject:myclickstream','row03','web','www.google.com'
0 row(s) in 0.0110 seconds

hbase(main):005:0> put 'mywebproject:myclickstream','row04','web','www.walmart.com'
0 row(s) in 0.0070 seconds

hbase(main):006:0> put 'mywebproject:myclickstream','row05','web','www.amazon.com'
0 row(s) in 0.0030 seconds

hbase(main):007:0> put 'mywebproject:myclickstream','row06','web','www.ebay.com'
0 row(s) in 0.0050 seconds

05) now lets put some data in the second column family 'websitedata'
hbase(main):009:0> put 'mywebproject:myclickstream','row01','websitedata','newandportaldata'
0 row(s) in 0.0040 seconds

hbase(main):010:0> put 'mywebproject:myclickstream','row02','websitedata','newandportalmediadata'
0 row(s) in 0.0040 seconds

hbase(main):011:0> put 'mywebproject:myclickstream','row03','websitedata','searhemailportalgoogleandroidmobilephone'
0 row(s) in 0.0040 seconds

hbase(main):012:0> put 'mywebproject:myclickstream','row04','websitedata','ecommercestoresretail'
0 row(s) in 0.0040 seconds

hbase(main):013:0> put 'mywebproject:myclickstream','row05','websitedata','ecommercestoresretailtvmediawebservice'
0 row(s) in 0.0040 seconds

hbase(main):014:0> put 'mywebproject:myclickstream','row06','websitedata','ecommercauctions'
0 row(s) in 0.0030 seconds
```

5. Let's scan it to check whatever we put is as expected:

```
hbase(main):015:0> scan 'mywebproject:myclickstream'
ROW                       COLUMN+CELL
 row01                     column=web:, timestamp=1425248071962, value=www.yahoo.com
 row01                     column=websitedata:, timestamp=1425248403602, value=newandportaldata
 row02                     column=web:, timestamp=1425248095238, value=www.yahoo.com
 row02                     column=websitedata:, timestamp=1425248425374, value=newandportalmediadata
 row03                     column=web:, timestamp=1425248140008, value=www.google.com
 row03                     column=websitedata:, timestamp=1425248470557, value=searhemailportalgoogleandroidmobilephone
 row04                     column=web:, timestamp=1425248185419, value=www.walmart.com
 row04                     column=websitedata:, timestamp=1425248515560, value=ecommercestoresretail
 row05                     column=web:, timestamp=1425248199257, value=www.amazon.com
 row05                     column=websitedata:, timestamp=1425248544111, value=ecommercestoresretailtvmediawebservice
 row06                     column=web:, timestamp=1425248216092, value=www.ebay.com
 row06                     column=websitedata:, timestamp=1425248574536, value=ecommercauctions
```

6. Let us try to get data for a single row with single column family:

```
hbase(main):016:0> get 'mywebproject:myclickstream','row06','websitedata'
COLUMN                          CELL
 websitedata:                    timestamp=1425248574536, value=ecommercauctions
1 row(s) in 0.0230 seconds

08) for multiple column family.

hbase(main):017:0> get 'mywebproject:myclickstream','row06'
COLUMN                          CELL
 web:                            timestamp=1425248216092, value=www.ebay.com
 websitedata:                    timestamp=1425248574536, value=ecommercauctions
2 row(s) in 0.0110 seconds
```

## How it works...

The data model of HBase is totally different to conventional RDBMS, but the logical separation is similar:

- When we create a namespace, it creates a logical separation of the entity within the cluster, specific access, based on the needs can be provided to make sure the logical separation is done with elegance.

- When we create a table, we associate the table with the namespace and then associate the respective column family.

- As we are making the put statement, we are passing the details of namespace, such as table name, rowID, and the column family where I want to insert or update.

- ▸ Similarly we can put data in other rows by changing the ID of the rows, if the same row ID is used then the version of the existing record will change and the old versions will be marked down. The latest version with the current timestamp is kept on the top for any further lookups. This allows the system to work with the true concept of MVCC.

- ▸ Similarly we are putting the data in the other column family, the rows + column family forms the uniqueness and hence till the time the column family is different we can keep inserting the data.

- ▸ To make sure all the `put` statements has gone through as planned we run a `scan` statement in step 06.

- ▸ The scan traverses the same path and we have to pass the exact details such as namespace, table name, row, and column family to get explicit details. Getting a full table scan we are using scan with namespace and table name, this allow the invocation to create a scan lookup on the entire rows agnostic to the number of rows and column families into it.

In case of a large table, it is not advisable to go for a full table scan, it's better to have a specific needs and rearrange the scan with range of rows.

## There's more...

In the preceding section we did not did not discuss the `delete` operations as we were more focused on the various components, which is used to run the `create`, `put` and `scan` statements.

Effective deleting of the records are equally importance to maintain the sanity of the systems and to allow periodic movement of data or purging of data, which is no longer required to fulfill the internal or external needs of the customer.

In HBase these are the following ways to delete a record:

- ▸ Records can be deleted for a specific version of a column

- ▸ Records can be deleted entirely on column basis, for all versions of a column

- ▸ You can also delete the entire family, for all columns of a particular column family

The `delete` process works in a way of **logical delete**. When `delete` is invoked, deleting an entire row, the internal subprocess of HBase creates a **tombstone** for each column family (not each individual column). For example, there is a query to delete a row. There are many ways to do it, the easiest way will be to provide the exact version and thus the record will be deleted. The other way will be to provide the timestamp and the recorder will be marked for delete. In case you have not provided the version or timestamp then the `currentTimeMillis` will be used as a default marker. This will allow a logical delete statement on the cells having version less than equal to the version we passed as a reference. As HBase is designed on the MVCC principal it never modifies data in place. This delete is never executed on storage file instantly but it's marked as logical delete formally know as tombstoning. Once major compaction is triggered during this time a cleanup process is triggered which deletes this data and the tombstones too.

There can be a scenario in which the version we used while deleting a row is greater than any value in the row then it's advisable to delete complete row. You can configure a `delete` operation on `hbase-site.xml` using `hbase.hstore.time.to.purge.deletes` property.

During major compaction `hbase.hstore.time.to.purge.delete` is checked and if it is not set to `0` then the internal process will purge all the records having tombstore including the records which are having timestamp marked for future.

 More details about the class and its specific methods can be found at `https://hbase.apache.org/apidocs/org/apache/hadoop/hbase/client/Delete.html`.

# HBase data model part 2

In the preceding section we discussed details about the core structure of the Hbase data model in this section we would like to go a step further deep to understand and do things, which will make your data model flexible, robust and scalable. And this is essential to know on an operation level too, as the cluster grows it becomes pivotal to take all consideration.

We should take the following steps to make it happen:

- Timestamps
- Versions
- Sort order
- Column metadata
- Joins

**Timestamps**: Every `put` in HBase is marked with a unique timestamp and this acts as a unique reference for a provided version of a value.

HBase associates timestamp by default mapping it with the respective region server. This default characteristic has a lot of flexibility and you can even specify timestamp value while putting date to the cell of that region server.

In case of multi-datacenter timestamp provides a way to avoid conflicts. In some use cases you can also use it to provide consistency of versions in particular to the data which spans for multiple regions. You as use the same timestamps to `insert/put` in both the tables and read the same timestamp when using `get()`.

>  However a lot of design time has gone for the timestamp and in rare case it needs custom manipulation, in case it is essential to do that, then it's advisable to do an encoding at application.

**Versioning**: This is core to HBase as its design is based on **MVCC** (**Multi versions concurrency control**). Whenever we *put* data to HBase a timestamp is associated with the data, this timestamp can be provided by the invoker or is generated automatically by the region servers. This timestamp must be unique for any given cell, as it's directly associated with the cell. With this design each write is assigned a write number, each data cell is written to a **memstore** with a write number and each write completes with a each write number.

Sort order is by default, HBase systems sorting precedence is first row then column family, then column qualifier and last is timestamp, Sorting is done in such a way that newest records are always returned first. Sort order is an important concept as this really speeds up the scan process in case and from application or client you don't need to pass a sort order in case you need the newest row or newest cell.

In some scenarios the HBase architecture imposes certain restriction for executing sort with some data value in ascending or descending order.

For example if we want to sort the details of URL with respect to their put dates in descending order or with respect to their DNS in descending order then there is no clear and effective solutions.

To overcome this, some form of secondary indexing needs to be done

**Column metadata**: This is stored inside the internal `KeyValue` instances of column family. This enables HBase to accommodate wider number of columns per row, but it can also store heterogeneous set of columns between rows, but this comes with an additional responsibility as you have to keep track of the column names.

**Joins**: This concept in HBase is slightly different then the usual RDBMS joins. In HBase you can achieve the same functionality by following ways:

- Denormalization
- Lookup-tables

## How to do it...

1. Login to your HBase cluster.

2. We will now discuss about timestamps. On your HBase shell type the following command:

```
hbase(main):003:0> scan 'mywebproject:myclickstream'
ROW                          COLUMN+CELL
 row01                       column=web:, timestamp=1425248071962, value=www.yahoo.com
 row01                       column=websitedata:, timestamp=1425248403602, value=newandportaldata
 row02                       column=web:, timestamp=1425248095238, value=www.yahoo.com
 row02                       column=websitedata:, timestamp=1425248425374, value=newandportalmediadata
 row03                       column=web:, timestamp=1425248140008, value=www.google.com
 row03                       column=websitedata:, timestamp=1425248470557, value=searhemailportalgoogleandroidmobilephone
 row04                       column=web:, timestamp=1425248185419, value=www.walmart.com
 row04                       column=websitedata:, timestamp=1425248515560, value=ecommercestoresretail
 row05                       column=websitedata:, timestamp=1425248544111, value=ecommercestoresretailtvmediawebservice
 row06                       column=web:, timestamp=1425248216092, value=www.ebay.com
 row06                       column=websitedata:, timestamp=1425248574536, value=ecommerceauctions
6 row(s) in 0.1160 seconds
```

3. I am assuming you are still connected to the HBase cluster. You can also specify the number of version you want to have in your table:

```
hbase(main):020:0> alter 'mywebproject:myclickstream','web','websitedata','websiteurls','websiteurlsclick', NAME =>'web', VERSIONS =>5
Updating all regions with the new schema...
0/1 regions updated.
1/1 regions updated.
Done.
Updating all regions with the new schema...
0/1 regions updated.
1/1 regions updated.
Done.
Updating all regions with the new schema...
0/1 regions updated.
1/1 regions updated.
Done.
Updating all regions with the new schema...
0/1 regions updated.
1/1 regions updated.
Done.
Updating all regions with the new schema...
0/1 regions updated.
1/1 regions updated.
Done.
0 row(s) in 12.0590 seconds
```

As shown in the preceding screenshot, it is very much possible to pass number of versions as a input parameter on a column family level. When max version number is reached HBase marks the older version as tombstone (logical deletions of records). By default HBase keeps 3 versions of cell data. However you can go for higher version if needed but this will increase the store file size, which will translate it to more storage overhead.

4. Let's discuss sort order.

   Secondary indexing is a way in which you want to reorganize your sort order if you want to customize it, we will discuss this in the MapReduce section or in Integration with Apache Phoenix client.

5. For column metadata use the following commands to connect to HBase shell:

   ```
   ./hbase shell -d
   ```

   -d is for debug option:

We will discuss joins in MapReduce section.

## How it works...

When we do a get, the recent timestamp of each cell is returned which in most the case it the most resent version of the data. But in some case you may not require this. You can use `Get.setMaxVerions()` to return more than one version, alternatively you can also use `Get.setTimeRange()` if you want other than latest versions.

When you run a `put` statement, the system always creates a new version of a cell in which the data resides logically and associates a default timestamp. This sits with the core architecture of true MVCC and also allows you to programmatically change the timestamp if you need it.

On each `put`, a new value is written for an existing cell, which in turn creates a new key-value payer by appending it to the store.

## There's more...

(**HBASE-2256**) discusses some scenarios in which if you invoke the `delete` operation and within milliseconds if you perform `put`, in rare scenarios row will miss a cell. This happens because the `delete` process marks a tombstone. And this tombstone record will be purged during the major compaction process. Now in case we deleted all the records which is less than or equal to **time** (**T**) and there is no major compaction happened during this time, which means the records are still there but with no reference, now during this time there is a `put` statement which will pose as if it's succeeded as there is no exception thrown, but in reality it's not succeeded an immediate `get` will have no effect. This issue can be avoided by incrementing timestamp for new `put` to a row.

# How HBase truly scales on key and schema design

In HBase schema design is one of the most critical part as it can be lifeline for a system which can grow on petabytes of data at a rapid pace.

> As the internal structure of HBase is designed to scale at a very high level of read and write the design of the data structure needs to use the same principles. It is essential to design the schema based on the access patterns of the applications like the row, key and the table structure must follow the same guiding thought. This defies the core principles on which the foundation of relational databases.

In HBase you design a denormalized table keeping in mind how the data will be effectively retrieved and inserted (`put` and `get`) by the applications and will perform with a consistency as the volume of data grows, so you need to plan in much advance.

You are much closer to the system with HBase as compared to the RDBMS.

It is essential to design the system which allows storage of very large volume of data is fault tolerant and is designed for high performance and scalability.

In doing so we must consider the following points:

- Row key design
- Supported data types
- Number of column families
- Number of versions
- Time to Live
- Keeping deleted cells
- Secondary indexes and alternative Query paths
- Column families in a table
- Columns in column family
- Data in column family
- Constrains
- Salting
- Tall Narrow VS Flat-Wide tables

**Row key design**:

HBase row keys are stored lexicographically and mapped to the column families. Column families are associated to list of column qualifiers, which is mapped to list of timestamps, which is an intern's maps to a cell, which has the pointer to the data which is kept in the HDFS or in memory. HBase implements MVCC and keeps the latest version as on the top and by defaults returns the latest version.

This design provides good performance on scan, which allows to store related rows. A poorly designed schema can lead to something known as hot spotting (it happens when a huge amount of client traffic is pointed to a few nodes in the cluster for all the operations, such as `read`, `write`, and other operations); this flood of requests causes the load of that region to increase exponentially and eventually causing the region to a standstill.

To overcome this, the row keys needs to be designed very carefully such that rows which needs to be in the same region stays together. And the data can be written to multiple region throughout the cluster.

Some of the other ways to design a better solution to avoid hot spotting are listed here:

- Salting: This can significantly improve read/write performance by presplitting the data into multiple regions. Although salting will yield better performance in most scenarios.
- Hashing
- Reversing the key

**Supported data types**:

Any data which is put in the HBase system is persistent and has multiple versions (varies based on the needs). This is achieved in a different way as RDBMS. The data model is a sorted nested map of maps and sits on top of the physical data model.

This model is very simple as per schemas goes. It provides very little facilities for mapping application-level meaning to physical layout. The only datatype this logical data model exposes is the humble byte[] and its encoding is a simple **no-op [3]**.

 While the byte [] datatype is sufficient, it's not very convenient for application developers and it's sometimes difficult to relate.

Let us take an example.

It will be convenient to have and item product number, bar code price as a byte[] datatype, but rather as a value conforming to the numeric type.

HBase requires that, I accept the burden of both datatype constraint maintenance and data value encoding into my application.

It's essential to use HBase data encodings for Java languages primitive types. These encodings are implemented in the methods on the bytes class.

 These methods allow us to transform the Java types into byte[]and back again. The caveat to this back and forth transformation is you have to sort the it every time which in the large dataset is a tedious task, as while transformation the sort order is lost always.

The core principle of sorted map of maps is extremely important in designing table layouts for effective read and write of your applications. The sort order influences physical layout of data on disk as is important to optimize the read and write to the disk, this also direct impact on data access patterns and latency.

In essence an effective schema design is the task of orchestrating your data physically so as to minimize the latency of the access patterns that are important to your application. This drives every aspect of designing a row key that orders well for the application.

The default encodings not promising the natural sorting of the values they represent in the data structure, it can become difficult to reason about application performance. HBase gives freedom to application developers to apply their own encoding that will represent the natural sorting of any data types they wish to use.

**Number of column families**:

In HBase, column families are stored in HFiles which are unique, keep the number of column families as small as possible. Thus it's essential for the performance reasons to reduce the number of column families to reduce the frequency of MemStore flushes, and the frequency of compactions. And, by using the smallest number of column families possible, we can improve the LOAD time and reduce disk consumption, as all the disk lookups are expensive in nature.

**Number of versions**:

In HBase version is a unique and are applied on each `put` and is cascaded on `{row,column,cell}`. It's very much possible to have multiple version of records exist at cell level wherein the row and columns are having same version. Version is a `long integer` datatype. It's stored in decreasing order, thus while scanning the latest comes first always.

In the early versions of HBase say 0.96, by design the number of version which we stored was 3, in new versions it's 1.

Its possible to set how many versions to keep while creating a table:

```
hbase> alter 'myclickstream', NAME => 'web1', MIN_VERSIONS => 2
```

By default, when doing get the latest version cell whose version has the largest value will be returned, if you have not specified a explicit version in your `get` query, in some scenarios this may or may not be the latest one written. The default behavior can be modified in the following ways:

- To return more than one version, see `Get.setMaxVersions()`
- To return versions other than the latest, see `Get.setTimeRange()`

To get latest version that is less than or equal to a given value, thus giving the *latest* state of the record at a certain point in time, just use a range from `0` to the desired version and set the `max versions` property to `1`.

**Time to Live (TTL)**:

TTL in HBase can be set at column family or at a cell level. Once the TTL is reached HBase marks a tombstone and by the HBase internal process these objects will be deleted will be taken up by the new dataset. In case there is a need to keep the data forever, we have to disable this TTL feature by setting `hbase.store.delete.expired.storefile`. The other way is to set the version to any other version than `0`.

Delete and TTL directly relates as TTL governs the physical `delete` operation of data. Delete checks for minimum version of data and the TTL. A careful consideration needs to be taken based on the application needs. For cases like backup, it's advisable to have a longer TTL and to keep a certain number of versions.

In some cases it's good to keep the TTL as follows:

- ▶ Expire it after 2 weeks
- ▶ Keep three versions of data

 During the `delete` invocation the cells become invisible and `scan` and `get` bypasses the deleted cells or the cells which has a tombstone marker.

There are various types of tombstone markers:

- ▶ Based on version `delete` marker, this tags a single version of a column for deletions
- ▶ Column family delete marker effects at a column family level
- ▶ Column delete marker deletes the entire column

HBase is very flexible thus it provides the flexibility to set time per cell basis.

Unit of cell TTL are in milliseconds rather in seconds. The cell TTL is governed by column family level TTL setting, which means a cell TTL cannot extent the parent column family level TTL.

**Keeping deleted cells**:

There are scenarios in which keeping the deleted cells is important and provides risk coverage. These can be cases such as:

- ▶ Software/hardware errors
- ▶ Data warehouse needs
- ▶ Backup needs

The `get/scan` commands will miss the deleted cell agnostic to the time range specified in the query.

There is an option for column families to keep deleted cells. In this scenario, the deleted marked cell scan still be retrieved even though it's having a tombstone. This can happen if the `get` or `scan` command is having a time range that is before the delete actually affects the cell. This gives us the opportunity to query the cells even in the presence of delete operations. This is referred as point in time queries.

Deleted cells abide by TTLs and stay below the maximum number of version specified.

The raw `scan` command provides the ability to see the deleted rows and cells. In the command prompt enter  the following command:

```
hbase> alter 'myclickstream', NAME => 'web1', KEEP_DELETED_CELLS => true
```

Using a Java client if we pass it the way it as shown in the following command, the flag in memory will be passed as `true` and this will be set. Later on these parameters will be flushed to the disk and will be persistent:

```
HcolumnDescriptor.setKeepDeletedCells(true);
```

**Secondary indexes and alternative query path**:

In HBase access of data uses a single index that is lexicographically sorted to the primary row key. For the use cases in which the records need to scan differently will result in all the rows against the filter. Secondary indexing, the columns you index form an alternate row key to allow point lookups and range scans along this new axis.

**Column families in a table:**

All column families are stored together, physically by design on the filesystem. This provides an inbuilt tuning capability at the storage layer; it is advised that all column family members have the same general access pattern and size characteristics. Thus it's advisable to keep the column families limited in a table and group then logically. The official recommendation for the number of column families per table is three or less.

**Columns versus column family**:

It is advisable to use few column families, as this opens lots of files that opens per region. When we separate data and `Meta` column logically we can get the best performance. The design of is always done based on the application access pattern.

**Data in column family**:

The data in column family depends upon the block size (64 KB is the default) of Hfile. This directly affects the size of the block index. The smaller the block size the larger will be index and hence will consume more memory. It's advisable to have a larger chunk of HFile to be loaded in the memory at once. Thus setting the block size to a large value provides better random read.

It also depends upon the block cache, aggressive caching, bloom filer, compression, TTL, cell versioning.

**Constrains**:

In HBase constrains are added before the tables is loaded using the following command:

```
Constrains. add(HTableDescriptor desc,Class<? Extends Constraint>...
constraints)
```

Alternatively the following command can also be used:

```
Constraints.add(HTableDescriptor,org.apache.hadoop.hbase.util.Pair...)
```

Constraints run in the order that they are added. Further, constrains impact write speed when it's used on cross-table references. But this can be done in practice.

 Implementing classes must have a nullary (no-args) constructor.

**Salting**:

In a large HBase cluster there is a problem of hotspotting. As discussed earlier, salting is one of the ways to bypass this problem, In case of salting in HBase it's not much about cryptography but about the randomness which we are trying to create by prefixing the random salted value to the key. By this we change the sorting nature and hence it will be distributed to different regions and hence hot spotting can be avoided.

Let us walk through and quick example that depicts how salting can spread wide load across the cluster.

Say you have 50 nodes, a cluster distributed as five regions, and keys as follows:

`Hello001`

`Hello002`

`Hello003`

`Hello004`

`Hello005`

So for all the rows staring with `H` they will go in the same region and hence created a imbalance in the region loading pattern, as the load starts growing the Zookeeper, which is responsible for the heartbeat of the region server, will start timing out and start throwing `YouAreDeadException` and finally it will create the hotspot.

The smarter way is to salt the keys with different salts such as `A`, `B`, `C`, `D`, and `E`. This will ensure it will go to five different regions. You can also use numbered prefixes. You can also do salting to keep the common data stay together for scanning or MapReduce processing:

`AHello001`

`BHello002`

`CHello003`

`DHello004`

`EHello005`

**Hashing**:

One-way hashing will also create a unique and will allow the rows to be always salted, which will eventually help to split the load across different region servers.

**Random key**:

This is a another way to achieve similar results. Random key also allows the keys to be distributed to different region servers; you can use a good hashing algorithm or can use `Maths.random()` Java class

**Tall-narrow versus flat-wide tables**:

**Tall-narrow table layout**: In the context of table design it means few columns but many rows:

| | Column Families : <qualifier> | |
|---|---|---|
| **Row** | clickstream:column_name | Actor:column_name |
| <type><login_id><Long. Max_VALUE-System. currentTimeMillis()> | Clickstream:homepage | Actor:address |
| | Clickstream:login | Actor:zip |

**Flat wide table layout**: This means few rows but many columns:

| | Column Families | |
|---|---|---|
| **Row** | clickstream:column_name | Actor:column_name |
| <type><login_id> | Clickstream:homepage | Actor:address |
| | Clickstream:login | Actor:zip |

Tall and narrow table design is more beneficial due to the following reasons:

► In flat-wide table design single row can expand and go beyond the maximum file/ region size and can work against the region split

► This is a guideline, every project/system needs some customizations please make changes to the system according to your custom needs

## How to do it...

1. Let us connect to the cluster which we have setup:

```
hbase(main):003:0> scan 'mywebproject:myclickstream'
ROW                        COLUMN+CELL
 row01                     column=web:, timestamp=1425248071962, value=www.yahoo.com
 row01                     column=websitedata:, timestamp=1425248403602, value=newandportaldata
 row02                     column=web:, timestamp=1425248095238, value=www.yahoo.com
 row02                     column=websitedata:, timestamp=1425248425374, value=newandportalmediadata
 row03                     column=web:, timestamp=1425248140008, value=www.google.com
 row03                     column=websitedata:, timestamp=1425248470557, value=searhemailportalgoogleandroidmobilephone
 row04                     column=web:, timestamp=1425248185419, value=www.walmart.com
 row04                     column=websitedata:, timestamp=1425248515560, value=ecommercestoresretail
 row05                     column=web:, timestamp=1425248199257, value=www.amazon.com
 row05                     column=websitedata:, timestamp=1425248544111, value=ecommercestoresretailtvmediawebservice
 row06                     column=web:, timestamp=1425248216092, value=www.ebay.com
 row06                     column=websitedata:, timestamp=1425248574536, value=ecommercauctions
6 row(s) in 0.0710 seconds
```

The row key marked in blue provides a clear mapping to the column family which is web in orange colour.

2. The preceding `scan` also shows the column families which are `web` and `websitedata`.

3. It also provides the number of column families which is 2 as `web` and `websitedata` is marked as column families. For number of versions we have to modify the `scan` query to give `RAW` data:

```
hbase(main):012:0> scan 'mywebproject:myclickstream',{RAW => true, VERSIONS => 2}
ROW                        COLUMN+CELL
 row01                     column=web:, timestamp=1425248071962, value=www.yahoo.com
 row01                     column=websitedata:, timestamp=1425248403602, value=newandportaldata
 row02                     column=web:, timestamp=1425248095238, value=www.yahoo.com
 row02                     column=websitedata:, timestamp=1425248425374, value=newandportalmediadata
 row03                     column=web:, timestamp=1425248140008, value=www.google.com
 row03                     column=websitedata:, timestamp=1425248470557, value=searhemailportalgoogleandroidmobilephone
 row04                     column=web:, timestamp=1425248185419, value=www.walmart.com
 row04                     column=websitedata:, timestamp=1425248515560, value=ecommercestoresretail
 row05                     column=web:, timestamp=1425266848775, value=www.amazon.com
 row05                     column=web:, timestamp=1425248199257, value=www.amazon.com
 row05                     column=websitedata:, timestamp=1425248544111, value=ecommercestoresretailtvmediawebservice
 row06                     column=web:, timestamp=1425248216092, value=www.ebay.com
 row06                     column=websitedata:, timestamp=1425248574536, value=ecommercauctions
6 row(s) in 0.0530 seconds
```

In the preceding example, when we ran the `scan` operation, we got six rows. The `row05` has two version as we `put` two rows with the same data but at different timestamps and the system created two different versions of it.

4. To get TTL we have to set the TTL first and then try to retrieve it using the `describe` command:

```
hbase(main):021:0> alter 'mywebproject:myclickstream',{NAME =>'web', TTL => 2592000, BLOCKCACHE => true}
Updating all regions with the new schema...
0/1 regions updated.
1/1 regions updated.
Done.
0 row(s) in 2.4130 seconds
```

In the preceding example, we have set the TTL for 2592000.

5. Now let's run a `describe` command to see the set TTL value:

```
hbase(main):022:0> describe 'mywebproject:myclickstream'
DESCRIPTION                                                                            ENABLED
 'mywebproject:myclickstream', {NAME => 'web', BLOOMFILTER => 'ROW', VERSIONS => '2', IN_MEMORY => true
 'false', KEEP_DELETED_CELLS => 'false', DATA_BLOCK_ENCODING => 'NONE', TTL => '2592000 SECONDS (
 30 DAYS)', COMPRESSION => 'NONE', MIN_VERSIONS => '0', BLOCKCACHE => 'true', BLOCKSIZE => '65536'
 , REPLICATION_SCOPE => '0'}, {NAME => 'websitedata', BLOOMFILTER => 'ROW', VERSIONS => '1', IN_ME
MORY => 'false', KEEP_DELETED_CELLS => 'false', DATA_BLOCK_ENCODING => 'NONE', TTL => 'FOREVER',
COMPRESSION => 'NONE', MIN_VERSIONS => '0', BLOCKCACHE => 'true', BLOCKSIZE => '65536', REPLICATI
ON_SCOPE => '0'}, {NAME => 'websiteurls', BLOOMFILTER => 'ROW', VERSIONS => '1', IN_MEMORY => 'fa
lse', KEEP_DELETED_CELLS => 'false', DATA_BLOCK_ENCODING => 'NONE', TTL => 'FOREVER', COMPRESSION
 => 'NONE', MIN_VERSIONS => '0', BLOCKCACHE => 'true', BLOCKSIZE => '65536', REPLICATION_SCOPE =>
 '0'}, {NAME => 'websiteurlsclick', BLOOMFILTER => 'ROW', VERSIONS => '1', IN_MEMORY => 'false',
KEEP_DELETED_CELLS => 'false', DATA_BLOCK_ENCODING => 'NONE', TTL => 'FOREVER', COMPRESSION => 'N
ONE', MIN_VERSIONS => '0', BLOCKCACHE => 'true', BLOCKSIZE => '65536', REPLICATION_SCOPE => '0'}
1 row(s) in 0.0640 seconds
```

6. Now let's do it for keeping deleted cell:

Let us delete the inserted record using the following command:

```
hbase(main):033:0> delete 'mywebproject:myclickstream','row05','web',timestamp=1425266848775
0 row(s) in 0.0210 seconds
```

We have to provide exact details such as namespace, table name, row ID, column family and the timestamp of the record we want to delete explicitly.

7. Now let's run the `scan` command with the `RAW` option and see the results:

```
hbase(main):034:0> scan 'mywebproject:myclickstream',{RAW => true, VERSIONS => 2}
ROW                     COLUMN+CELL
 row01                   column=web:, timestamp=1425248071962, value=www.yahoo.com
 row01                   column=websitedata:, timestamp=1425248403602, value=newandportaldata
 row02                   column=web:, timestamp=1425248095238, value=www.yahoo.com
 row02                   column=websitedata:, timestamp=1425248425374, value=newandportalmediadata
 row03                   column=web:, timestamp=1425248140008, value=www.google.com
 row03                   column=websitedata:, timestamp=1425248470557, value=searhemailportalgoogleandroidmobilephone
 row04                   column=web:, timestamp=1425248185419, value=www.walmart.com
 row04                   column=websitedata:, timestamp=1425248515560, value=ecommercestoresretail
 row05                   column=web:, timestamp=1425266848775, type=DeleteColumn
 row05                   column=web:, timestamp=1425266848775, value=www.amazon.com
 row05                   column=web:, timestamp=1425248199257, value=www.amazon.com
 row05                   column=websitedata:, timestamp=1425248544111, value=ecommercestoresretailtvmediawebservice
 row06                   column=web:, timestamp=1425248216092, value=www.ebay.com
 row06                   column=websitedata:, timestamp=1425248574536, value=ecommercauctions
6 row(s) in 0.0200 seconds
```

It still shows the record in the RAW option. This record is marked as a tombstone; the record will live in the system till the TTL time and will be cleared once the time expires.

8. Secondary index we will cover when we will cover Apache Phoenix.

9. Column families are covered in all the preceding queries, in our example:

```
hbase(main):035:0> alter 'mywebproject:myclickstream','web','websitedata','websiteurls','websiteurlsclick',{TTL => 2592000, BLOCKCACHE => true}
```

10. Data size in column families can be seen by using the following command:

```
hbase(main):036:0> describe 'mywebproject:myclickstream'
DESCRIPTION                                                                    ENABLED
'mywebproject:myclickstream', {NAME => 'web', BLOOMFILTER => 'ROW', VERSIONS => '2', IN_MEMORY => true
 'false', KEEP_DELETED_CELLS => 'false', DATA_BLOCK_ENCODING => 'NONE', TTL => '2592000 SECONDS (
30 DAYS)', COMPRESSION => 'NONE', MIN_VERSIONS => '0', BLOCKCACHE => 'true', BLOCKSIZE => '65536'
, REPLICATION_SCOPE => '0'}, {NAME => 'websitedata', BLOOMFILTER => 'ROW', VERSIONS => '1', IN_ME
MORY => 'false', KEEP_DELETED_CELLS => 'false', DATA_BLOCK_ENCODING => 'NONE', TTL => 'FOREVER',
COMPRESSION => 'NONE', MIN_VERSIONS => '0', BLOCKCACHE => 'true', BLOCKSIZE => '65536', REPLICATI
ON_SCOPE => '0'}, {NAME => 'websiteurls', BLOOMFILTER => 'ROW', VERSIONS => '1', IN_MEMORY => 'fa
lse', KEEP_DELETED_CELLS => 'false', DATA_BLOCK_ENCODING => 'NONE', TTL => 'FOREVER', COMPRESSION
 => 'NONE', MIN_VERSIONS => '0', BLOCKCACHE => 'true', BLOCKSIZE => '65536', REPLICATION_SCOPE =>
 '0'}, {NAME => 'websiteurlsclick', BLOOMFILTER => 'ROW', VERSIONS => '1', IN_MEMORY => 'false',
KEEP_DELETED_CELLS => 'false', DATA_BLOCK_ENCODING => 'NONE', TTL => 'FOREVER', COMPRESSION => 'N
ONE', MIN_VERSIONS => '0', BLOCKCACHE => 'true', BLOCKSIZE => '65536', REPLICATION_SCOPE => '0'}
1 row(s) in 0.0880 seconds
```

## See also

▸ Some interesting concepts and case studies are located at this URL:

```
http://hbase.apache.org/book.html - perf.schema
```

▸ For details about allowing CF to retain deleted rows:

```
https://issues.apache.org/jira/browse/HBASE-4536
```

▸ For details about column family, you can refer to the below API details:

```
http://hbase.apache.org/apidocs/org/apache/hadoop/hbase/
HColumnDescriptor.html
```

▸ For salted tables:

```
http://phoenix.apache.org/salted.html
```

```
http://www.gwms.com.tw/TREND_HadoopinTaiwan2012/1002download/
A4.pdf
```

# 6
# HBase Clients

In this chapter, we are going to cover the following recipes:

- HBase REST and the Java client
- Working with Apache Thrift
- Working with Apache Avro
- Working with Protocol Buffer
- Working with Pig and using Shell

## Introduction

In this chapter, we will consider the communication between HBase using different types of clients. We will also discuss briefly when which client is suitable and why.

It's very much possible to use HBase without the use of Java. There are two main ways to access the data: REST based and using Thrift API. Also one of the priorities was to decouple the HBase client application with HBase server-side components. The HBase client can write to different clusters having two different versions and should work seamlessly; that is to say that a client running on version A and a server running on version A2 will be able to communicate.

## HBase REST and Java Client

HBase provides various communication mechanisms for communicating with the datastore, and it's also designed to solve different types of scenario that can occur.

Using the REST server, we are channeling all the requests to `HTablePool`, which provides efficiency in the following ways:

- Efficient connection pool management.
- If there is a case where an object is short-lived, it goes through the entire lifecycle of connection creation, such as connection preparation, preparing metadata, and then the actual transaction. This is totally avoided as the connection object is readily available.
- Use of caching of the **RegionServer** information provides significant benefits.
- In case of less but large size requests, REST is better:

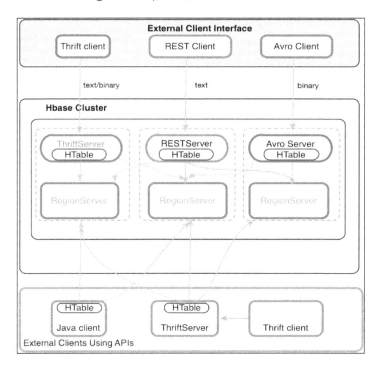

## How to do it...

Let's connect to the cluster that we created earlier and make sure that all the components are working.

The structure of the call will be as follows:

Let's log in to the HBase Master by executing the following command:

1. Before we start the rest services on port 8080, let's check whether everything is working as expected by taking a look on the mater configuration.

   Create a table by using the following command:

   ```
   create 'mywebproject:myclickstream', {NAME => 'web', BLOOMFILTER
   => 'ROW', VERSIONS => '2', IN_MEMORY => 'false', KEEP_DELETED_
   CELLS =>'false',DATA_BLOCK_ENCODING => 'NONE', TTL => '2592000',
   COMPRESSION => 'NONE', MIN_VERSIONS => '0', BLOCKCACHE => 'true',
   BLOCKSIZE => '65536', REPLICATION_SCOPE => '0'},
    {NAME => 'websitedata', BLOOMFILTER => 'ROW', VERSIONS => '1',IN_
   MEMORY => 'false', KEEP_DELETED_CELLS => 'false', DATA_BLOCK_
   ENCODING => 'NONE', TTL =>'2147483647', COMPRESSION => 'NONE',
   MIN_VERSIONS => '0', BLOCKCACHE => 'true', BLOCKSIZE => '65536',
   REPLICATION_SCOPE => '0'},
    {NAME => 'websiteurls', BLOOMFILTER => 'ROW',VERSIONS => '1',
   IN_MEMORY => 'false', KEEP_DELETED_CELLS => 'false', DATA_BLOCK_
   ENCODING => 'NONE', TTL =>'2147483647', COMPRESSION => 'NONE',
   MIN_VERSIONS => '0', BLOCKCACHE => 'true', BLOCKSIZE => '65536',
   REPLICATION_SCOPE => '0'},
    {NAME => 'websiteurlsclick', BLOOMFILTER => 'ROW', VERSIONS
   => '1', IN_MEMORY => 'false', KEEP_DELETED_CELLS => 'false',
   DATA_BLOCK_ENCODING => 'NONE',TTL =>'2147483647', COMPRESSION =>
   'NONE', MIN_VERSIONS => '0', BLOCKCACHE => 'true', BLOCKSIZE =>
   '65536', REPLICATION_SCOPE => '0'}
   ```

By pointing your browser to `http://master: :60010/tablesDetailed.jsp`, you will see the following details of the table:

2. Now we can start the JSON interface engine:

```
./hbase-daemon.sh start rest -p 8080
In essence, it's the <.hbase-daemon> <command> <protocol> -p
<port> and the actual port on which this service will run, <8080>
```

Once you invoke the following

starting REST, logging to `/opt/HbaseB/hbase-0.98.5-hadoop2/logs/hbase-hadoop-rest-rchoudhry-linux64.yourmachine.out`

This means the REST interface is ready to listen on the port specified, `8080`.

Let's test the setup by invoking the following commands:

This shows a number of tables, which are sitting in the Hbase landscape. In case you don't find the respective t

You can create it by using the following command:

```
Create 'mywebproject:myclickstream', {NAME => 'web', BLOOMFILTER
=> 'ROW', VERSIONS => '2', IN_MEMORY => 'false', KEEP_DELETED_
CELLS =>'false',DATA_BLOCK_ENCODING => 'NONE', TTL => '2592000',
COMPRESSION => 'NONE', MIN_VERSIONS => '0', BLOCKCACHE => 'true',
BLOCKSIZE => '65536', REPLICATION_SCOPE => '0'},
  {NAME => 'websitedata', BLOOMFILTER => 'ROW', VERSIONS => '1',IN_
MEMORY => 'false', KEEP_DELETED_CELLS => 'false', DATA_BLOCK_
ENCODING => 'NONE', TTL =>'2147483647', COMPRESSION => 'NONE',
MIN_VERSIONS => '0', BLOCKCACHE => 'true', BLOCKSIZE => '65536',
REPLICATION_SCOPE => '0'},
  {NAME => 'websiteurls', BLOOMFILTER => 'ROW',VERSIONS => '1',
IN_MEMORY => 'false', KEEP_DELETED_CELLS => 'false', DATA_BLOCK_
ENCODING => 'NONE', TTL =>'2147483647', COMPRESSION => 'NONE',
MIN_VERSIONS => '0', BLOCKCACHE => 'true', BLOCKSIZE => '65536',
REPLICATION_SCOPE => '0'},
  {NAME => 'websiteurlsclick', BLOOMFILTER => 'ROW', VERSIONS
=> '1', IN_MEMORY => 'false', KEEP_DELETED_CELLS => 'false',
DATA_BLOCK_ENCODING => 'NONE',TTL =>'2147483647', COMPRESSION =>
'NONE', MIN_VERSIONS => '0', BLOCKCACHE => 'true', BLOCKSIZE =>
'65536', REPLICATION_SCOPE => '0'}
```

3. Let's run another command:

```
[hadoop@rchoudhry-linux64 ~]$ curl http://master:8080/version
rest 0.0.3 [JVM: Oracle Corporation 1.8.0_05-25.5-b02] [
OS: Linux 2.6.32-131.0.15.el6.x86_64 amd64] [Server: jetty/6.1.26]
[Jersey: 1.8]
```

4. Let's run a more significant command, which provide

```
[hadoop@rchoudhry-linux64 ~]$ curl http://master:8080/
mywebproject:myclickstream/schema
{ NAME=> 'mywebproject:myclickstream', IS_META => 'false',
COLUMNS => [ { NAME => 'web', BLOOMFILTER => 'ROW', VERSIONS
=> '2', IN_MEMORY => 'false', KEEP_DELETED_CELLS => 'false',
DATA_BLOCK_ENCODING => 'NONE', TTL => '2592000', COMPRESSION =>
'NONE', MIN_VERSIONS => '0', BLOCKCACHE => 'true', BLOCKSIZE =>
'65536', REPLICATION_SCOPE => '0' }, { NAME => 'websitedata',
BLOOMFILTER => 'ROW', VERSIONS => '1', IN_MEMORY => 'false',
KEEP_DELETED_CELLS => 'false', DATA_BLOCK_ENCODING => 'NONE',
TTL => '2147483647', COMPRESSION => 'NONE', MIN_VERSIONS => '0',
BLOCKCACHE => 'true', BLOCKSIZE => '65536', REPLICATION_SCOPE =>
'0' }, { NAME => 'websiteurls', BLOOMFILTER => 'ROW', VERSIONS =>
'1', IN_MEMORY => 'false', KEEP_DELETED_CELLS => 'false', DATA_
BLOCK_ENCODING => 'NONE', TTL => '2147483647', COMPRESSION =>
'NONE', MIN_VERSIONS => '0', BLOCKCACHE => 'true', BLOCKSIZE =>
'65536', REPLICATION_SCOPE => '0' }, { NAME => 'websiteurlsclick',
BLOOMFILTER => 'ROW', VERSIONS => '1', IN_MEMORY => 'false',
KEEP_DELETED_CELLS => 'false', DATA_BLOCK_ENCODING => 'NONE',
TTL => '2147483647', COMPRESSION => 'NONE', MIN_VERSIONS => '0',
BLOCKCACHE => 'true', BLOCKSIZE => '65536', REPLICATION_SCOPE =>
'0' } ] }
```

5. This provides all of the information about the internal schema, table, and the details of the schema.

6. You can also try plain format by using the following command:

```
[hadoop@rchoudhry-linux64 bin]$ curl -H "Accept: text/plain"
http://master:8080/version
rest 0.0.3 [JVM: Oracle Corporation 1.8.0_05-25.5-b02] [OS: Linux
2.6.32-131.0.15.el6.x86_64 amd64] [Server: jetty/6.1.26] [Jersey:
1.8]
```

7. For an XML format:

```
[hadoop@rchoudhry-linux64 bin]$ curl -H "Accept: text/xml" http://
master:8080/version
<?xml version="1.0" encoding="UTF-8" standalone="yes"?><Version
JVM="Oracle Corporation 1.8.0_05-25.5-b02" Jersey="1.8"
OS="Linux 2.6.32-131.0.15.el6.x86_64 amd64" REST="0.0.3"
Server="jetty/6.1.26"/>[hadoop@rchoudhry-linux64 bin]$
```

8. The following class (`HBaseRegularClient`) is a generic call that will allow us to add the respective data. It can also be used for scanning, getting a single row, and so on. Refer to the *There's more...* section for details:

```
public static void main(String[] agrs) {
  try {
    String tableNameUsed = "mywebproject:mybrowsedata";
    String[] familys = { "web", "websitedata" };
    HBaseRegularClient.creatTable(tableNameUsed, familys);


    // add record www.google.com
    HBaseRegularClient.addRecord(tableNameUsed, "www.google.
com", "web", "", "best");
HBaseRegularClient.addRecord(tableNameUsed, "www.google.com",
"websitedata", "", "search");
    HBaseRegularClient
        .addRecord(tableNameUsed, "www.google.com",
"websitedata", "gmail", "email");
HBaseRegularClient.addRecord(tableNameUsed, "www.google.com",
"websitedata", "google+",
        "hangout");
    // add record www.yahoo.com
    HBaseRegularClient.addRecord(tableNameUsed, "www.yahoo.com",
"web", "", "secondbest");
HBaseRegularClient.addRecord(tableNameUsed, "www.yahoo.com",
"websitedata", "email",
        "good email system");

System.out.println("||===========get www.google.com
record========||");
HBaseRegularClient.getOneRecord(tableNameUsed, "www.google.com");

System.out.println("||===========show all record========||");
    HBaseRegularClient.getAllRecord(tableNameUsed);

System.out.println("||===========del www.yahoo.com
record========||");
HBaseRegularClient.delRecord(tableNameUsed, "www.yahoo.com");
    HBaseRegularClient.getAllRecord(tableNameUsed);

System.out.println("||===========show all record========||");
    HBaseRegularClient.getAllRecord(tableNameUsed);
  } catch (Exception e) {
    e.printStackTrace();
  }
}
```

Take care while using this class in production where the table has a huge dataset. This is just an example.

9. Now let's discuss the REST Java client:

```
package Col;
// Please change the package accordingly
//Java IO class
import java.io.IOException;
// Hbase specific class
import org.apache.hadoop.hbase.client.Get;
import org.apache.hadoop.hbase.client.Result;
import org.apache.hadoop.hbase.client.ResultScanner;
import org.apache.hadoop.hbase.client.Scan;
import org.apache.hadoop.hbase.rest.client.Client;
import org.apache.hadoop.hbase.rest.client.Cluster;
import org.apache.hadoop.hbase.rest.client.RemoteHTable;
import org.apache.hadoop.hbase.util.Bytes;

public class RestHbaseClent {

  private static RemoteHTable table;//
  /* has three Constructurs we are using
    * RemoteHTable(Client client, String name)
    * https://hbase.apache.org/apidocs/org/apache/hadoop/hbase/
rest/client/RemoteHTable.html
   */
  public static void main(String[] args) throws Exception {
    getDataFromHbaseRest();
  }

  public static void getDataFromHbaseRest() {
    ResultScanner scanner = null;// it needs to be initialized to
null
    Cluster hbaseCluster = new Cluster();//Creating and cluster
object
    hbaseCluster.add("172.28.182.45", 8080);//passing the IP and
post
    // Create Rest client instance and get the connection
    Client restClient = new Client(hbaseCluster);//pass the
cluster object to the client
    table = new RemoteHTable(restClient, "mywebproject:myclickstre
am");// Makes a Remote Call
    Get get = new Get(Bytes.toBytes("row02"));//Gets the row in
question
```

```
    Result result1=null;// initializing it to null
    try {
      result1 = table.get(get);// getting the table and the
connection object
      byte[] valueWeb = result1.getValue(Bytes.toBytes("web"),
Bytes.toBytes("col01"));
      byte[] valueWeb01 = result1.getValue(Bytes.toBytes("web"),
Bytes.toBytes("col02"));
      /*
       * getting the  colum family: column qualifire values
       * */
      byte[] valueWebData = result1.getValue(Bytes.
toBytes("websitedata"), Bytes.toBytes("col01"));
      byte[] valueWebData01 = result1.getValue(Bytes.
toBytes("websitedata"), Bytes.toBytes("col02"));
      /*
       * getting the  colum family: column qualifire values
       * */
      String valueStr = Bytes.toString(valueWeb);
      String valueStr1 = Bytes.toString(valueWeb01);
      String valueWebdataStr = Bytes.toString(valueWebData);
      String valueWebdataStr1 = Bytes.toString(valueWebData01);

      System.out.println("GET: \n" + " web: " + valueStr + "\n
web: " + valueStr1+"\n "+"Webdata: "+valueWebdataStr);
    } catch (IOException e1) {
    // TODO Auto-generated catch block
    e1.printStackTrace();
    }finally{
    /*make sure the resultset is set to null before exiting the
program
      * In case it's needed, keep the object, but whenever the
object is removed from the
      * rs, please null it. It's a good programming practice.
      */
    if(!result1.isEmpty());
    result1=null;
    }
    ResultScanner rsScanner = null;
    try {
      Scan s = new Scan();
      s.addColumn(Bytes.toBytes("web"), Bytes.toBytes("col01"));
      s.addColumn(Bytes.toBytes("web"), Bytes.toBytes("col02"));
```

```
        rsScanner = table.getScanner(s);

        for (Result rr = rsScanner.next(); rr != null; rr =
rsScanner.next()) {
            System.out.println("Found row : " + rr);
        }
    } catch (Exception e) {
        e.printStackTrace();
    } finally {
        // Make sure you close your scanners when you are done!
        rsScanner.close();
    }
  }
}
```

I am assuming your classpath has all the respective JARs needed to compile the Java class and to run it. If not, add the following to your project classpath:

```
lib
├── commons-configuration-1.8.jar
├── commons-lang-2.6.jar
├── commons-logging-1.1.1.jar
├── hadoop-core-1.0.0.jar
├── hbase-0.92.1.jar
├── log4j-1.2.16.jar
├── slf4j-api-1.5.8.jar
├── slf4j-log4j12-1.5.8.jar
└── zookeeper-3.4.3.jar
```

10. When you run the Java class, you will get the following result:

```
GET:
 web: www.yahoo.com
 web: www.google.com
 Webdata: Ecommerce Website
Found row : keyvalues={row02/web:col01/1427044333953/Put/vlen=13/
mvcc=0, row02/web:col02/1427044353631/Put/vlen=14/mvcc=0}
```

## How it works...

Let's walkthrough the Java class, which gives us a very good idea of how this interface works:

1. When we started the JSON server at port 8080, the series of interface is invoked, making HBase data, which is sitting in the HDFS, accessible to the remote caller.

2. When we create an object of Cluster class and add the HBase Server details along with the port on which the JSON server is running, we are binding the IP to the port which is listening for any client invocation.

3. Now we connect to `RemoteTable` and pass the rest client details along with the table details.

4. Then we pass the row which we want to extract along with the get request. The get pulls the data in bytes, which need to be converted to a `byteArray` object.

5. This byte array is then type casted to String, and hence, we get the string value ready to be printed on the console.

6. We pass this to `System.out.println` and thus the values, which reside in the HBase `row02` to the specific column family, is printed.

## There's more...

In the previous section, we did not did not discuss regular operations, which can be done by a Java class using the `HBaseAdmin` class:

```
//Regular java classes
import java.io.IOException;
import java.util.ArrayList;
import java.util.List;
//Hadoop/Hbase related classes
import org.apache.hadoop.conf.Configuration;
import org.apache.hadoop.hbase.HBaseConfiguration;
import org.apache.hadoop.hbase.HColumnDescriptor;
import org.apache.hadoop.hbase.HTableDescriptor;
import org.apache.hadoop.hbase.KeyValue;
import org.apache.hadoop.hbase.MasterNotRunningException;
import org.apache.hadoop.hbase.ZooKeeperConnectionException;
import org.apache.hadoop.hbase.client.Delete;
import org.apache.hadoop.hbase.client.Get;
import org.apache.hadoop.hbase.client.HBaseAdmin;
import org.apache.hadoop.hbase.client.HTable;
import org.apache.hadoop.hbase.client.Result;
import org.apache.hadoop.hbase.client.ResultScanner;
import org.apache.hadoop.hbase.client.Scan;
```

```java
import org.apache.hadoop.hbase.client.Put;
import org.apache.hadoop.hbase.util.Bytes;

public class HBaseRegularClient {

  private static Configuration conf = null;
  /**
   * Initialization the Hbase config file as static so that it remain
in memory.
   */
  static {
    conf = HBaseConfiguration.create();
  }

  /**
   * Create a table in case the table is not there. Else prints table
already exist conf is the
   * configuration file object which needs to be passed, hbase-site.
xml
   */
  public static void creatTable(String tableNameUsed, String[]
familys) throws Exception {
    HBaseAdmin admin = new HBaseAdmin(conf);
    if (admin.tableExists(tableNameUsed)) {
      System.out.println("opps…table already exists!");
    } else {
      @SuppressWarnings("deprecation")
      HTableDescriptor tableDesc = new (tableNameUsed);
      for (int i = 0; i < familys.length; i++) {
        tableDesc.addFamily(new HColumnDescriptor(familys[i]));
      }
      admin.createTable(tableDesc);
      System.out.println("create table " + tableNameUsed + " Done.");
      // Table is created
    }
  }

  /**
   * Method to delete tables @ String tableNameUsed as an input
parameter First it disables the
   * table as Hbase does not allow the table to be deleted directly
Delete a table
   */
  public static void deleteTable(String tableNameUsed) {
```

```
    try {
      @SuppressWarnings("resource")
      HBaseAdmin admin = new HBaseAdmin(conf);
      admin.disableTable(tableNameUsed);
      admin.deleteTable(tableNameUsed);
      System.out.println("delete table " + tableNameUsed + " ok.");
    } catch (MasterNotRunningException e) {
      e.printStackTrace();
    } catch (ZooKeeperConnectionException e) {
      e.printStackTrace();
    }catch (Exception e) {
      e.printStackTrace();
    }
  }

  /**
   * Put (or insert) a row
   */
  public static void addRecord(String tableNameUsed, String rowKey,
String family,
      String qualifier, String value) {
    HTable table = null;
    try {
      table = new HTable(conf, tableNameUsed);
      Put put = new Put(Bytes.toBytes(rowKey));
      put.add(Bytes.toBytes(family), Bytes.toBytes(qualifier), Bytes.
toBytes(value));
      table.put(put);
      System.out.println("insert recored " + rowKey + " to table " +
tableNameUsed + " ok.");
    } catch (Exception e) {
      e.printStackTrace();
    } finally {
      try {
        table.close();
      } catch (IOException e) {
        // TODO Auto-generated catch block
        e.printStackTrace();
      }
    }
  }

  /**
   * Delete a row
```

```
        */
      public static void delRecord(String tableNameUsed, String rowKey) {
        @SuppressWarnings("resource")
        HTable table = null;
        try {
          table = new HTable(conf, tableNameUsed);

          List<Delete> list = new ArrayList<Delete>();
          Delete del = new Delete(rowKey.getBytes());
          list.add(del);
          table.delete(list);
        } catch (IOException e) {
          // TODO Auto-generated catch block
          e.printStackTrace();
        } finally {
          try {
            table.close();
          } catch (IOException e) {
            // TODO Auto-generated catch block
            e.printStackTrace();
          }
        }
        System.out.println("del recored " + rowKey + " ok.");
      }


      /**
       * Get a row
       */
      @SuppressWarnings("deprecation")
      public static void getOneRecord(String tableNameUsed, String rowKey)
    {
        HTable table;
        Result rs = null;
        try {
          table = new HTable(conf, tableNameUsed);
          Get get = new Get(rowKey.getBytes());
          rs = table.get(get);
          for (KeyValue kv : rs.raw()) {
            System.out.print(new String(kv.getRow()) + " ");
            System.out.print(new String(kv.getFamily()) + ":");
            System.out.print(new String(kv.getQualifier()) + " ");
            System.out.print(kv.getTimestamp() + " ");
            System.out.println(new String(kv.getValue()));
          }
```

```
    } catch (IOException e) {
      // TODO Auto-generated catch block
      e.printStackTrace();
    } finally {
      if (!rs.isEmpty()) rs = null;
    }
  }

  /**
   * Scan (or list) a table
   */
  @SuppressWarnings({ "deprecation", "resource" })
  public static void getAllRecord(String tableNameUsed) {
    ResultScanner ss = null;
    try {
      HTable table = new HTable(conf, tableNameUsed);
      Scan s = new Scan();
      ss = table.getScanner(s);
      for (Result r : ss) {
        for (KeyValue kv : r.raw()) {
          System.out.print(new String(kv.getRow()) + " ");
          System.out.print(new String(kv.getFamily()) + ":");
          System.out.print(new String(kv.getQualifier()) + " ");
          System.out.print(kv.getTimestamp() + " ");
          System.out.println(new String(kv.getValue()));
        }
      }
    } catch (IOException e) {
      e.printStackTrace();
    } finally {
      if (ss != null) ss.close();
    }
  }

  public static void main(String[] agrs) {
    try {
      String tableNameUsed = "mywebproject:mybrowsedata";
      String[] familys = { "web", "websitedata" };
      HBaseRegularClient.creatTable(tableNameUsed, familys);

      // add record www.google.com
      HBaseRegularClient.addRecord(tableNameUsed, "www.google.com",
"web", "", "best");
```

```
        HBaseRegularClient.addRecord(tableNameUsed, "www.google.com",
    "websitedata", "", "search");
        HBaseRegularClient
            .addRecord(tableNameUsed, "www.google.com", "websitedata",
    "gmail", "email");
        HBaseRegularClient.addRecord(tableNameUsed, "www.google.com",
    "websitedata", "google+",
            "hangout");
        // add record www.yahoo.com
        HBaseRegularClient.addRecord(tableNameUsed, "www.yahoo.com",
    "web", "", "secondbest");
        HBaseRegularClient.addRecord(tableNameUsed, "www.yahoo.com",
    "websitedata", "email",
            "good email system");

        System.out.println("||===========get www.google.com
    record========||");
        HBaseRegularClient.getOneRecord(tableNameUsed, "www.google.
    com");

        System.out.println("||==========show all record========||");
        HBaseRegularClient.getAllRecord(tableNameUsed);

        System.out.println("||==========del www.yahoo.com
    record========||");
        HBaseRegularClient.delRecord(tableNameUsed, "www.yahoo.com");
        HBaseRegularClient.getAllRecord(tableNameUsed);

        System.out.println("||==========show all record========||");
        HBaseRegularClient.getAllRecord(tableNameUsed);
    } catch (Exception e) {
        e.printStackTrace();
    }
  }
}
```

# Working with Apache Thrift

In this section, we will discuss Apache Thrift, Avro, and will briefly touch on the Protocol buffer software framework, for scalable cross-language services development, which combines a software stack with a code generation engine to build services that work efficiently and seamlessly between C++, Java, Python, PHP, other languages.

It won't be possible to discuss each topic in depth, but we will try to discuss some use cases.

We will start with Apache Thrift first; the Thrift framework is widely used, and is used for scalable cross-language services development, combining a software stack with a code generation engine to build services that work efficiently and seamlessly between C++, Java, Python, PHP, Ruby, Erlang, Perl, Haskell, C#, Cocoa, JavaScript, Node.js, Smalltalk, OCaml Delphi, and other languages.

## How to do it...

Let's connect to the cluster that we have set up:

1.  Download the latest Thrift by using Wget.

    ```
    http://mirror.sdunix.com/apache/thrift/0.9.2/thrift-0.9.2.tar.
    gz
    ```

2.  Untar it using the following command:

    ```
    tar xvf thrift-0.9.2.tar.gz
    ```

3.  Now a folder will be created with `thrift-0.9.2`.

4.  You can run `./configure` in case there is no dependency thrown this process will complete with success.

 There can be dependency like g++ compiler or JDK versions, and so on. You have to resolve it before you run make.

5.  Once Thrift is installed, use:

    ```
    thrift --gen <language> <Thrift filename>
    thrift –gen java  /src/main/resources/org/apache/hadoop/hbase/
    thrift/Hbase.thrift.
    In our case we used
    thrift -r --gen py HbaseB.thrift
    ```

6.  Now it's time to start the Thrift server:

    ```
    cd to /opt/HbaseB/hbase-0.98.5-hadoop2/bin
    ./hbase thrift start
    ```

    You can also check whether everything went through successfully.

7. On the VI editor, open the `HbaseClientForThrift.py` file:

```
__author__ = 'r0choud'
#import thrift libraries
#! /usr/bin/env python
import sys
import os
import time
from thrift.transport import TTransport
from thrift.transport import TSocket
from thrift.transport import THttpClient
from thrift.protocol import TBinaryProtocol
from hbase import THBaseService
from hbase.ttypes import *
# Add path for local "gen-py/hbase" for the pre-generated module
gen_py_path = os.path.abspath('gen-py')
sys.path.append(gen_py_path)
print "Connecting from Python to HBase using thrift"
host = "172.28.182.45" # Hbase Master to connect
port = 9090 # Port to connect to
framed = False
try:
    socket = TSocket.TSocket(host, port) # Passing host and post
details to the R=TSocket
    if framed:
        transport = TTransport.TFramedTransport(socket)
    else:
        transport = TTransport.TBufferedTransport(socket)
    protocol = TBinaryProtocol.TBinaryProtocol(transport)

        # Getting Thrift client handle and instance
    client = THBaseService.Client(protocol)
        #Opening socket Connection with HBase
    transport.open()
    table = "mywebproject:mybrowsedata" # passing the table
details
    # Creating PUT call by using TPut
    put = TPut(row="row02", columnValues=[TColumnValue(family="web
",qualifier="site",value="www.yahoo.com")])
    print "Putting Data to the web column family:", put
    # Put Data in HBase using thrift client
    client.put(table, put)
    # Create the GET call
    get = TGet(row="row02")
    print "Retrieving Data :", get
```

```
      # Retrieve Data from HBase using thrift client
      result = client.get(table, get)
      print "Result:", result
      #Closing socket connection with HBase
      transport.close()
except IOError, e:
      if hasattr(e, 'code'): # Error
        print 'error code: ', e.code
      elif hasattr(e, 'reason'): # Error
       print "can't connect, reason: ", e.reason
      else:
        raise
finally:
      transport.close() # closing the connection in finally
section to make sure the connection is always closed
```

8.  Now the client-side code is ready.

9.  Let's log in to the HBase cluster and run the following command:

10. Now run the preceding Python `HbaseClientForThrift.py` file by Python `HbaseClientForThrift.py`.

11. This will create a namespace; `mywebproject`.

12. Under the namespace, it will create a table: `mybrowsedata`.

13. In this table, on `row02` and column `"web"`, with a qualifier as site, the values inserted will be `www.yahoo.com`.

## How it works...

1.  When we start the HBase Thrift server, it registers the thrift APIs and forms a broker.

2.  When the client invokes an RPC call using Python Thrift lib, it has a host and associated port on which the HBase Thrift server is listing.

3.  This allows the socket APIs which make a socket connection to the HBase Thrift server.

4.  Once a secure transport socket is open, it will invoke the corresponding namespace.

5.  Once the namespace is located, it invokes the table which is looked up by the client.

6.  Once the table is associated to the invoking thread, the execute task is performed a column family: qualifier and at a row, cell level.

7.  Hence, the data is PUT into the respective cell with a version number and a timestamp.

8.  Once the PUT call is over, in the same open socket, a GET call is initiated by passing the row number `"row02"`.

9. By invoking `client.get(Table. Get)`.

10. Then we iterate over the results and print the results on the console.

## There's more...

Some interesting concepts and case studies are located at the following URLs:

`http://thrift.apache.org/docs/features`

`https://thrift.apache.org/tutorial/py`

`http://wiki.apache.org/hadoop/Hbase/ThriftApi`

# Working with Apache Avro

Avro is created with a vision to provide a language-independent serialization system. Avro allows us to process and share data with an array of languages like C, C++, C#, Java, Python, Perl, PHP, and Ruby.

The schema of Avro in JSON and are encoded in binary format. A datafile of Avro essentially contains metadata where the schema is stored. The scalability is backed into the Avro system, as the datafile supports compression and can be split based on need. The serialized data is in a compact binary format that doesn't require proxy objects or code generation. Instead of using generated proxy libraries and strong typing, Avro relies on the schemas that are sent, along with the serialized data.

Including schemas with the Avro messages allows any application to deserialize the data. All the major primitive data types are supported. Complex data types such as records, enums, arrays, and maps are also supported. It's optional to generate code in Avro; the data can be written or read, or can be used in RPC (remote procedure calls) without generating classes or code.

 In this section, we will consider more on the basics. A very detailed explanation is beyond the scope of this chapter/book.

## How to do it...

1. Let's download a compatible/stable version (which is compatible with the Hadoop, HDFS, and HBase versions).

 Direct integration of HBase and Avro was removed in HBase 0.98. Thus, we will work with the Hadoop ecosystem.

2. Download the stable version of Avro (`http://avro.apache.org/docs/1.7.5/`).

   `http://archive.apache.org/dist/avro/avro-1.7.5/java/avro-1.7.5.jar` and `http://archive.apache.org/dist/avro/avro-1.7.5/java/avro-tools-1.7.5.jar`.

   `http://archive.apache.org/dist/avro/avro-1.7.5/c/avro-c-1.7.5.tar.gz` for C.

   `http://archive.apache.org/dist/avro/avro-1.7.5/cpp/avro-cpp-1.7.5.tar.gz` for C++.

   `http://archive.apache.org/dist/avro/avro-1.7.5/php/avro-php-1.7.5.tar.bz2` for PHP.

   `http://archive.apache.org/dist/avro/avro-1.7.5/py/avro-1.7.5.tar.gz` for Python.

3. Alternatively, you can use Apache Maven to download the JAR files and their dependencies:

```xml
<dependencies>
        <dependency>
            <groupId>org.apache.avro</groupId>
            <artifactId>avro</artifactId>
            <version>1.7.5</version>
        </dependency>
        <dependency>
            <groupId>org.apache.avro</groupId>
            <artifactId>avro-tools</artifactId>
            <version>1.7.5</version>
        </dependency>
</dependencies>
```

4. Create a project in Eclipse (you can use other IDEs too). For the purposes of very large audiences, we are considering Eclipse; this project must have support from Maven.

5. Now create a `pom.xml` and save it.

6. The `pom.xml` must contain the following:

```
<dependencies>
        <dependency>
            <groupId>org.apache.avro</groupId>
            <artifactId>avro</artifactId>
            <version>1.7.5</version>
        </dependency>
        <dependency>
            <groupId>org.apache.avro</groupId>
            <artifactId>avro-tools</artifactId>
            <version>1.7.5</version>
        </dependency>
    </dependencies>
    <project xmlns="http://maven.apache.org/POM/4.0.0"
    xmlns:xsi="http://www.w3.org/2001/XMLSchema-instance"
    xsi:schemaLocation="http://maven.apache.org/POM/4.0.0
    http://maven.apache.org/xsd/maven-4.0.0.xsd">
    <modelVersion>4.0.0</modelVersion>
    <groupId>com.hbaseb.avroexample</groupId>
    <artifactId>avroHbaseB</artifactId>
    <version>0.0.1-SNAPSHOT</version>
    <packaging>jar</packaging>
    <name>avroSample</name>
    <url>http://maven.apache.org</url>
    <properties>
        <project.build.sourceEncoding>UTF-</project.build.
sourceEncoding>
    </properties>
    <dependencies>
        <dependency>
            <groupId>junit</groupId>
            <artifactId>junit</artifactId>
            <version>4.12</version>
            <scope>test</scope>
        </dependency>

        <dependency>
            <groupId>org.apache.avro</groupId>
            <artifactId>avro</artifactId>
            <version>1.7.5</version>
        </dependency>

        <dependency>
```

```
            <groupId>org.apache.avro</groupId>
            <artifactId>avro-tools</artifactId>
            <version>1.7.5</version>
        </dependency>

        <dependency>
            <groupId>org.apache.logging.log4j</groupId>
            <artifactId>log4j-api</artifactId>
            <version>2.2</version>
        </dependency>
        <dependency>
            <groupId>org.apache.logging.log4j</groupId>
            <artifactId>log4j-core</artifactId>
            <version>2.2</version>
        </dependency>
    </dependencies>
</project>
```

7. Now let's create a source folder where the schema will reside, for example `src/main/hbaseb/avro`, and then finish.

8. Now let's create a schema file, say, `mysiteUrl.asvc`.

9. At this point, we can add the JSON data to define the schema as follows:

```
{
    "namespace":"com.hbaseb.avroexample.model",
    "type":"record",
    "name":"Mywebsitedata",
    "fields":[
        {
            "name":"webURL",
            "type":"string"
        },
        {
            "name":"name",
            "type":"string"
        },
        {
            "name":"data",
            "type":"int"
        },
        {
            "name":"size",
            "type":"int"
        }
```

10. Now we can compile the schema; there are two ways to do it:
    - ❏ Using the Avro JAR tool
    - ❏ Using the Maven plugin method

    We will use the command-line option

11. Go to the directory where you have kept the Avro jars of point it the jar files from your shell:

```
sudo -jar avro-tools-1.7.5.jar pass the following as an argument
complile
schema
src/main/avro/avroSample.avsc
src/main/java
```

12. This will generate a Java file class as `Mywebsitedata` at the following location: `src/main/java` folder `com.hbaseb.avroexample.model`, as follows:

```
/**
 * Autogenerated by Avro
 *
 * DO NOT EDIT DIRECTLY
 */
package com.example.avroSample.model;
@SuppressWarnings("all")
@org.apache.avro.specific.AvroGenerated
public class Mywebsitedata extends org.apache.avro.specific.
SpecificRecordBase
    implements org.apache.avro.specific.SpecificRecord {

  public static final org.apache.avro.Schema SCHEMA$ = new org.
apache.avro.
Schema.Parser().parse("{\"type\":\"record\",\"name\":\"Mywebsiteda
ta\",
\"namespace\":\"com.hbaseb.avroexample.
model\",\"fields\":[{\"name\":
\"webURL\",\"type\":\"string\"},{\"name\":\"name\",\"type\":\"i
nt\"},{
\"name\":\"data\",\"type\":\"int\"},{\"name\":\"size\",
\"type\":\"int\"}]}");
  public static org.apache.avro.Schema getClassSchema() { return
SCHEMA$; }
  @Deprecated public java.lang.CharSequence webURL;
  @Deprecated public java.lang.CharSequence name;
  @Deprecated public int data;
```

```
    @Deprecated public int size;

    /**
     * Default constructor.  Note that this does not initialize
fields
     * to their default values from the schema.  If that is desired
then
     * one should use {@link \#newBuilder()}.
     */
    public Mywebsitedata() {}

    /**
     * All-args constructor.
     */
    public Mywebsitedata(java.lang.CharSequence webURL,
        java.lang.CharSequence name, java.lang.Integer data,
        java.lang.Integer size) {

    this.webURL = webURL;
    this.name = name;
    this.data = data;
    this.size = size;

    }
    /* some code... */
}
```

13. Let's write some code that builds objects using the generated classes, assigns values to their properties, and serializes the objects to a file:

```
Mywebsitedata mywebsite = Mywebsitedata.newBuilder().
setname("Google.com")
                .setwebURL("www.google.com").setData(1024)
                setSize(8).build();
        DatumWriter<Mywebsitedata> dw =
            new SpecificDatumWriter<Mywebsitedata>(Mywebsitedata.
class);
        DataFileWriter<Mywebsitedata> fw =
            new DataFileWriter<Mywebsitedata>(dw);

        try {
            fw.create(mywebsite.getSchema(), outputFile);
            fw.append(mywebsite); // data added to the file using
append
```

```
                fw.close();
        } catch (IOException e) {
            LOGGER.error("Error <"+ outputFile.getAbsolutePath() +
    ">.", e);
        }
```

14. Similarly, you can deserialize with the schema:

```
DatumReader<Mywebsitedata> dr =
        new SpecificDatumReader<Mywebsitedata>(Mywebsitedata.
class);
    try {
        DataFileReader<Mywebsitedata> fr =
            new DataFileReader<Mywebsitedata>(opf, dr);

        Mywebsitedata mywebsite = null;

        if (fileReader.hasNext()) {
            mywebsite = fr.next(mywebsite);
        }

    } catch (IOException e) {
        LOGGER.error("Error  <"+ opf.getAbsolutePath() + ">.", e);
    }
```

15. Now we must integrate it with the Hadoop ecosystem.

    To do this, let's open `pom.xml` and add the following lines as a dependency:

```xml
<dependency>
            <groupId>org.apache.avro</groupId>
            <artifactId>avro-mapred</artifactId>
            <version>1.7.5</version>
        </dependency>
        <dependency>
            <groupId>org.apache.hadoop</groupId>
            <artifactId>hadoop-core</artifactId>
            <version>2.2.0</version>
        </dependency>
    </dependencies>
```

16. Let's write `AvroMapper` and `AvroReducer`:

```java
AvroMapper
package com.hbaseb.avroexample.mapReduce;

import java.io.IOException;
```

```
import org.apache.avro.mapred.AvroCollector;
import org.apache.avro.mapred.AvroMapper;
import org.apache.avro.mapred.Pair;
import org.apache.hadoop.mapred.Reporter;

import com.hbaseb.avroexample.model.Mywebsitedata;

/**
 * Class class will count the number of models of automobiles
found.
 */
public final class WebSiteMapper extends
        AvroMapper<Mywebsitedata, Pair<CharSequence, Integer>> {

    private static final Integer ONE = Integer.valueOf(1);

    @Override
    public void map(Mywebsitedata datum,
            AvroCollector<Pair<CharSequence, Integer>> collector,
            Reporter reporter) throws IOException {

        CharSequence name = datum.getName();

        collector.collect(new Pair<CharSequence, Integer>(name,
ONE));

    }

}
Reducer
package com.hbaseb.avroexample.mapReduce;

import java.io.IOException;

import org.apache.avro.mapred.AvroCollector;
import org.apache.avro.mapred.AvroReducer;
import org.apache.avro.mapred.Pair;
import org.apache.hadoop.mapred.Reporter;

public class ModelCountReducer extends
        AvroReducer<CharSequence, Integer, Pair<CharSequence,
Integer>> {

    /**
```

```
     * This method "reduces" the input
     */
    @Override
    public void reduce(CharSequence name, Iterable<Integer>
values,
            AvroCollector<Pair<CharSequence, Integer>> collector,
Reporter reporter)
            throws IOException {

        int sum = 0;

        for (Integer value : values) {
            sum += value.intValue();
        }

        collector.collect(new Pair<CharSequence, Integer>(name,
sum));

    }

}
```

17. Let's create a class that executes Mapper and reducer classes using `AvroJob`:

```
ackage com.hbaseb.avroexample.mapReduce;

import java.io.File;

import org.apache.avro.Schema;
import org.apache.avro.Schema.Type;
import org.apache.avro.mapred.AvroJob;
import org.apache.avro.mapred.Pair;
import org.apache.hadoop.conf.Configured;
import org.apache.hadoop.fs.Path;
import org.apache.hadoop.mapred.FileInputFormat;
import org.apache.hadoop.mapred.FileOutputFormat;
import org.apache.hadoop.mapred.JobClient;
import org.apache.hadoop.mapred.JobConf;
import org.apache.hadoop.util.Tool;
import org.apache.logging.log4j.LogManager;
import org.apache.logging.log4j.Logger;

import com.hbaseb.avroexample.model.Mywebsitedata;;
```

```
public class NameCountApp extends Configured implements Tool {

    private static final Logger LOGGER = LogManager
            .getLogger(ModelNameCountApp.class);

    private static final String JOB_NAME = "NameCountAppJob";

    @Override
    public int run(String[] args) throws Exception {

        JobConf job = new JobConf(getConf(),NameCountApp.class);
        job.setJobName(JOB_NAME);

        FileInputFormat.setInputPaths(job, new Path(args[0]));
        FileOutputFormat.setOutputPath(job, new Path(args[1]));

        AvroJob.setMapperClass(job, ModelCountMapper.class);
        AvroJob.setReducerClass(job, ModelCountReducer.class);

        AvroJob.setInputSchema(job, Automobile.getClassSchema());
        AvroJob.setOutputSchema(
                job,
                Pair.getPairSchema(Schema.create(Type.STRING),
                        Schema.create(Type.INT)));

        JobClient.runJob(job);

        return 0;

    }

    /**
     * Creates an instance of this class and executes it to
provide a call-able
     * entry point.
     */
    public static void main(String[] args) {

        if (args == null || args.length != 2) {
            throw new IllegalArgumentException(
                    "Two parameters must be supplied , " +
                    "input directory and output directory
location.");
```

```
            }

        new File(args[0]).mkdir();
        new File(args[1]).mkdir();

        int result = 0;

        try {
            result = new NameCountApp().run(args);
        } catch (Exception e) {
            result = -1;
            LOGGER.error("An error occurred while running the
example", e);
        }

        if (result == 0) {
            LOGGER.info("SUCCESS");
        } else {
            LOGGER.fatal("FAILED");
        }

    }
}
```

18. Now, to run this example, select Java application and click new. Enter the name of the class as project main class (`NameCountApp`), provide the input and output locations of the directory from where the program will read the input and will output it to.

Now run the example.

You can see the output in the `/output` directory.

## How it works...

1. Avro is coupled with the schema, which has the format of the message defined in JSON. Avro uses this schema while reading/writing data. It also provides a concise format of the serialized object.

2. The second step is to compile the schema using the Avro library; we have used the JAR method. When we compile the schema with reference to the Avro lib, we also provide the path of `avsc` and the location of the Java folder where the Java file will be created.

3. The created Java file contains a public static final `org.apache.avro.Schema SCHEMA$ = new org.apache.avro.`

   `Schema.Parser().parse()`, which parsed the variable we placed in the schema, and we defined earlier.

4. It also passed these variables to the constructor of public `Mywebsitedata(java.lang.CharSequence webURL,`

   `java.lang.CharSequence name, java.lang.Integer data, java.lang.Integer size).`

5. Now we build the objects using the class which was just generated by the Avro process. The values are assigned to the objects before the `build()` method is invoked, which returns the instance.

6. For writing, `DatumWrite` is used to write data from the object through the `DataFileWriter`, which writes the data based on the grammar specified in the schema.

7. At this point, objects are added to the file using the `append()` method (step 14).

8. At this point, the data is written to the file in a serialized format.

9. At step 15, we are deserializing the content of the file into an object with `Mywebsitedata`. We use `DataumReader` that reads the content using `DataFileReader`.

10. After this, we are integrating it with the Hadoop process by writing a mapper and a reducer.

11. We list this dependency in the `pom.xml`, which is used as a reference to invoke the Hadoop lib for `MapReduce`.

12. We are using three classes to do this: `AvroMapper`, `AvroReducer`, and the `NameCountApp` class, which invokes the `MapReduce` job.

13. This triggers a sequence of events; when we run the program by invoking the main method, the Reducer collects the `map()` data and invokes the `reduce()`, and thus produces the result.

## There's more...

http://blog.cloudera.com/blog/2011/07/avro-data-interop/

http://www.javarants.com/2010/06/30/havrobase-a-searchable-evolvable-entity-store-on-top-of-hbase-and-solr/

http://avro.apache.org/docs/current/

http://ndolgov.blogspot.com/2010/12/apache-avro-serialization-without-code.html

https://www.igvita.com/2010/02/16/data-serialization-rpc-with-avro-ruby/

http://files.meetup.com/1634302/CHUG-ApacheAvro.pdf

http://ganges.usc.edu/pgroupW/images/a/a9/Serializarion_Framework.pdf

# Working with Protocol buffer

Protocol buffer was created to be smaller, faster, and simpler, and must provide an automated mechanism to serialize structured data. You decide the structure, then you can use the generated source code to read and write data to various streams and to many languages. You can change your data structure without breaking the old format.

As compared to XML serialization, it is:

- Simpler.

- Generates DAO classes, which works well for the programmers.

- Footprint is 3 to 10 times smaller.

- It is 20 to 100 times faster, which is a big benefit.

- Much simpler, thus less ambiguous.

- **Efficiency**: Protocol buffers are generally much more efficient at transmitting the same amount of data than Java binary serialization.

- **Portability**: Java binary serialization is not widely implemented outside Java, as far as I'm aware (unsurprisingly). Robustness in the face of unrelated changes. Unless you manually specify the serializable UUID, you can end up making breaking changes without touching data at all in Java. Backward and forward.

- **Compatibility**: Old code can read data written by new code. New code can read data written by old code. (You still need to be careful, and the implications of changes are slightly different between proto2 and proto3, but basically, protobuf makes this a lot easier to reason about than Java.)

- It's a lot easier to accidentally introduce non-serializable members into Java binary serialization, as proto descriptor files are all about serialization. You can't refer to an arbitrary class, and so on.

## How to do it...

1. Download the Jar file from the following location and add it to the project build path.

   Alternatively, you can build it from scratch too: `https://github.com/google/protobuf/releases/download/v2.6.1/protobuf-2.6.1.tar.gz`

   Then perform the following:

   ```
   sudo ./configure
   sudo make
   sudo make check
   sudo make install
   ```

It may ask for additional libs to be installed if it's not able to find the dependent lib.

```
https://repo1.maven.org/maven2/com/google/protobuf/protobuf-
java/2.6.1/protobuf-java-2.6.1.jar
```

2. Create a `.proto` file, the definition at `/u/HbaseB/hbase-0.98.5-hadoop2` location.

3. Let's see the structure of the file:

```
option java_package = "chap6.pb"; // its a package definition
option java_outer_classname = "CounterProtos";// it indicated that
the name of the classfile
option java_generic_services = true;
option java_generate_equals_and_hash = true;
option optimize_for = SPEED;

message CountRequest { // its a request message aggregate
containing a set of typed fileds
  // data types are available as field types, including bool,
int32,
  //float, double, and string.
}

message CountResponse { // its a request message initializing
count response
// required means its a must
  required int64 count = 1 [default = 0];
}

service RowCountService {
  rpc getMyRowCount(CountRequest)
    returns (CountResponse);
  rpc getMyCellCount(CountRequest)
    returns (CountResponse);
}
```

In Java, your generated classes will be placed in a `namespace` matching the package name.

Now let's compile the proto file that we just created:

**`protoc -I=$SRC_DIR --java_out=$DST_DIR $SRC_DIR/Counter.proto`**

4. This generates a `CounterProtos` public final class in the `chap6.pb` package.

5. Let's write a class that will use the auto-generated class, and we will override the methods as needed:

```
package chap6.pb;
// core protocol buffer classed
import com.google.protobuf.RpcCallback;
import com.google.protobuf.RpcController;
import com.google.protobuf.Service;
// our generated class
import coprocessor.generated.CounterProtos;
// Hbase specific classed
import org.apache.hadoop.hbase.Cell;
import org.apache.hadoop.hbase.CellUtil;
import org.apache.hadoop.hbase.Coprocessor;
import org.apache.hadoop.hbase.CoprocessorEnvironment;
import org.apache.hadoop.hbase.client.Scan;
import org.apache.hadoop.hbase.coprocessor.CoprocessorException;
import org.apache.hadoop.hbase.coprocessor.CoprocessorService;
import org.apache.hadoop.hbase.coprocessor.
RegionCoprocessorEnvironment;
import org.apache.hadoop.hbase.filter.Filter;
import org.apache.hadoop.hbase.filter.FirstKeyOnlyFilter;
import org.apache.hadoop.hbase.protobuf.ResponseConverter;
import org.apache.hadoop.hbase.regionserver.InternalScanner;
// core java classes
import java.io.IOException;
import java.util.ArrayList;
import java.util.List;


public class MyCount extends CounterProtos.CountService
  implements Coprocessor, CoprocessorService {

  private RegionCoprocessorEnvironment env;

  @Override
  public void start(CoprocessorEnvironment env) throws IOException
{
    if (env instanceof RegionCoprocessorEnvironment) {
      this.env = (RegionCoprocessorEnvironment) env;
    } else {
```

```
      throw new CoprocessorException("Must be loaded on a table
region!");
    }
  }

  @Override
  public void stop(CoprocessorEnvironment env) throws IOException
{
    // nothing to do when coprocessor is shutting down
  }

  @Override
  public Service getService() {
    return this;
  }

  @Override
  public void getMyRowCount(RpcController controller,
    CounterProtos.CountRequest request,
    RpcCallback<CounterProtos.CountResponse> done) {
    CounterProtos.CountResponse response = null;
    try {
      long count = getMyCountFromRowCell(new FirstKeyOnlyFilter(),
false);
      response = CounterProtos.CountResponse.newBuilder().
setCount(count).build();
    } catch (IOException ioe) {
      ResponseConverter.setControllerException(controller, ioe);
    }
    done.run(response);
  }

  @Override
  public void getMyCellCount(RpcController controller,
    CounterProtos.CountRequest request,
    RpcCallback<CounterProtos.CountResponse> done) {
    CounterProtos.CountResponse response = null;
    try {
      long count = getMyCountFromRowCell(null, true);
      response = CounterProtos.CountResponse.newBuilder().
setCount(count).build();
    } catch (IOException ioe) {
```

```
        ResponseConverter.setControllerException(controller, ioe);
      }
      done.run(response);
    }

  /**
    * Helper method  getMyCountFromRowCell to count rows or cells.
    * @param filter is an optional filter instance.
    * @param countCell
    * @returns count
    * @throws IOException When something fails with the scan.
    */
  private long getMyCountFromRowCell(Filter filter, boolean
countCells)
    throws IOException {
      long count = 0;
      Scan scan = new Scan();// for scanning
      scan.setMaxVersions(1);// taking max number to scan
      if (filter != null) {
        scan.setFilter(filter);
      }
      try (
        InternalScanner scanner = env.getRegion().getScanner(scan);
        // getting the regions to scan
      ) {
        List<Cell> results = new ArrayList<Cell>();
        boolean hasMore = false;
        byte[] lastRow = null;
        do {
          hasMore = scanner.next(results);
          for (Cell cell : results) {
            if (!countCells) {
              if (lastRow == null || !CellUtil.matchingRow(cell,
lastRow)) {
                lastRow = CellUtil.cloneRow(cell);
                count++;
              }
            } else count++;
          }
          results.clear();
        } while (hasMore);
      }
      return count;
    }
  }
```

This completes the integration of the Protocol buffer with Hbase. You can run this class and if all configurations are correct, you can invoke the respective methods and get the results.

For support of dynamic compressor endpoints with protocol buffer-based RPC, there was a patch added in `HBASE-5448` this allows.

 **CounterProtos** is not added due to the space constraints.

This discussion is the tip of the iceberg; however, much larger discussion is beyond the scope of this book.

## There's More...

http://blog.zahoor.in/2012/08/protocol-buffers-in-hbase/

https://developers.google.com/protocol-buffers/docs/proto

# Working with Pig and using Shell

In addition to the previously mentioned clients, some very useful clients which can be used in various scenarios are Pig and HBase shell.

Using Pig comes with a unique integration process, in which `HbaseStorage` is used to read and write data to HBase tables. But it does allow you to do it in a bulk loading fashion. If the data is already present in HBase, then the reads are much faster as compared to pulling it from the HDFS.

## How to do it...

The process is as follows:

1. You let Pig know the table, column families, individual columns, or even the entire column family.

2. The column family may contain various sets of columns and their values, hence it's essential to cast it to their Pig map type.

3. The load location string needs to be the name of the table that needs to be loaded.

4. Then we have to specify the exact column name, which is needed to pull the data. When the entire column family needs to be extracted, then we provide the column family and an asterisk.

5.  In case you are looking to get a subset of the value, you can provide a number *, say 50* after the column family.

6.  `HBaseStorage` allows the data to be stored in HBase. While storing data in Hbase, you specify the table name as the location string, similar to what we do in load. To be precise, the constructor arguments are also similar to the load case. The first describes the mapping of Pig fields to the HBase table, which uses the same `column_family:column` syntax as in load.

7.  Any Pig value can be mapped to a column. A Pig map can be mapped to a column family saying `column_family:*`. A point to be noted is that the row key is not referenced in this argument, but it is assumed to be the first field in the Pig tuple. The only valid option in the optional second argument in the store case is -caster.

>  These conditions are only valid from version 0.9 or later.

## How it works...

1.  When you create a table using the DDL, you create it with a `HBaseHCatStorageHandler`, specifically as follows:

    ```
    TBLPROPERTIES (hbase.table.name, hbase.column.mapping,hcat.hbase.
    output.bulkMode=true);
    ```

2.  Then you specify `A=LOAD USING PigStorage -DUMP A`

3.  Then you specify `STORE A Into 'TABLE_NAME'` using `org.apache.hcatalog.pig.HCatStorer()`

4.  Now, we use Pig to populate the HBase table via `Hcatalog` bulkload using pig – `useHcatalog` NAME of the file created earlier, say `mytestURL.bulkload.pig`

5.  At this point, the data is loaded in the HBase table.

## There's more...

http://pig.apache.org/docs/r0.9.1/api/org/apache/pig/backend/hadoop/hbase/HBaseStorage.html

The previous section talks about the API-level details with `LOAD` and `STORE`-level implementation.

I feel this chapter will be insufficient without talking about some core transactions of HBase Shell commands.

I will try to categorize it as follows:

- Basic shell commands:
    - ❑ `Hbase> version`: To get the version of Hbase
    - ❑ `Hbase>whoami`: Similar to using shell, it gives the owner
    - ❑ `Hbase>status`: Shows cluster status

- Table management commands/data Manipulations:
    - ❑ `List`: Lists all the tables in HBase
    - ❑ `Show_filters`: Shows all the filters in HBase
    - ❑ `Describe`: Describes the name of the table passed.
    - ❑ `Create`: Creates a table, various configuration options can be provided at create time and it lives with the table till the table is alive
    - ❑ `alter`: Alters column families' schema
    - ❑ `disable`: Disables the name of the table which is specified in the command line
    - ❑ `Disable_all`: Disables all the tables which match the regular expression
    - ❑ `Disable_all 'k.*'`
    - ❑ `Is_disable`: Checks if the table passed in is disabled or not
    - ❑ `Drop`: Drops the table whose name is passed as a parameter
    - ❑ `Drop_all`: Drops all the tables matching reg expressions (`drop_all'k.*'`).
    - ❑ `Count`: Counts the row in the table.
    - ❑ `Get`: Gets row, cell.
    - ❑ `Scan`: Scans a table; filters can be specified to limit the returns. Filter can be specified in two ways using filterString or using the entire package name. It also supports custom formatting.
    - ❑ `Truncate`: Disables, drops, and recreates the specified table.

- Cluster management tools:
    - ❑ `flush`: Flushes all the regions in passed `table '(flush 'mywebsite')`
    - ❑ `REGIONNANE: major_compaction`: Runs compactions on row or tables which are passed (`major_compation 'k1'`)
    - ❑ `move`: Moves a region (`move 'ENCIDED_REGIONNAME','SERVER'`)
    - ❑ `split`: Splits the entire table (`split 'tableName,' , split 'region_name','slitKey'`)

- ❏  Hlog_roll: Rolls the log writer (hlog_roll)

- ❏  zk_dump: Dumps status of the HBase cluster as been seen by ZooKeepr

- ❏  List_peers: Lists all replication peer clusters (list_peers)

- ❏  Enable_peer: Restarts the replication to the specified peer cluster (enable_peer '1')

There are many such commands; however, I have only listed a few important ones.

# 7

# Large-Scale MapReduce

In this chapter, we will consider how to write MapReduce jobs, how to design a large-scale MapReduce using HBase, how the internals of it work, and how to optimize the HBase framework to do it. In doing so, we will discuss the following:

- ▸ MapReduce frameworks
- ▸ When to use MapReduce and when not to
- ▸ Case study with example code and explanations

## Introduction

HBase provides various ways to leverage the potential of MapReduce based on the stack and the architecture you are going to use.

Before we start, let's do a quick revisit to the components, which will be used in MapReduce:

- ▸ Record reader
- ▸ Mapper
- ▸ Combiner
- ▸ Practitioner

- ▸ Shuffle and sort
- ▸ Reduce
- ▸ Output format

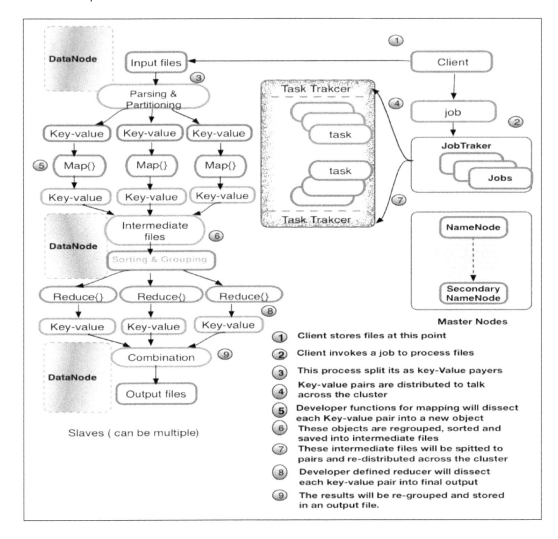

- ▸ **Record reader**: The core responsibility of a record reader is to analyze the data and then parse the data in key-value. The key is the location in the index and the value is the data that is composed of records.

- ▸ **Mapper**: Mapper executes each key-value pair that we got from the records. The design of the key and values depends on what we are planning to achieve from it. The key is the data we will use to group the values.

- **Combiner**: Combiner is an alternative localized reducer; the main advantage is the ability to group data during the mapping process. It gathers all the in-between keys that are parsed from the previous process (Mapper) and invokes a custom method to rearrange values in a granular scope of that specific mapper. It drastically reduces the data, which is moved around the network because by this; you can generate intermediate counts and then sum these counts to achieve the final results. Combiner is very useful when extreme performance is of prime importance.

In some cases, combiners are not guaranteed to execute.

- **Partitioner**: Partitioner collects all the intermediate key/value pairs once the mapper finishes the mapping operation and shards based on the reducer's capacity. Partitioner performs a job of modularizing the entire effort based on the reducers configured. It performs modulus operations by the number of reducers, thereby randomly distributing the keyspace per reducer. The partitioner gives an option of customization; this is extremely useful in sorting operations. Once the data is partitioned, it's saved on the local disk or file system.

- **Shuffle and sorting**: During the initiation process of reducer task shuffles and sorts, the output files generated are downloaded to local reducers, which is the next process in the pipeline. Based on this process, the reducer proceeds with the gathered data as input dataset and invokes a reduce job, one per group. The reduced dataset can be organized, cleaned, and merged in different ways. On completion of the previous process, it pipes the arrogated key/value pair in the predefined (as configured) format as an output.

- **Output format**: The output format transforms the final key/value pair, which it gets after the reduce process, and then writes to a file with the help of a record writer. As per the design, it always generates a tab-separated key-value; the records are separated by a newline character. This can be customized based on the need, and the data can be changed into various formats. All the data is persisted to HDFS agnostic to the output format.

Like the record reader, customizing your own output format is outside the scope of this book since it simply deals with I/O.

## Getting Ready...

Before we start working with MapReduce jobs in HBase, some of the essential components we will require are as follows:

Classes details, JAR files to be involved:

- `CellCounter`: This job counts the cell in an HBase table and is invoked during the process of map/reduce phase.

- `CellCreator`: This is a facade to create cells for HFileOutputFormat.

- `CopyTable`: As the name implies, this tool is utilized for copying a table to an alternative one with a distinctive setup.

- `Export`: This is used to export an HBase table.

- `GroupingTableMapper`: This extracts grouping columns from the input record.

- `HFileOutputFormat2`: This writes HFiles.

- `HRegionPartitioner<KEY,VALUE>`: This is used to partition the output keys into groups of keys.

- `IdentityTableMapper`: This passes the given key and record as it is to the reduce phase.

- `IdentityTableReducer`: This is a convenience class that simply writes all the values (which must be Put or Delete instances) passed to it out to the configured HBase table.

- `Import`: This imports data written by Export.

- `ImportTsv`: This tool imports data from a TSV file.

- `KeyValueSortReducer`: This emits sorted KeyValues.

- `LoadIncrementalHFiles`: This is a tool to load the output of `HFileOutputFormat` into an existing table.

- `MultiTableInputFormat`: This converts HBase tabular data from multiple scanners into a format that is consumable by Map/Reduce.

- `MultiTableInputFormatBase`: This is a base for MultiTableInputFormats.

- `MultiTableOutputFormat`: This is a Hadoop output format that writes to one or more HBase tables.

- `PutCombiner<K>`: This tool combines Puts.

- `PutSortReducer`: This emits sorted Puts.

- `RowCounter`: This is a job with a just a map phase to count rows.

- `SimpleTotalOrderPartitioner<VALUE>`: This is a partitioner that takes start and end keys and uses bigdecimal to figure which reduce a key belongs to.

- `TableInputFormat`: This converts HBase tabular data into a format that is consumable by Map/Reduce.

- `TableInputFormatBase`: This is a base for TableInputFormats.

- `TableMapper<KEYOUT,VALUEOUT>`: This extends the base Mapper class to add the required input key and value classes.

- `TableMapReduceUtil`: This is a utility tool for TableMapper and TableReducer.

- `TableOutputCommitter`: This is a small committer class that does not do anything.

- `TableOutputFormat<KEY>`: This converts Map/Reduce output and writes it to an HBase table.

- ▶ `TableRecordReader`: This iterates over an HBase table data, returns (ImmutableBytesWritable, Result) pairs.

- ▶ `TableRecordReaderImpl`: This iterates over an HBase table data, returns (ImmutableBytesWritable, Result) pairs.

- ▶ `TableReducer<KEYIN,VALUEIN,KEYOUT>`: This extends the basic reducer class to add the required key and value input/output classes.

- ▶ `TableSnapshotInputFormat:TableSnapshotInputFormat`: This allows a MapReduce job to run over a table snapshot.

- ▶ `TableSplit:`A table split corresponds to a key range (low, high) and an optional scanner.

- ▶ `TextSortReducer`: This emits sorted KeyValues.

- ▶ `TsvImporterMapper`: This writes table content out to files in HDFS.

- ▶ `TsvImporterTextMapper`: This writes table content out to map output files.

- ▶ `WALInputFormat`: Simple `InputFormat` for WAL files.

- ▶ `WALPlayer`: This is a tool to replay WAL files as an M/R job.

- ▶ `Mapper class`: (TestChap07Mapper) should extend the TableMapper class. The `TableMapper` class takes `KEYOUT` (the type of the key) and `VALUEOUT` (the type of the value).

- ▶ The map method of the Mapper class takes the rowkey of the Hbase table as an input key.

- ▶ Defined input key is the `ImmutableByteWritable` object.

The `org.apache.hadoop.hbase.client.Result` object contains the input values as column/column-families from the HBase table.

## How to do it...

The following is the code in the file:

```
public static class TestChap07Mapper extends TableMapper<ImmutableByte
sWritable, Put>
  {
  public void map(ImmutableBytesWritable row, Result value, Context
context) throws IOException, InterruptedException
{
context.write(row, resultToPut(row,value));
}
private static Put resultToPut(ImmutableBytesWritable key, Result
result) throws IOException
{
```

```
Put myPut = new Put(key.get());
for (KeyValue mykv : result.raw())
{
 myPut.add(mykv);
}
return myPut; // returning the put object which has key-values
}
}
```

▶ The Mapper class (`TestChap07Mapper`) should extend the `TableReducer` class.

▶ The output key is defined as NULL.

▶ The output value is defined as the `org.apache.hadoop.clent.Put` object.

```
public static class TestChap07MTableReducer extends
TableReducer<Text, IntWritable, ImmutableBytesWritable>  {
public static final byte[] CF = "cf".getBytes();
//getting the data from the column family as bytes
  public static final byte[] COUNT = "count".getBytes();
// getting the count in bytes
  public void reduce(Text key, Iterable<IntWritable> values,
Context context) throws IOException, InterruptedException {
    int i = 0; //initializing it to 0
    for (IntWritable myVal : values) {
      i += myVal.get();
    }
    Put myPut = new Put(Bytes.toBytes(key.toString()));
//converting the respective keys to string format
    myPut.add(CF, COUNT, Bytes.toBytes(i));
// adding column family byte array , COUNT as a byte array,
getting the valuer in byte)
    context.write(null, myPut);
  }
}
```

▶ Configure the `org.apache.hadoop.hbase.client.Scan` object and optionally define parameters such as start row, stop row, row filter, columns, and the column-families for the scan object.

▶ Set the record caching size (the default is 1, which is not preferred for MapReduce) for scan object.

▶ Set the block cache for scan object as false. This is done because timeouts can happen while executing the Map tasks; this can happen when we are processing batch records and it takes a very long time during which the client requests the RegionServer for the next dataset.

- Define the input table using the `TableMapReduceUtil.initTableMapperJob` method. This method takes the source table name, scan object, the Mapper class name, `MapOutputKey`, `MapOutputValue`, and the job object.
- Define the input table using `TableMapReduceUtil.initTableReducerJob`. This method takes the target table name, the reducer class name and the job object.

HBase works with MapReduce in the following ways:

- Using DataSource to feed the job
- Using data sink to store the job results
- Or using both data sink and DataSource

Let's connect to the cluster we created earlier and make sure all the components are working.

The structure of the call will be as follows.

Let's log in to the HBase Master by executing the following command:

```
Create 'myTest07MapRedcue','cf01'
put'myTest07MapRedcue','20150425#1','cf01:hits,'20000'
'myTest07MapRedcue','20150425#2','cf01:hits','40000'
```

1. The mapper class is the class that extends the TableMapper:

```
public class TestChap07Mapper extends TableMapper {

 @Override
 public void map(ImmutableBytesWritable rowKey, Result columns,
Context context)
    throws IOException, InterruptedException {

  try {
   // get rowKey and convert it to string
   String inKey = new String(rowKey.get());
   // set new key having only hits
   String outKey = inKey.split("#")[0];
   // get hits column in byte format first and then convert it to
string (as it is stored as string from hbase shell)
   byte[] bHits = columns.getValue(Bytes.toBytes("cf1"), Bytes.
toBytes("hits"));
   String sHits = new String(bHits);
   Integer hits = new Integer (sHits);
   // hist values
   context.write(new Text(outKey), new IntWritable(hits));
  } catch (RuntimeException e){
   e.printStackTrace();
```

```
      }
     }
    }
```

2. Now let's work with the reducer class:

```
public class TestChap07Reducer extends TableReducer{

 @Override
 public void reduce(Text key, Iterable values, Context context)
   throws IOException, InterruptedException {
  try {
   int reducerSum = 0;
   // loop through different hits vales and add it to sum
   for (IntWritable hits : values) {
    Integer intHitss = new Integer(hits.toString());
    reducerSum += intHitss;
   }

   // create hbase put with rowkey as date
   Put insHBase = new Put(key.getBytes());
   // insert sum value to hbase from the above
   insHBase.add(Bytes.toBytes("cf1"), Bytes.toBytes("reducerSum"),
Bytes.toBytes(reducerSum));
   // writes data to Hbase table
   context.write(null, insHBase);

  } catch (Exception e) {
   e.printStackTrace();
  }
 }
}
```

3. Now let's work on the driver class:

```
public class TestChap07Driver
{
 public static void main(String[] argvs) throws Exception {
 Configuration myConf = new Configuration();

 // define scan and define all the column families to scan
 // in our case we have just one
 Scan myScan = new Scan();
```

```
myScan.addFamily(Bytes.toBytes("cf1"));

Job myJob = new Job(myConf);

    myJob.setJarByClass(TestChap07Driver.class);
// define input hbase table
    TableMapReduceUtil.initTableMapperJob(
    "hitstest1", myScan,TestChap07Mapper.class,Text.
class,IntWritable.class,
        myJob);
// define output table
    TableMapReduceUtil.initTableReducerJob(
      "hitstest2",
      TestChap07Reducer.class,
      myJob);
    myJob.waitForCompletion(true);
  }
}
```

4.  At this stage, the classes are ready to be executed with Hadoop, MapReduce, and HBase JARs. This requires `classpath` setting and changes in `hbase-site.xml`.

5.  This can be done by adding `hbase-site.xml` to the `$HADOOP_HOME/conf/` directory and adding the HBase JAR to the `$HADOOP_HOME/lib` directory. However, it requires the Hadoop cluster to be restarted.

6.  Let's use the following command:

    **$ HADOOP_CLASSPATH=/path/to/hbase-protocol.jar:/path/to/ hbase/conf hadoop jar MyJob.jar MyJobMainClass $ HADOOP_ CLASSPATH=$(hbase mapredcp):/path/to/hbase/conf hadoop jar MyJob. jar TestChap07Driver $ HADOOP_CLASSPATH=$(hbase classpath) hadoop jar MyJob.jar TestChap07Driver**

7.  Now let's see the changes in the table by scanning the table using the HBase shell command:

    **hbase(main):010:0> org.apache.hadoop.hbase.util.Bytes.toInt("\x00\ x00\x00\xS2".to_java_bytes)**

    ```
    => 60000
    ```

## How it works...

Let's walk through the code so that we can have a clear idea at each step as to what is happening:

- At step 1, we created a table that can be used for manipulation of the data; let's say the table `myTest07MapRedcue` contains the counts of the hits my website is getting. This table has a cf (column family) as cf1 and an identifier as hits, which stores the data as value.

- At step 2, we create a class `TestChap07Mapper` using any standard IDE, say Eclipse. This class extends the TableMapper, which works as an invoker to the MapReduce framework. The `mapper` class with the help of the framework. It splits the value based on the hashtag. It grabs the data from the cf by using the identifier 'hits' and then the count of hits and holds it in the **outkey;** when we create an object of cluster class and add the HBase server details along with the port on which the JSON server is running, we are binding the IP to the port, which is listening for any client invocation.

- Now at stage 3, the reduce class `TestChap07Reducer`, which extends `TableReducer`, provides the framework of communication to the MapReduce design. We get the hit data, sum it, and insert it back to the table.

- Step 4 has a driver class that connects the Mapper and the reducer class and creates invocation sequence, which is in line with the MapReduce pattern. This byte array is then type casted to String, and hence, we get the String value ready to be printed on the console.

- At step 5 and 6, we can see the results of the invocation by scanning the table.

## There's more...

With **Pig** and **Hive** coming as high-level languages, this provides an abstraction on the MapReduce landscape. Thus, a fundamental question comes to mind: what is the value of MapReduce? The answer is very simple: to understand the basic building block on the MapReduce framework and the details of its low-level working. There are use-cases/scenarios that Pig or Hive cannot solve but which can still be solved using the pure Java-based MapReduce. As the Hadoop/HBase ecosystem matures more, there is a possibility that most of the work can be done using Pig and Hive.

## When not to use MapReduce

▸ When computation depends on previous computed values

▸ Full text indexing or when ad-hoc searching is required

▸ When an algorithm depends upon shared global state

▸ When joining an algorithm for log processing

▸ For lightweight solutions

Some alternatives to MapReduce frameworks can be found at the following:

▸ `http://static.googleusercontent.com/media/research.google.com/en/us/pubs/archive/35650.pdf`

▸ `http://static.googleusercontent.com/media/research.google.com/en/us/pubs/archive/41378.pdf`

Let's take the case where we will talk about how to use MapReduce on multiple tables:

1. Create two tables:

```
Create 'myTest07WebSite','cf01'
Create 'myTest07SiteHits','cf01'
```

2. Put data into these tables by the following commands:

   ❑ First table:

```
put 'myTest07WebSite','2015042601#01','cf02:sWebSite','1001'
put 'myTest07WebSite','2015042601#02','cf02:sWebSite','1002'
put 'myTest07WebSite','2015042601#03','cf02:sWebSite','1003'
```

   ❑ Second table:

```
put 'myTest07SiteHits','2015042601#01','cf01:sWebSi
te','12001'
put 'myTest07SiteHits','2015042601#02','cf01:sWebSite',
'12002'
put 'myTest07SiteHits','2015042601#03','cf01:sWebSite',
'12003'
```

3. Now we will use these tables as input tables and write a MapReduce, which will merge these two tables and put them in the third table:

```
Create 'myTest07SiteHitsPlusWebSite','cf03'
```

4. Let's create a class `MyTestMapper`.

```
Public class com.hbasebook.chap07.mywebsite.WebSiteMapReduceJob
```

Import statement is removed to bring more clarity to the code. Take a look at the code in detail by downloading it from the Packt location.

```
public class TableWebsiteMapper extends TableMapper<Text, IntWritable>
{
    private static byte[] websiteTable =Bytes.
toBytes("myTest07WebSite'");
    private staticbyte[] siteHitTable=Bytes.
toBytes("myTest07SiteHits'");

    byte[] site;
    String website;
    Integer wsite;
    String siteHit;
    Integer csiteHit;
    Text mapperKey;
    IntWritable mapperValue;

    @Override
    public void map(ImmutableBytesWritable rowKey, Result columns,
Context context) {
        // get table name
        TableSplit cSplit = (TableSplit)context.getInputSplit();
        byte[] mytableName = cSplit.getTableName();
        try {
            if (Arrays.equals(mytableName, websiteTable)) {
                String mydate = new String(rowKey.get()).split("#")
[0];
mySite = columns.getValue(Bytes.toBytes("cf02"), Bytes.
toBytes("wsite"));
                website = new String(mySite);
                wsite = new Integer(website);
                mapperKey = new Text("s#" + mydate);
                mapperValue = new IntWritable(wsite);
                context.write(mapperKey, mapperValue);
            } else if (Arrays.equals(mytableName, siteHitTable)) {
                String mydate01 = new String(rowKey.get());
mySite = columns.getValue(Bytes.toBytes("cf01"), Bytes.
toBytes("csiteHit"));
                siteHit = new String(mySite);
                Integer csiteHit = new Integer(siteHit);
                mapperKey = new Text("w#"+ mydate01 );
                mapperValue = new IntWritable(csiteHit);
                context.write(mapperKey, mapperValue);
            }
```

```
        } catch (Exception e) {
            e.printStackTrace();
        }
    }
}
```

Now let's go for the reducer class:

**com.hbasebook.chap07.mywebsite.WebSiteMapReduceJob**

Import statement is removed to bring more clarity to the code. Take a look at the code in detail by downloading it from the Packt location.

```
public class TableWebsiteReducer extends TableReducer<Text,
IntWritable, ImmutableBytesWritable>{
    @Override
    public void reduce(Text key, Iterable<IntWritable> values,
Context context)  {
        if (key.toString().startsWith("s")) {
            Integer wsiteVisit = 0;
            for (IntWritable website : values) {
                wsiteVisit = wsiteVisit + new Integer(website.
toString());
            }
            Put myPut = new Put(Bytes.toBytes(key.toString()));
            myPut.add(Bytes.toBytes("cf02"), Bytes.
toBytes("twebsite"), Bytes.toBytes(wsiteVisit));
            try {
                context.write(null, myPut);
            } catch (IOException e) {
                e.printStackTrace();
            } catch (InterruptedException e) {
                e.printStackTrace();
            }
        } else {// going for site hit numbers
            Integer wsiteVisit = 0;
            for (IntWritable website : values) {
                wsiteVisit = wsiteVisit + new Integer(website.
toString());
            }
            Put myPut = new Put(Bytes.toBytes(key.toString()));
            myPut.add(Bytes.toBytes("cf02"), Bytes.
toBytes("twebsite"), Bytes.toBytes(wsiteVisit));
            try {
                context.write(null, myPut);
            } catch (IOException e) {
                e.printStackTrace();
```

```
            } catch (InterruptedException e) {
                e.printStackTrace();
            }
        }
    }
}
```

Now let's plan for the MapReduce Job:

```
com.hbasebook.chap07.mywebsite.WebSiteMapReduceJob
public class TableWebsiteJob extends Configured implements Tool {
    @Override
    public int run(String[] arg0) throws Exception {
        List<Scan> mainSiteScan = new ArrayList<Scan>();
        Scan siteScan = new Scan();
        siteScan.setAttribute("scan.attributes.table.name", Bytes.
toBytes("myTest07WebSite"));
    System.out.println(siteScan.getAttribute("scan.attributes.table.
name"));
        mainSiteScan.add(siteScan);
        Scan webSitehitScan = new Scan();
        webSitehitScan.setAttribute("scan.attributes.table.name",
Bytes.toBytes("myTest07SiteHits"));// lookup for the table which we
have created and is having the site hit data.
    System.out.println(webSitehitScan.getAttribute("scan.attributes.
table.name"));
        mainSiteScan.add(webSitehitScan);

        Configuration myConf = new Configuration();
        Job myJob = new Job(myConf);
// will get the server details of Hbase/hadoop
        job.setJarByClass(TableWebsiteJob.class);
 // setting the class name to the job
        TableMapReduceUtil.initTableMapperJob(
                mainSiteScan, // tables to read from
                TableWebsiteMapper.class,
                Text.class,
                IntWritable.class,
                myJob);
        TableMapReduceUtil.initTableReducerJob(
                "myTest07SiteHitsPlusWebSite",
                TableWebsiteReducer.class,
                myJob);
        myJob.waitForCompletion(true);
        return 0;
// totalhit is the third table which will receive the data
    }

    public static void main(String[] args) throws Exception {
        TableWebsiteJob runWebHitJob = new TableWebsiteJob();
```

```
        runWebHitJob.run(args);
// invoking the class
    }
}
```

There are two HBase Scans to scan the inputs from two tables. I am grabbing the data from these tables and pushing it in a list to the `TableMapReduceUtil.initTableReducerJob` method to ready from multiple tables. Package the file to `hbaseWebsite.jar`.

Execute the command as listed next:

**Hadoop jar hbaseWebsite.jar com.hbasebook.chap07.mywebsite. WebSiteMapReduceJob**

The job will take a few seconds to complete depending on the data size in the table.

Once the Job is complete, please re-log in to the HBase shell:

```
    hbase(main):006:0> scan 'mywebproject:myTest07SiteHitsPlusWebSite'
ROW                                COLUMN+CELL
 S#20150531                               column=cf1: twebsite,
timestamp= 1425248403602, value=\x00\x00\x01\x92
 w#20150531                               column=cf1: twebsite,
timestamp= 1425248425374, value=\x00\x00\x00\x94
 s#20150531
column=cf1: twebsite, timestamp= 1425248470557, value=\x00\x00\x01\x98
 s#20150531                               column=cf1: twebsite,
timestamp= 1425248515560, value=\x00\x00\x01\x9D
4 row(s) in 0.0410 seconds
hbase(main):035:0> org.apache.hadoop.hbase.util.Bytes.toInt("\x00\x00\
x01\x92                                                      ".to_
java_bytes)
=> 4
hbase(main):036:0> org.apache.hadoop.hbase.util.Bytes.toInt("\x00\x00\
x00\x94".to_java_bytes)
=> 3
hbase(main):037:0> org.apache.hadoop.hbase.util.Bytes.toInt("\\x00\x00\
x01\x98".to_java_bytes)
=> 4
hbase(main):038:0> org.apache.hadoop.hbase.util.Bytes.toInt("\x00\x00\
x01\x9D ".to_java_bytes)
=> 4
```

It is also possible to work on multiple tables using `MutliTableOutputFormat`. This can happen based on a flexible design in which the Hadoop output can be written to more than one HBase table. In this case, the table name acts as a key and the value can be a `PUT` or `DELETE` instance. It's mandatory to have pre-existing tables as the `PUT` and `DELETE` invoked can be done on a valid column family.

In some desired condition, we can set `WAL_OFF` in `WAL_PROPERTY`. This will not invoke the WAL pipeline, and hence, WAL will be off. WAL is always set to ON by default.

> We need to be extra careful and disable write-ahead logs for those use cases where it's possible to lose data due to region server failure. And the process can be rerun to achieve the same objectives (for example, bulk import process).

In some scenarios/cases, it's possible to connect to an RDBMS using a custom build reducer.

Careful consideration needs to be given for the number of reducer jobs as more reducers will cerate more simultaneous connections to the RDBMS.

## See also...

- https://highlyscalable.wordpress.com/2012/02/01/mapreduce-patterns/
- https://www.mapr.com/blog/mapreduce-design-patterns-implemented-apache-spark
- https://www.amazon.com/dp/B00RP13B6M/ref=dp-kindle-redirect?_encoding=UTF8&btkr=1
- https://www.youtube.com/watch?v=1nIWZq-9iRQ

# 8
# HBase Performance Tuning

In this chapter, we will discuss various options to improve the performance of HBase even if the data is continuously growing in size in an exponential way.

We will also discuss the components that can be reconfigured to optimize the throughput both from hardware and software perspectives. In doing so, we will discuss the following recipes in detail. It's of utmost importance to know what the load patterns are, what CPU-intensive footprints are, which of them are IO intensive, and which systems will bring network chattiness in the infrastructure; and plan it in advance.

- ▶ Working with the infrastructure/operating systems
- ▶ Working with the Java virtual machine
- ▶ Changing the configurations of components
- ▶ Working with HDFS

## Introduction

As the usage of HBase is becoming a more real-time-based, it's important to make sure that HBase performs the read and write at a consistent speed agnostic to the scale at which it is running:

| Type of work | Usage patterns | Remarks |
|---|---|---|
| Data intensive | IO, Network | Copying data from HDFS |
| Text searching | CPU, IO, Network | Locating different sets of data |

| Type of work | Usage patterns | Remarks |
|---|---|---|
| Machine learning | CPU, IO, Network | Grouping, categorizing, applying models |
| MapReduce, indexing, grouping | IO, CPU, Networking | Filtering, realigning, combining |
| Master, slave, region server, Zookeeper communication | Network, CPU, IO | Communicating between different systems, load balancing |

In doing so, we need to make sure that all the distributed components perform at a benchmark that is executable on the Linux-based OS.

The list of distributed components is as follows:

- Hardware
- OS (Linux, REH6.5)
- JVM/Java 1.7.0_10 and above
- HDFS
- Read/write on the OS
- Region servers
- Master servers/HMaster
- Client servers/HClient
- Zookeeper
- Table design
- Large-scale data compression
- Heavy-volume-based Map Reduce (which we will discuss throughout this chapter)

# Working with infrastructure/operating systems

Infrastructure design plays an important role in HBase optimization and performance. An HBase engineer is pivotal for making the right choices during the initial phase of the design as once the data grows exponentially, it starts bringing in operational challenges. In addition to this, the infrastructure should perform to the predefined performance criteria as the cluster transitions from small to medium and from medium to large.

## Getting ready...

HBase works in the master-slave pattern, wherein a master comprises HDFS NameNode, MapReduce JobTracker, and HBase Master, and the slave contains HDFS DataNode, the MapReduce TaskTrackers, and the HBase region servers. It's better to collocate DataNode HBase region server, which helps in data locality and hence increases the performance of the system as the data does not cross the network.

HBase also requires managing a separate component of ZooKeeper; this manages the HBase cluster.

It's always better to separate the slave nodes from the master nodes because of the frequent decommissioning and maintenance of the slaves. A large cluster form the master will have a separate rack with NameNode, Secondary NameNode, JobTracker, and HBase master.

The slave nodes will be on a different rack, preferably connecting with a 1 GB Ethernet switch wherein each rack switch will be connected to a cluster switch.

- ▸ **Balanced workload**: In a true large production environment, balanced workload means that the various resources are distributed uniformly across various job types, which are CPU, disk I/O, or Network I/O intensive.

- ▸ **Compute intensive**: The jobs that are more I/O intensive will require more computing power to do the work in hand. Usually, the slaves are more compute intensive and require more RAM and CPU to store the heap data while processing.

- ▸ **I/O intensive**: Usually, a MapReduce job (such as sorting) does not need a lot of compute power but is more I/O bound to the cluster (for example, if you have a lot of cold data). Hadoop clusters loading this cold data and trying to get this to a hot zone take up a lot of I/O. For this type of workload, we recommend investing in more disks per box.

- ▸ For a small cluster (10 to 50 nodes):

| Master/Slave | Cluster | Storage | Number of cores | Memory in GB | Network |
|---|---|---|---|---|---|
| Masters | Balanced and/or HBase cluster | Four to eight 2 TB disks | Dual Quad | 32 | 1 GB Ethernet |
| Slave | Balanced workload | Four to eight 2 TB disks | Dual Quad | 32 | |
| | HBase cluster | Eight to twelve 2 TB disks | Dual Quad | 64 | |

For medium to large clusters (50 to 1,000 nodes):

| Master/ Slave | Cluster | Storage | Number of cores | Memory in GB | Network |
|---|---|---|---|---|---|
| Masters | HBase cluster | Four to eight 2 TB disks | Dual Quad | 64 | Dual 1 GB links for all nodes in a 20 node rack and 2 x 10 GB interconnect links per rack going to a pair of central switches |
| Slave | Balanced workload | Four to eight 2 TB disks | Dual Quad | 32 | |
| | Compute-intensive workload | Eight to twelve 2 TB disks | Dual Hexa Quad | 64 | |
| | HBase clusters (region servers) | Sixteen 2 TB disks | Dual Hexa Quad | 96-128 | |
| | I/O intensive workload | Sixteen 1 TB disk | Dual Quad | 64 | |

- ▸ **Choosing servers**: For medium and large clusters, entry-level servers are a good choice as they provide good parallelization capabilities. It's good to have a hardware that fits into low rack units, typically, 1U or 2U servers.

- ▸ **Memory sizing**: It's essential to provide an adequate amount of memory (RAM) to optimize the processors so that there is no memory swapping, as swapping degrades performance. When swapping starts, it means that the system is trying to acquire more memory and the RAM is full. The system is actively involved in disk I/O to push the inactive files to the swap allocated space on the physical disk. The right amount of memory depends upon the ratio of processors versus the size of the memory. In most of the scenarios, the preceding table will work and will require some fine tuning in some unique situations.

- ▸ **Processors**: It's advisable to use four socket medium clock speed processors. This depends upon the size of the cluster; if the need is to have a large cluster, then 2-octo-core will be a better choice. The slaves can have four quad cores per machine for zookeeper, you can live with two quad cores.

- ▸ **Network**: The biggest performance hit in HBase comes from switching hardware which is serving the traffic. It's also pivotal when you expand your capacity due to the growth of the cluster. There can be various situations that can arise due to this:

- ▸ HBase hotspot regions

- ▸ Slowness due to network starvation

- ▸ Slowness due to high processor usage

We can use various strategies to overcome such issues based on the situations, such as the following:

- ▸ Single switch
- ▸ Multiple switch
- ▸ Multiple rack

The objective is to optimize the usage of network and all the different nodes to communicate between themselves and with the master in the most effective ways by providing high performance at a relatively low price. A 1 GB dedicated link will be sufficient for a very large cluster.

The core of the network design is to foresee various scenarios and use cases that a cluster will go thought during its lifetime and bake in the elasticity to expand as needed, in some cases reserve the burst capacity, if needed.

A large HBase cluster should be separated from the other web application networks by using a dedicated switch. As the usage pattern is data intensive and requires data modeling, high processing speeds, when clubbed with the regular web applications, will degrade the performance of the web/app. The HBase administrate of the architects should discuss and work with the network team and get the switch that suffices the needs of the HBase cluster. These devices should be monitored 24x7 for the usage and capacity.

The core of the design is keeping in mind that there will be growth and there can be additional racks, which can be added on demand or on the fly in this HBase/Hadoop cluster. Revisiting the network design once everything is setup is very expensive and can lead to unavailability of services.

Is a critical piece in the HBase/Hadoop landscape, especially for the NameNode and SecondaryNameNode servers and masters. For large clusters, we will always use primary and secondary NameNode servers pointing to the same storage.

The NameNode server is very important and is the heart of the Hadoop/HBase system. This is the core reason to keep it on a highly reliable storage system as it stores namespaces and edits log journaling .Thus, in these scenarios, it's good to go for RAID hardware or any other equivalent storage system.

To make it fully HA, we must plan the HBase master to have two local storage volumes and two on the remote. This can be planned as 1 TB each but must have the capacity to grow till petabyte.

- ▸ **Planning an expansion**: It's relatively easy to expand a Hadoop/HBase cluster by adding new servers to the cluster or rack or by increasing the memory footprint. As the expansion happens, there is lot of rebalancing done to sync the data, and this can impact the performance of the system.
    - ❑ Plan for expansion in the network in advance.

❑ Plan for more memory on the master servers as the traffic grows. The server must have the capacity to accommodate more CPUs and memory if needed.

❑ Plan for some free capacity in the data center near the HBase cluster.

▶ **Operating system**: HBase is primarily designed to work with most Unix- and Linux-based systems. Running HBase on windows in not production-tested; thus it's not recommended by the Apache foundation.

The Linux/Unix OSes on which it's recommended are as follows:

▶ CentOS

▶ Fedora

▶ Debian

▶ Ubuntu

▶ Red Hat Enterprise

▶ Some version of Solaris

▶ Storage and file system tuning

On some occasions, there can be high I/O usage, and this can result in swapping, which can lead to the system being unresponsive.

Log in to the node and set up the swap size as zero:

```
Vm.swappiness to 0 in /etc/sysctl.conf
Vm.swappiness=0
```

The `atime` and `noatime` settings: Linux OS records every piece of information of the file, such as when it was created, accessed, or modified. All these activities come at a cost. The ext2 file system works differently and has the capacity to avoid the access time and not record it entirely. This can be configured by the super user easily. This gives significant performance benefits if you are considering frequently accessed files (`var/spool/news directory`) to the overall performance of OS.

## How to do it...

We can use the `noatime` mount options to achieve this. This is done for every line that is bound to a file system in the `/etc/fstab` file. Once this is done, all the reads preformed will bypass the updates to the `atime` information associated with the file. The objective is to avoid writes to the disk where only reads are performed and hence avoid the entire cycle of write operations on the disk, thus boosting the performance.

In the following example, we will do the setup using the `noatime` option in our `/chroot` filesystem.

Do `vi` to the `fstab file /etc/fstab` and add in the line that refers to the `/chrootfile`
system. The `noatime` option after the default option is shown as follows:

```
/dev/sda7   /chroot        ext2    defaults,noatime        1   2
```

> This change doesn't need a reboot of the system. To make sure the
> changes are effective immediately, you have to remount the existing
> file system. This can be done using the following command.
> **root@yourname] /#mount -oremount /chroot/**

**bdflush**: This parameter is directly related to the virtual memory of the Linux kernel.

The `/proc/sys/vm/bdflush` file holds this information.

Edit the `/etc/sysctl.conf` file:

```
Vm.bdflush=100 1200 128 512 15 500 60 20 2
```

The first parameter is `100(is nfract)`; the default value is 50. This controls the maximum
number of dirty buffers in the buffer cache. A higher value means the kernel can hold writes
for a longer time, but it also implies that it will do so when the memory is low. A lower value
balances the I/O more effectively.

The second parameter is `1200 ndirty`; the default value is `500`. We have changed it to
1200 to get burst I/O. A small value can slow down the bdflush process and thus lead to
memory shortage. A higher value will delay the frequent flush or write to the disk and hence
improve the performance.

The third parameter `128 nrefill` is the number of buffers that bdflush will add to the list of
free buffers when `refill_freelist()` is invoked by the kernel.

The fourth parameter is not currently used.

The fifth parameter is `interval`; by default, the value is 500. This value is used by the kernel
to pause between the `kupdate` flush. We have set it low to reduce this pause.

The sixth parameter is `Age_buffer`. By default, the value is 3000. It's the delay in the kernel
to flush the normal buffer. We have reduced it to 500.

The seventh parameter is `nfract_sync` and has a default value of 60. It's measured in
terms of percentage. Once this percentage is achieved, the kernel activates the bdflush of the
buffered cache synchronously.

The eighth parameter, `nfract_stop_bdflush`, has a default value of 20. This indicates
when the kernel will stop the bdflush process.

The ninth parameter is not used; hence we need to keep it as 2.

Schedulers: The scheduler is a critical component in the stack of OS. This I/O or disk scheduling is a comprehensive terminology. This process determines the timings and frequency of the I/O operation on storage device. It's part of OS kernel and is invoked by the OS. It's also termed as the I/O elevator.

A completely fair queuing or `cfq` is what comes as a default I/O scheduler. This algorithm separates invocation into three parts: real-time, best effort, and idle. The cfq process applies its algorithm on historical access patterns. This process waits for the complete new I/O making other processes wait even if they are ready to proceed. This process is best suited for desktop and cannot work well with RAID controllers. This core design is not applicable to high performance I/O operations and thus cannot be used by HDFS, Hadoop/HBase systems.

Noop scheduler is used when deploying on iSCI over HBA (hardware-based RAID).

 ▸  Solid state drive(SSD) based storage uses a deadline scheduler:

```
Cat /sys/block/sda/queue/scheduler
```

Echo deadline> sys/block/sda/queue/scheduler

The `nr_request` can be used to optimize the number of read and write requests that can be queued for a given time. The default used is 128; this can be changed to 1024 to increase the scheduler depth and gain performance:

```
Echo 1024> /sys/block/sda/queue/nr_requests
```

> The values and the performance results may vary. It's very much required to do a deep dive into all the parameters and do multiple rounds of performance testing on various loads. These are some of the recommendations that can be done if needed.

Filesystem: ZFS and XFS are very advanced file systems and are very highly recommended, reliable, and recoverable.

In case these file systems are not available, ext3 and ext4 are also pretty robust, reliable and scale.

Ext4 provides integrity as the default by providing two options.

By changing the following values, the XSF file system performance can be optimized:

Nobarrier

Logbufs=8

Allocsize=2M

Logbside=256k

These settings need to be added in /etc/fstab so that it persists and the changes become oblivious to the restart of the servers.

Kernel and network tuning:

> ▸ Note that in practice, the first thing is to see is whether there are any issues related to the network and whether the performance benchmarking is giving these symptoms. We must match these values with the current system configuration to make sure that the configuration is not causing any degradation in the system performance:

```
Ethtool -k eth0 lro off
Ethtool -k eth0 tso off


The above two can be added in the /etc/rc.local
In ect/sysctl.conf
We can change the value of the following :
Net.ipv4.tcp_modrate_rcvbuf =1
Net.ipv4.tcp_keepalive_intvl=30
Net.ipv4.tcp_tw_reuse=1II
Net.ipv4.tcp_window_scaling=1
Net.ipv4.tcp_stack=1
Net.ipv4.tcp_fin_timeout=15
net.ipv4.tcp_max_syn_backlog = 40000
net.core.somaxconn = 40000
net.core.wmem_default = 8388608
net.core.rmem_default = 8388608
```

I/O tuning:

In some scenarios, certain parts of the cluster get more I/O as compared to other sections in the cluster and this creates wait time or spikes in the I/O activities.

We have used these settings in our cluster and it seems to be working fine:

```
Vm.dirty_ratio=40
Vm.dirty_expire_centisecs=200
Vm.dirty_writeback_centisecs=100
Vm.dirty_bytes=0
Vm.dirty_background_ratio=0
Vm.dirty_background_bytes=209715200
```

These settings will change based on the RAM, processing power, caching, and other infrastructure-related components. You need to plan a proper benchmarking process to make sure it doesn't impact adversely.

Number of open files: This is a kernel setting done at the OS level.

The number of open files plays a very important role in the I/O performance. This can increase the performance by changing the file-max value. It's directly related to the RAM available on the machine. In case you have too less, you may get a "too many open files" error.

Say for 4 GB of RAM, set it to (4x1024)/4=1024 x 256=262144.

```
With sudo su -  or root access you can edit the following file and place
this number:
```

```
/proc/sys/fs/file-max
```

To make the change permanent, edit the /etc/sysctl.conf file and add the following:

```
fs.file-,max = 262144
```

```
To make it immediately effective, you can fire the following command:
```

```
/etc/rc.d/init.d/network restart
```

This will allow you to restart the network communication, thus making it permanent.

# Working with Java virtual machines

Working with Java virtual machines is one of the key areas of performance tuning as JVM optimization task can be very tricky and depends on many factors.

There are a lot of factors that can directly impact the performance of HBase as each query has to pass through the JVM.  The main reason it impacts the performance is the optimization of JVM so that the garbage collection threads don't trigger stop the world GC (garbage collections) and does the GC efficiently even at varying load.

It's also essential to understand the GC process and how it works. There are various design choices such as serial versus parallel, concurrent versus stop the world, compaction versus non-compaction vs copying. Similarly, various performance matrices need to be calculated to make sure we get optimum performance, which includes throughput, GC overheads, pause time, frequency of collections, footprint, and promptness.

Our discussion will be limited to the improvement areas and what changes we can do to improve the performance as this topic is beyond the scope of this chapter.

We will talk more about the G1 or Garbage First (G1) collection process as we consider JDK1.7.X onwards.

## Getting ready...

The principles of garbage collections are slightly different in G1 as compared to CMS (concurrent mark sweep); some details are as follows. It's essential to understand the core concept to make a better performance choice while doing performance tuning.

| Garbage First (G1) | Concurrent Mark Sweep (CMS) |
|---|---|
| In G1, it's done logically. This is done by dividing the total heap space into number of regions, and the regions are then identified as young or old. | Young and old generation heap space are physically differentiated. |
| Recently allotted objects are more likely to have a week reference and become garbage compared to the objects that have survived the scavenging process and become older objects. Pointer modification is another process that we have to take into consideration. In the case of a new object; this is due to the initialization process. | It provides collector completeness without imposing any order on region choice for collection sets. |
| In case of G1, the liveliness of the objects in various region comes into picture. G1 collects the data with minimum liveliness as it will be fast in releasing the heap space. Live objects remains in the region get copied to another region that has enough space to accommodate the objects. GC pause time is one of the main reasons for latency fluctuations. Thus, reduction in pause time with G1 improves the HBase performance. | In CMS, objects are formed in young generations first. Then during the garbage collection process, the leftover objects are moved to the survivor space, and the objects that survive the next minor GC move to the old generation space. |

When using HBase we need to think of two main in-memory objects: BlockCache and Memstore as shown next. The block cache used in HBase is nothing but a representation of LruBlockCache, which helps HBase use large byte arrays and thus enables HBase to hold bigger blocks. The GC process looks at the non-referenced objects and tries to remove them (GC them) and reallocate the memory process:

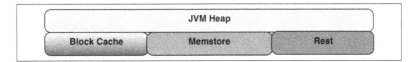

To get optimum results, you have to fine-tune the following parameters:

| Parameter to be tuned | Reasons for tuning | Remarks / Recommendations |
|---|---|---|
| -XX:+UseG1GC | Use of G1 Garbage collections | |
| –XX:G1HeapRegionSize=n | This sets the size of individual regions. The default value is decided ergonomically based on the heap size, The minimum is 1 MB and the maximum is 32 MB. | In this case, as we have taken -Xms32g and –Xmx32g, we can take 32 MB. |
| -XX:InitiatingHeapOccupancyPercent=n | Percentage of heap occupied to initiate the concurrency GC process. The zero value indicates constant a GC process, the default value is 45. | We should keep this as a default of 45 levels. |
| XX:MaxGCPauseMillis=n | This sets a soft goal for the JVM and JVM and makes the best effort to honor this goal. | For better performance, you have to do a series of tests, and based on this, you should finalize it; generally 100 ms is good enough. |
| -XX:+ParallelRefProcEnabled | If it's turned on, GC uses multiple threads to process the references during Young and mixed GC. | For HBase, the GC remarking time is reduced to 75%, and the overall GC pause time is reduced to 30%. |
| -XX:-ResizePLAB and -XX:ParallelGCThreads | PLAB- Promotion local allocation buffer is used during young collections where multithread env are in play. PLAB makes sure the thread doesn't compete with data structure that shares the same memory space.<br><br>For Parallel GC threads, we need a fixed number of GC threads. The recommended formula for this is 8 + (logical processors-8)(5/8). | Say you have 16 logical processors. Thus the value should be<br><br>$8+(16-8)\times(5/8)=13$. |

| Parameter to be tuned | Reasons for tuning | Remarks / Recommendations |
|---|---|---|
| -XX:G1NewSizePercent | This is the percentage of heap to be used as the minimum for young generation size; the default value is 5. Keeping it below 3 may give better performance. | In various test scenarios, the lower value of 1 and 2 gave better performance.<br><br>Note that it depends upon the heap size, thus needs extensive testing before we conclude. Please test your env, and based on the data, make the changes. |

## How to do it...

During the startup of HBase, you can pass these parameters in HBase_SHELL_OPTS:

```
HBASE_SHELL_OPTS="-verbose:gc -XX:+UseG1GC --XX:G1HeapRegionSize=32 -XX:MaxGCPauseMillis=100 \
-XX:+ParallelRefProcEnabled  -XX:-ResizePLAB -XX:ParallelGCThreads=13 -XX:G1NewSizePercent=1 \
-XX:+PrintGCApplicationStoppedTime -XX:+PrintGCDateStamps \
-XX:+PrintGCDetails -Xloggc:$HBASE_HOME/logs/gc-hbase.log" ./bin/hbase shell
```

Alternatively you can also set this up in ~/.bashrc. This will be applied once you are entering or logging in to the shell.

## See also

For further reading, please refer to the following links:

http://www.oracle.com/technetwork/java/javase/memorymanagement-whitepaper-150215.pdf

http://www.oracle.com/technetwork/articles/java/g1gc-1984535.html

http://www.oracle.com/technetwork/java/javase/tech/vmoptions-jsp-140102.html#G1Options

http://citeseerx.ist.psu.edu/viewdoc/download?doi=10.1.1.63.6386&rep=rep1&type=pdf

# Changing the configuration of components

In this section, we will discuss the configuration changes that can help us improve the overall performance of HBase.

## Getting ready...

Let's start with `hbase-site.xml`:

**`hbase.hregion.max.filesize:`**

The first step is to think in advance how to split the regions, which can be done using this parameter (hbase.hregion.max.filesize). In this scenario, the size of the one of the store in the region is constantly monitored by the HBase internal process. Once the internal process detects that the size is greater than what was specified by this parameter, it splits the region. The default value is 10 GB.

**`hbase.regionserver.handler.count:`**

This is primarily used to govern the incoming request to the user tables. This allocates the listener threads, which intercept the call to the user tables. In case of very high volume cluster, it's important to increase it. The default is 10.

 A proper estimation needs to be done to fine-tune this setting based on the usage patterns and the scenarios for which the cluster is used. In some cases, it may negatively impact the cluster and may cause excessive GC.

**Compaction**: In case of compaction, we have to discuss both the scenarios: major compaction and minor compaction.

**Major compaction**: It will pick smaller StoreFiles, merge them into one, and generate a single StoreFile per store, which helps in performance. It's highly recommended to do major compaction manually.

**Minor compaction**: Minor compaction picks up all the store files in the store and writes them as one. A major difference with major compaction is that it never removes the deleted or expired cells whereas major dose.

Major compaction can be set by `hbase.hregion.majorcompaction`.

**Region splitter**: This is nothing but a process of pre-splitting the tables and creating split points with the row key space. HBase allows you to create a table with a specified number of pre-split regions. In case there is an existing table and there is a need to do a split, you can execute a network IO safe rolling split.

There is a note of caution: pre-split in some cases may cause uneven distribution of load due to large rows. In case you are doing the split at runtime or on a preexisting table, there are chances that the split points were not considered properly and the new split may distribute the load unevenly causing the cluster to underperform.

▸ `hbase.client.write.buffer`: Whenever the client requests a change, this request is routed to a region server instantly. However, it is advisable to programmatically control this for better performance. In some scenarios, the client caches the changes and flushes these changes in batches to the region server to minimize the network chattiness and optimize the use of batch flushing, hence increasing the performance. This is controlled by an auto flush flag and can be changed by turning it off. Once this flag is turned off, the changes will be cached till the time flush-commit is invoked or the buffer side exceeds the configured size.

▸ `hbase.client.scanner.caching`: This is used to fetch the rows when calling the next scanner if it's not consuming the local memory.

 Check the value of scanner timeout before making any changes here.

## How to do it...

Open `hbase-site.xml` in edit mode:

```
Sudo su -
Cd $HBASE_HOME/conf
vi hbase-site.xml
change the following for hbase.regionserver.handler.count :
<property>
<name>hbase.regionserver.handler.count</name>
<value>64<value>
</property>
```

 It is advisable to keep the value low when the payload for each request is going to be large. It's a good practice to keep the handler count approximately matching the CPU count.

For hbase.hregion.max.filesize, the default value is 10737418240. Changing it to a smaller size increases the performance. The recommendation is to keep it at 10 GB:

```
<property>
  <name>hbase.hregion.max.filesize</name>
  <value>1073741824</value>
</property>
```

For hbase.hregion.majorcompaction, setting the value to zero will disable all major compactions:

```
<property>
  <name>hbase.hregion.majorcompaction</name>
  <value>0</value>
</property>
```

For hbase.client.write.buffer, the default value is 2097152.

A larger buffer consumes more memory both on the client and server sides, but it reduces the RPC (remote procedure calls), hence providing performance benefits. In this case, we have increased it to four times the default size:

```
<property>
  <name>hbase.client.write.buffer</name>
  <value>8388608</value>
</property>
```

For hbase.client.scanner.caching, the default value is 100. Increasing the cache size increases the performance of large reads as this allows more rows to be fetched when calling next on a scanner.

In most of the scenarios, the following size suits the needs:

```
<property>
  <name>hbase.client.scanner.caching</name>
  <value>10000</value>
</property>
```

## See also

For further reading, refer to the following article:

```
http://hortonworks.com/blog/apache-hbase-region-splitting-and-
merging/
```

# Working with HDFS

To get the best performance from HBase, it is essential to get optimal performance from Hadoop/HDFS.

There are various parameters we can look at, but we will limit ourselves to make sure we get the benefits.

Multiple disk mount point:

```
Df.datanode.data.dir  -> use all attached disks to data node.
Block Side(DFS) =128 MB
Local file system buffer
Io.file.buffer.size=131072 (128k)
Io.sort.factor=50 to 100
Data Node and NameNode  conconcurry
Dfs.namenode.handler.count(131072)
Dfs..datanode,max.transfer.tthread 4096
```

Give HDFS as many paths as possible to spread the disk I/O around and to increase the capacity of HDFS.

## How to do it...

Please open the `dfs.block.size` section from `dfs-site.xml` and `mapred.min.split.size` from `mapred.max.split.size` in `mapred-site.xml`.

The split of the input size and the total input data size can be changed and can be mapped to the block size.

This also helps us reduce the number of map tasks. If the map task is reduced, the performance will increase. This also reduces the cost involved in merging the map's output segment.

Based on my observations, 256M is a good number to process.

## See also....

https://www.cmg.org/wp-content/uploads/2013/04/m_97_3.pdf

https://blog.cloudera.com/blog/2009/12/7-tips-for-improving-mapreduce-performance/

# 9
# Performing Advanced Tasks on HBase

In this chapter, we will consider some advanced topics where Hbase is used extensively in the industry. We will walk through the following topics:

- Machine learning using Hbase
- Real-time data analysis using Hbase and Mahout
- Full text indexing using Hbase

## Machine learning using Hbase

Before we dive deep into the details of Hbase/Hadoop, Mahout, and machine learning, it's vital to discuss and highlight some important concepts, which will be used in this chapter.

**Data science**—in software engineering terms—is an operation of a set of programs that churns a large quantity of data to evaluate supervised or unsupervised learning models and provides a valuable tool to data scientists or systems through which decisions can be made.

The most important aspect is applying programming/algorithms that provide a cleaner dataset on which the next program can be synthesized. This also allows us to look at different patterns that can change as the size of data grows. Thus, it's important to use some form of machine learning that can adapt as the size of data grows exponentially.

There are various use cases that can be solved with different types of machine learning techniques:

- ▸ Supervised learning
- ▸ Unsupervised learning
- ▸ Recommender system
- ▸ Model efficacy

The use of such techniques can be applied to solve a vast array of problems in different industry segments, such as retail, healthcare, defense, weather, space, traffic, oil and gas, financial services, and other forms of engineering.

We will use Mahout and Apache open source platforms to do this.

 A detailed discussion on this topic is out of scope of this book; you can check `https://mahout.apache.org/general/books-tutorials-and-talks.html` for more details.

We will also discuss some other important topics such as optimizing transaction management, real-time data analysis, and full text-based indexing using the Hadoop/Hbase platform.

 We will only consider integrating Mahout/Hadoop with an external data source; there may be scenarios such as using a flat file data source or connecting with different DBs, but we will limit ourselves to one data source.

## Getting ready

1. Before we start, we need a community edition of RDBMS (MySQL).
2. We will install MySQL in a Red Hat Linux environment.
3. Download and configure the MySQL Java connector.
4. Configure it to work with Sqoop and the HDFS/Hadoop setup. In our scenario, Sqoop is already set up; we need to reconfigure it to make sure that it works with the integration of the MySQL Java connector.

## How to do it...

We will discuss a couple of ways to do it:

- ▶ Get the data from an RDBMS and then parse it
- ▶ Use a Hadoop/Hbase cluster
- ▶ Use a plain Java class

### RDBMS

1. Let's get the MySQL community edition: `https://dev.mysql.com/downloads/mysql/`

   If you don't have an Oracle account, then you will have to create one.

   The following is the version that we have used:

   | Variable_name | Value |
   |---|---|
   | innodb_version | 5.7.16 |
   | protocol_version | 10 |
   | slave_type_conversions | |
   | tls_version | TLSv1,TLSv1.1 |
   | version | 5.7.16 |
   | version_comment | MySQL Community Server (GPL) |
   | version_compile_machine | x86_64 |
   | version_compile_os | redhat-linux-gnu |

   Once you install MySQL, you can run the following command and you will see the preceding result:

   ```
   ./mysql -u root --password=yourmysqlrootpassword -e 'SHOW
   VARIABLES LIKE "%version%"'
   ```

   Alternatively, you can connect to the server and execute the following commands:

   ```
   mysql> SELECT VERSION();
   +-----------+
   | VERSION() |
   +-----------+
   | 5.7.16    |
   +-----------+
   1 row in set (0.01 sec)


   mysql -u root -p -e 'STATUS'
   ```

```
./mysql -u root --password=yourmysqlrootpassword -e 'STATUS'
```

```
mysql: [Warning] Using a password on the command line interface
can be insecure.
```

```
--------------
```

```
./mysql  Ver 14.14 Distrib 5.7.16, for redhat-linux-gnu
(x86_64) using  EditLine wrapper
```

```
Connection id:420
Current database:
Current user:root@localhost
SSL:Not in use
Current pager:stdout
Using outfile:''
Using delimiter:;
Server version:5.7.16 MySQL Community Server (GPL)
Protocol version:10
Connection:Localhost via UNIX socket
Server characterset:latin1
Db      characterset:latin1
Client characterset:utf8
Conn.   characterset:utf8
UNIX socket: /tmp/mysql.sock
Uptime:1 hour 16 min 53 sec
```

```
Threads: 1  Questions: 28  Slow queries: 0  Opens: 108  Flush
tables: 1  Open tables: 101  Queries per second avg: 0.006
```

```
--------------
```

> We will set up a single-node Hadoop/Hbase machine. This will help us kickstart development much faster, or we will use our existing cluster that we build earlier.

Jdk: /usr/lib/jvm/jdk1.8.0_05/bin/java

Hadoop: hadoop-2.2.0

Maven: 3.0.4

Mahout: mahout-distribution-0.9

In our case, most of the setup is already done; we need to integrate the new lib of Mahout.

2. Let's go to the following location:

```
/opt/HbaseB/mahout-distribution-0.9
```

3. Now let's take a sample dataset using a simple wget command.

4. From the shell prompt, create a folder:

```
mkdir /mahout-data
```

Let's do 'cd' `mahout-data` that will bring you to the `mahout-data` folder. This will copy the file to the `data` folder.

5. Once the file has been copied, use ls from the `mahout-data` folder that you created in step 4:

```
[hadoop@rchoudhry-linux64 mahout-data]$ ls -ltr
total 4816
drwxr-x---. 2 hadoop hadoop    4096 Mar 31  2015 ml-100k
-rw-rw-r--. 1 hadoop hadoop 4923869 Mar 31  2015 ml-100k.zip
-rw-rw-r--. 1 hadoop hadoop 4923869 Mar 31 14:34 ml-100k.zip
```

6. `unzip ml-100k.zip` to extract the zipped folder. The ZIP file is in the `mahout-data` folder:

```
unzip ml-100k.zip
```

This creates the following `ml-100k` folder:

```
drwxr-x---. 2 hadoop hadoop    4096 Mar 31 14:33 ml-100k
-rw-rw-r--. 1 hadoop hadoop 4923869 Mar 31 14:34 ml-100k.zip
```

These are the files that will be listed:

```
[hadoop@rchoudhry-linux64 ml-100k]$ ls -ltr
total 15776
-rwxr-x---. 1 hadoop hadoop      643 Jul 19  2000 mku.sh
-rwxr-x---. 1 hadoop hadoop      716 Jul 19  2000 allbut.pl
-rw-r-----. 1 hadoop hadoop    22628 Jul 19  2000 u.user
-rw-r-----. 1 hadoop hadoop      193 Jul 19  2000 u.occupation
-rw-r-----. 1 hadoop hadoop   236344 Jul 19  2000 u.item
-rw-r-----. 1 hadoop hadoop       36 Jul 19  2000 u.info
-rw-r-----. 1 hadoop hadoop      202 Jul 19  2000 u.genre
```

```
-rw-r-----. 1 hadoop hadoop 1979173 Jul 19  2000 u.data
-rw-r-----. 1 hadoop hadoop  392629 Mar  8  2001 u1.test
-rw-r-----. 1 hadoop hadoop 1586544 Mar  8  2001 u1.base
-rw-r-----. 1 hadoop hadoop  395225 Mar  8  2001 u2.test
-rw-r-----. 1 hadoop hadoop 1583948 Mar  8  2001 u2.base
-rw-r-----. 1 hadoop hadoop  396627 Mar  8  2001 u3.test
-rw-r-----. 1 hadoop hadoop 1582546 Mar  8  2001 u3.base
-rw-r-----. 1 hadoop hadoop  397295 Mar  8  2001 u4.test
-rw-r-----. 1 hadoop hadoop 1581878 Mar  8  2001 u4.base
-rw-r-----. 1 hadoop hadoop  397397 Mar  8  2001 u5.test
-rw-r-----. 1 hadoop hadoop 1581776 Mar  8  2001 u5.base
-rw-r-----. 1 hadoop hadoop 1792501 Mar  8  2001 ua.base
-rw-r-----. 1 hadoop hadoop  186672 Mar  8  2001 ua.test
-rw-r-----. 1 hadoop hadoop 1792476 Mar  8  2001 ub.base
-rw-r-----. 1 hadoop hadoop  186697 Mar  8  2001 ub.test
-rw-r-----. 1 hadoop hadoop    6403 Mar 31 14:33 README
```

Before we go into the details, let's discuss the data that we got from the ZIP file:

| File name | Type of data | Separation parameter | Remarks |
|---|---|---|---|
| u.users | User_id<br>Age<br>Gender<br>Occupation<br>Zipcode<br>timestamp | Pipe delimited | This is used to identify the user uniquely; in a real use case, we can use the address as well to identify the actor specifically.<br><br>Note: We need to consider the privacy act for that location before placing it specifically in the algorithms. |
| u.item | Movie_id<br>Title of the move<br>Release date<br>Video_release_data<br>Imdb_url<br>Cat_unkwon | Pipe delimited | This provides the details of the movies, URLs, when it will be released in theatres, and their releases as a video. |

| File name | Type of data | Separation parameter | Remarks |
|-----------|--------------|----------------------|---------|
| u.data | User_id<br>Movie_id<br>Rating<br>timestamp | Space delimited | This provides a relationship between the movie and user along with its rating. |

7. Let's create a folder, `mahout-data`, in the Hadoop cluster.

8. This is the file structure that needs to be created. Use the following commands to create a file structure:

```
./hdfs dfs -mkdir /mahout-data

./hdfs dfs -mkdir /mahout-data/tmpDir

./hdfs dfs -mkdir /mahout-data/out

./hdfs dfs -mkdir /mahout-data/userFilelocation
```

The resultant file structure will look as follows:

```
drwxr-xr-x   - hadoop supergroup          0 2015-08-16 22:50 /
mahout-data/out

drwxr-xr-x   - hadoop supergroup          0 2015-08-22 16:37 /
mahout-data/tmpDir

-rw-r--r--   2 hadoop supergroup    1979173 2015-08-16 17:55 /
mahout-data/u.data

drwxr-xr-x   - hadoop supergroup          0 2015-08-22 16:39 /
mahout-data/userFilelocation
```

9. After creating the folder, point your browser to `http://<datanode>:50075/browseDirectory.jsp?namenodeInfoPort=50070&dir=/&nnaddr=<namenode>:8020`.

   You can see the folder in the following format:

Goto : |/|        go

| Name | Type | Size | Replication | Block Size | Modification Time | Permission | Owner | Group |
|------|------|------|-------------|------------|-------------------|------------|-------|-------|
| app-logs | dir | | | | 2015-08-16 14:34 | rwxrwxrwt | hadoop | supergroup |
| hbase | dir | | | | 2015-03-15 18:12 | rwxr-xr-x | hadoop | supergroup |
| mahout-data | dir | | | | 2015-08-22 16:39 | rwxr-xr-x | hadoop | supergroup |
| tmp | dir | | | | 2014-09-08 16:00 | rwxrwx--- | hadoop | supergroup |
| user | dir | | | | 2014-10-17 10:12 | rwxr-xr-x | hadoop | supergroup |

10. Now, let's copy the file to the Hadoop cluster:

```
./hdfs dfs -put /opt/HbaseB/hadoop-2.2.0/mahout-data/ml-100k/u.
data /mahout-data/
```

Once you run this command and click on mahout-data, you will see the following files/directories:

Goto : /mahout-data    go

Go to parent directory

| Name | Type | Size | Replication | Block Size | Modification Time | Permission | Owner | Group |
|------|------|------|-------------|------------|-------------------|------------|-------|-------|
| out | dir | | | | 2015-08-16 22:50 | rwxr-xr-x | hadoop | supergroup |
| tmpDir | dir | | | | 2015-08-22 16:37 | rwxr-xr-x | hadoop | supergroup |
| u.data | file | 1.89 MB | 2 | 256 MB | 2015-08-16 17:55 | rw-r--r-- | hadoop | supergroup |
| userFilelocation | dir | | | | 2015-08-22 16:39 | rwxr-xr-x | hadoop | supergroup |

The `u.data` file has all the data that needs to be processed:

```
/hadoop jar /opt/HbaseB/mahout-distribution-0.7/mahout-core-0.7-
job.jar org.apache.mahout.cf.taste.hadoop.item.RecommenderJob -s
SIMILARITY_COOCCURRENCE --input /mahout-data/u.data -output /
mahout-data/output/myoutoutdata --similarityClassname SIMILARITY_
PEARSON_CORRELATION
```

This job runs for 10 to 20 minutes and completes, it also creates a file, `myoutputdata`.

11. Now run the following command to merge the file:

```
hdfs dfs -getmerge myoutputdata myoutoutdata.txt
```

```
[hadoop@rchoudhry-linux64 bin]$  ./hdfs dfs -cat /mahout-data/out/myoutput
16/05/30 18:05:01 WARN util.NativeCodeLoader: Unable to load native-hadoop library for your platform... using builtin-java classes when
le
1       [845:5.0,550:5.0,546:5.0,25:5.0,531:5.0,529:5.0,527:5.0,31:5.0,515:5.0,514:5.0]
2       [546:5.0,288:5.0,11:5.0,25:5.0,531:5.0,527:5.0,515:5.0,508:5.0,496:5.0,483:5.0]
3       [137:5.0,284:5.0,508:4.8327274,248:4.826923,285:4.80597,845:4.754717,124:4.7058825,319:4.703242,293:4.6792455,591:4.6629214]
4       [748:5.0,1296:5.0,546:5.0,568:5.0,538:5.0,508:5.0,483:5.0,475:5.0,471:5.0,876:5.0]
5       [732:5.0,550:5.0,9:5.0,546:5.0,11:5.0,527:5.0,523:5.0,514:5.0,511:5.0,508:5.0]
6       [739:5.0,9:5.0,546:5.0,11:5.0,25:5.0,531:5.0,528:5.0,527:5.0,526:5.0,521:5.0]
7       [879:5.0,845:5.0,751:5.0,750:5.0,748:5.0,746:5.0,742:5.0,739:5.0,735:5.0,732:5.0]
8       [742:5.0,550:5.0,546:5.0,566:5.0,568:5.0,527:5.0,31:5.0,523:5.0,515:5.0,514:5.0]
9       [739:5.0,550:5.0,546:5.0,11:5.0,527:5.0,523:5.0,514:5.0,511:5.0,508:5.0,498:5.0]
10      [732:5.0,9:5.0,546:5.0,11:5.0,25:5.0,529:5.0,528:5.0,527:5.0,526:5.0,523:5.0]

[hadoop@rchoudhry-linux64 bin]$
```

The response that we get is that `10` users have `10` recommendations. The results are not in the tabular format. For clarity, let's try to put it in a table:

| User ID | Recommendation for movie_id | Score |
|---------|------------------------------|-------|
| 10 | 732 | 5 |
| 10 | 9 | 5 |
| 10 | 546 | 5 |
| 10 | 11 | 5 |
| 10 | 25 | 5 |
| 10 | 529 | 5 |
| 10 | 528 | 5 |
| 10 | 527 | 5 |
| 10 | 526 | 5 |
| 10 | 523 | 5 |

`10 is a→ Key`

`[732:5.0,9:5.0,546:5.0,11:5.0,25:5.0,529:5.0,528:5.0,527:5.0,526:5`
`.0,523:5.0]is the value → value`

In case you want to change the size of the recommender of item similarity, you can change the following section of `genRecommender.` `recommend(user , count)`, but you have to recompile the class and run the preceeding job using this class. Refer to the `ItemRecommender` class as follows:

```
Recommender recommender =   newGenericItemBasedRecomm
ender(model, itemSimilarity);
```
```
Recommender genRecommender = new
genRecommender(recommender); List<RecommendedItem>
recommendations =   genRecommender.recommend(10, 10);
```

## A plain Java program (static)

For this, we will use the same `u.data` file that we downloaded previously.

We will need the following libraries:

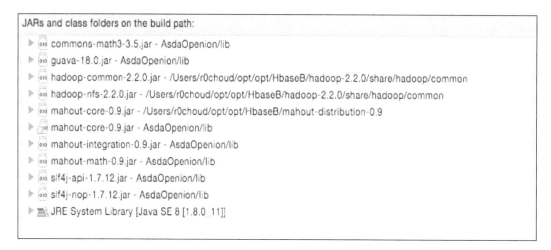

These libraries can be downloaded from the Internet.

1. We will set up a Java project in Eclipse. However, it can be done using some other IDE, such as NetBeans, Intellij, and so on.

2. Let's create two folders—one for a library in which all the preceding libraries need to be copied and a data folder where the preprocessed data and the post-processed data need to be kept.

3. Create two classes, `MyUDataConvertor` and `MyItemBasedRecommendor`. The `MyUDataConvertor` class will be used to clean the data and make it consumable for the next recommender class. We will also create an interface class, which will keep all the constants that will be implemented in `MyUDataConvertor`.

 You can also convert it using a Unix command in case you are using a Unix system. This way, you don't have to write Java code.

The raw data looks as follows:

```
L-SB830T7FFT-M:data r0choud$ cat u.txt | more
196      242      3      881250949
186      302      3      891717742
22       377      1      878887116
244      51       2      880606923
166      346      1      886397596
298      474      4      884182806
115      265      2      881171488
253      465      5      891628467
305      451      3      886324817
6        86       3      883603013
62       257      2      879372434
286      1014     5      879781125
200      222      5      876042340
210      40       3      891035994
224      29       3      888104457
303      785      3      879485318
122      387      5      879270459
```

On the Unix prompt, you can run the following command; it will pipe the file to `myu.txt` and shred the last column that we don't want. We are specifying it in the command, as follows:

`cat u.txt | cut -f1,2,3 | tr "\\t" "," > myu.txt`

```
186,302,3
22,377,1
244,51,2
166,346,1
298,474,4
115,265,2
253,465,5
305,451,3
6,86,3
62,257,2
286,1014,5
200,222,5
210,40,3
224,29,3
303,785,3
```

This will convert the raw data to an input format that can be inputted to the `MyItemRecommendor` class:

```java
import java.io.BufferedReader;
import java.io.BufferedWriter;
import java.io.FileReader;
import java.io.FileWriter;
```

```java
import java.io.IOException;

public class MyUDataConvertor implements RecommendationInf {

  public MyUDataConvertor() {
    // TODO Auto-generated constructor stub
  }

  /**
   * @param args
   */
  public static void main(String[] args) {
    BufferedReader br = null;
    BufferedWriter bw = null;
    try {
      br = new BufferedReader(new FileReader(DATA_FILE_LOCATION));
      /*
       * This BufferReader will get the data from FileReader which
will actually read it from the
       * u.txt file
       */
      bw = new BufferedWriter(new FileWriter(DATA_NEW_FILE_
LOCATION));
      String line; // creating a string object as line.
      while ((line = br.readLine()) != null) {
        // the above while statement will read the data line by
line till there is no more line to
        // be read
        String[] values = line.split("\\t", -1);
        // this will split the line and remvoe the tabs
        bw.write(values[0] + "," + values[1] + "," + values[2] +
"\n");
        // this will write the file from bw and will push with ","
separated format.
      }
    } catch (Exception e) {
      e.printStackTrace();
    } finally {
      try {
        br.close();// close the buffer reader
      } catch (IOException e) {
        e.printStackTrace();
      }
      try {
```

```
        bw.close();// will close the buffer writer.
      } catch (IOException e) {
        e.printStackTrace();
      }
    }

  }

}
```

Interface that is used in the preceding class:

```
public interface RecommendationInf {
 public static String DATA_FILE_LOCATION = "data/u.txt";
 public static String DATA_NEW_FILE_LOCATION = "data/myu.txt";
 public static int NUMBER_OF_RECORDS=8;
 public static int NUMBER_IN_A_BATCH=16;
}
```

Once we run the preceding class, this will create a `myu.txt` file.

4.  Now we will write the MyItemRecommendor class, as follows:

```
import java.io.File;
import java.io.IOException;
import java.util.List;
import org.apache.mahout.cf.taste.model.DataModel;
import org.apache.mahout.cf.taste.recommender.RecommendedItem;
import org.apache.mahout.cf.taste.impl.model.file.FileDataModel;
import org.apache.mahout.cf.taste.common.TasteException;
import org.apache.mahout.cf.taste.impl.common.
LongPrimitiveIterator;
import org.apache.mahout.cf.taste.impl.recommender.
GenericItemBasedRecommender;
import org.apache.mahout.cf.taste.impl.similarity.
EuclideanDistanceSimilarity;
import org.apache.mahout.cf.taste.impl.similarity.
LogLikelihoodSimilarity;
import org.apache.mahout.cf.taste.impl.similarity.
PearsonCorrelationSimilarity;
```

```
import org.apache.mahout.cf.taste.impl.similarity.
TanimotoCoefficientSimilarity;

public class ItemBasedRecommendation implements RecommendationInf
{

  public ItemBasedRecommendation() {
    // TODO Auto-generated constructor stub
  }
  /**
   * @param args
   */
  public static void main(String[] args) {
    /*
     * we will execute one method at a time to make sure we are
able
     * to capture the results as needed.
     *
     */
    //ItemBasedRecommendation.executeLogLikelihoodSimilarity();
    //ItemBasedRecommendation.
executeTanimotoCoefficientSimilarity();
    ItemBasedRecommendation.executePearsonCorrelationSimilarity();
    //ItemBasedRecommendation.executeEuclideanDistanceSimilarity();
  }
  public static void executeLogLikelihoodSimilarity()
  {
    DataModel dm =null;
    try {
     dm= new FileDataModel(new File(DATA_NEW_FILE_LOCATION));
      GenericItemBasedRecommender recommender =
         new GenericItemBasedRecommender(dm, new
LogLikelihoodSimilarity(dm));
      // Using LogLikelihoodSimilarity as the Algorithm.
      int x = 1;
      for (LongPrimitiveIterator items = dm.getItemIDs(); items.
hasNext();) {
        long itemId = items.nextLong();
        List<RecommendedItem> recommendations = recommender.
mostSimilarItems(itemId, NUMBER_OF_RECORDS);// batch of
        for (RecommendedItem recommendation : recommendations) {
          System.out.println("|"+itemId + "|" + recommendation.
getItemID() + "|"+ recommendation.getValue()+"|");
          // Printing the ItemId , recommendation based ItemId ,
actual recommendations
```

```
        }
        x++;// this will allow us to keep increasing till we reach
16
        if (x > NUMBER_IN_A_BATCH) System.exit(1); // generate
recommendation for first 16 items only then the exit
                                        // will be fired to
        // exit the loop
      }
    } catch (IOException e) {
      System.out.println("Error happen while i/o operation.");
      e.printStackTrace();
    } catch (TasteException e) {
      System.out.println("There was a Taste Exception.");
      e.printStackTrace();
    }finally{
      executeCleanUp(dm);
    }
  }
  public static void executeTanimotoCoefficientSimilarity()
  {
    DataModel dm = null;
    try {
      dm = new FileDataModel(new File(DATA_NEW_FILE_LOCATION));
      GenericItemBasedRecommender recommender = new
GenericItemBasedRecommender(dm, new TanimotoCoefficientSimilarity(
dm));
      // Using LogLikelihoodSimilarity as the Algorithm.
      int x = 1;
      for (LongPrimitiveIterator items = dm.getItemIDs(); items.
hasNext();) {
        long itemId = items.nextLong();
        List<RecommendedItem> recommendations = recommender.
mostSimilarItems(itemId, NUMBER_OF_RECORDS);// batch of

// 8
        for (RecommendedItem recommendation : recommendations) {
          System.out.println("|"+itemId + "|" + recommendation.
getItemID() + "|"
                + recommendation.getValue()+"|");
          // Printing the ItemId , recommendation based ItemId ,
actual recommendations
        }
        x++;// this will allow us to keep increasing till we reach
16
```

```
            if (x > NUMBER_IN_A_BATCH) System.exit(1); // generate
recommendation for first 16 items only then the exit
                                    // will be fired to
        // exit the loop
      }
    } catch (IOException e) {
      System.out.println("Error happen while i/o operation.");
      e.printStackTrace();
    } catch (TasteException e) {
      System.out.println("There was a Taste Exception.");
      e.printStackTrace();
    }finally{
      executeCleanUp(dm);
    }
  }
  public static void executePearsonCorrelationSimilarity()
  {
    DataModel dm =null;
    try {
      dm = new FileDataModel(new File(DATA_NEW_FILE_LOCATION));
      GenericItemBasedRecommender recommender = new
GenericItemBasedRecommender(dm, new PearsonCorrelationSimilarity(
dm));
      // Using LogLikelihoodSimilarity as the Algorithm.
      int x = 1;
      for (LongPrimitiveIterator items = dm.getItemIDs(); items.
hasNext();) {
        long itemId = items.nextLong();
        List<RecommendedItem> recommendations = recommender.
mostSimilarItems(itemId, NUMBER_OF_RECORDS);// batch of

// 8
        for (RecommendedItem recommendation : recommendations) {
          System.out.println("|"+itemId + "|" + recommendation.
getItemID() + "|"
              + recommendation.getValue()+"|");
          // Printing the ItemId , recommendation based ItemId ,
actual recommendations
        }
        x++;// this will allow us to keep increasing till we reach
16
        if (x > NUMBER_IN_A_BATCH) System.exit(1); // generate
recommendation for first 16 items only then the exit
                                    // will be fired to
        // exit the loop
```

```
      }
    } catch (IOException e) {
      System.out.println("Error happen while i/o operation.");
      e.printStackTrace();
    } catch (TasteException e) {
      System.out.println("There was a Taste Exception.");
      e.printStackTrace();
    }finally{
      executeCleanUp(dm);
    }
  }
  public static void executeEuclideanDistanceSimilarity()
  {
    DataModel dm =null;
    try {
     dm= new FileDataModel(new File(DATA_NEW_FILE_LOCATION));
      GenericItemBasedRecommender recommender =
          new GenericItemBasedRecommender(dm, new EuclideanDistanc
eSimilarity(dm));
      // Using LogLikelihoodSimilarity as the Algorithm.
      int x = 1;
      for (LongPrimitiveIterator items = dm.getItemIDs(); items.
hasNext();) {
        long itemId = items.nextLong();
        List<RecommendedItem> recommendations = recommender.
mostSimilarItems(itemId, NUMBER_OF_RECORDS);// batch of
        for (RecommendedItem recommendation : recommendations) {
          System.out.println("|"+itemId + "|" + recommendation.
getItemID() + "|"+ recommendation.getValue()+"|");
          // Printing the ItemId , recommendation based ItemId ,
actual recommendations
        }
        x++;// this will allow us to keep increasing till we reach
16
        if (x > NUMBER_IN_A_BATCH) System.exit(1); // generate
recommendation for first 16 items only then the exit
                                    // will be fired to
        // exit the loop
      }
    } catch (IOException e) {
      System.out.println("Error happen while i/o operation.");
      e.printStackTrace();
    } catch (TasteException e) {
      System.out.println("There was a Taste Exception.");
```

```
        e.printStackTrace();
      }finally{
        executeCleanUp(dm);
      }
    }
  }
  /*
   * This methods will do a cleanup the data
   * as we get out of the every method
   */
  public static void executeCleanUp(DataModel dm)
  {
    try {
      if(dm.getNumItems()!=0)
        dm=null;
    } catch (TasteException e) {
      // TODO Auto-generated catch block
      e.printStackTrace();
    }
  }
}
```

Let's run both the classes, one by one, in your Eclipse IDE against your project JDK, that is, JDK1.8.

The first class will produce the following file. By creating the file, `movies.csv`.

 If you are using Excel for Mac, you can open this `myu.txt` file in Excel; it will look exactly like the following file. Alternatively, you can open it in a raw text format using the VI editor.

```
 1 196,242,3
 2 186,302,3
 3 22,377,1
 4 244,51,2
 5 166,346,1
 6 298,474,4
 7 115,265,2
 8 253,465,5
 9 305,451,3
10 6,86,3
11 62,257,2
12 286,1014,5
13 200,222,5
14 210,40,3
```

5. Now, we can run our `ItemBasedRecommendation` class; this will create a recommended dataset, as follows:

```
//ItemBasedRecommendation.executeLogLikelihoodSimilarity();
ItemBasedRecommendation.executeTanimotoCoefficientSimilarity();  ──────▶   we are using
//ItemBasedRecommendation.executePearsonCorrelationSimilarity();              TanimotoCoefficientSimilarity
}
public static void executeLogLikelihoodSimilarity()
{
    DataModel dm =null;
    try {
    dm= new FileDataModel(new File(DATA_NEW_FILE_LOCATION));
    GenericItemBasedRecommender recommender =
        new GenericItemBasedRecommender(dm, new LogLikelihoodSimilarity(dm));
    // Using LogLikelihoodSimilarity as the Algorithm.
    int x = 1;
    for (LongPrimitiveIterator items = dm.getItemIDs(); items.hasNext();) {
        long itemId = items.nextLong();
        List<RecommendedItem> recommendations = recommender.mostSimilarItems(itemId, NUMBER_OF_RECORDS);// batch of
        for (RecommendedItem recommendation : recommendations) {
            System.out.println("|"+itemId + "|" + recommendation.getItemID() + "|"+ recommendation.getValue()+"|");
            // Printing the itemId , recommendation based ItemId , actual recommendations
        }
        x++;// this will allow us to keep increasing till we reach 16
        if (x > NUMBER_IN_A_BATCH) System.exit(1); // generate recommendation for first 16 items only then the exit
                                    // will be fired to
        // exit the loop
    }
    } catch (IOException e) {
        System.out.println("Error happen while i/o operation.");
        e.printStackTrace();
    } catch (TasteException e) {
        System.out.println("There was a Taste Exception.");
        e.printStackTrace();
```

```
Markers  Properties  Servers  Data S...  ...s Explorer  Snippets  ...  sole 🖾  ...GitRepositories  ...bug
<terminated> ItemBasedRecommendation (1) [Java App...  ...ion] /Library/Java/JavaVirtualM...  ...es/jdk1.8.0_11.jdk/Contents/Home...  .java (Sep 13, 2016 3:35:49 AM)
|115|0.58256881|
|11|12|0.55379191|
|11|8|0.5492731|
|111|17|0.53419596|
|11|00|0.5118111|
|11|40|5|0.50472591|
|11|15|5|0.50193051|
|117|0.4991110|
|2|233|0.53614455|
|2|231|0.49180331|
|2|403|0.48878923|
|2|62|0.474285721|
|2|550|0.46875|
|2|168|0.45604396|
|2|226|0.45588234|
|2|161|0.45041323|
```

the date is based on itemId.recommendationId. recommendation value

group of 8 recommendation used for TanimotoCoefficientSimilarity

8 itemid , recommendedId, recommended value using PearsonCorrelationSimilarity

Similarly, you can run the following command:

```
ItemBasedRecommendation.executeEuclideanDistanceSimilarity() to
use Euclide based alogorithm.
```

## There's more...

http://ganges.usc.edu/pgroupW/images/a/a9/Serializarion_Framework.pdf

# Real-time data analysis using Hbase and Mahout

The data, which is readily available using different data streams, needs to be parsed and converted to a meaningful format, which essentially creates value for the business. Hbase integration with Mahout provides the stream that allows us to do clustering in machine learning, which is a way of programmatically orchestrating similar sets of data in a more organized and meaningful way.

Let's say that you have a fruit tasting session where you have different types of fruits, and you want to group people who liked apples, bananas, watermelons, and so on. A small set of data will look staggered, so we have to create some sort of algorithm to do it programmatically. Here is how the data will look before clustering and after clustering. In this section, we can access the underlying data using direct invocation from the Java client.

This can be done in analysis for the purpose of exposing the data in various forms to the data scientist, data analysis team, and customer as well; for example, we can use this type of clustering for pattern analysis for energy consumption of a household, expense analysis, segment of companies performance, and so on.

In Mahout, there are various ways to do this; we will discuss only a few, as others are beyond the scope of this book:

- ▶ K-means
- ▶ Centroid generation using canopy clustering
- ▶ Fuzzy k-means clustering
- ▶ Dirichlet clustering

▸ Latent Dirichlet allocation clustering

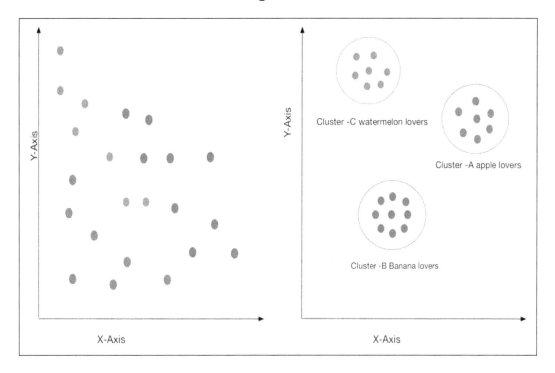

K-means is a simple and generic algorithm that can be customized for the clustering.

Before we start, a k-means cluster is associated with a cluster center known as the mean or centroid. Each point is assigned to the cluster with the closest centroid. Here, K is the number of clusters that must be specified; this sometimes gives an appearance that we are setting a hard limit and may impact the quality of data. However, k-means is used widely in the industry and has served its purpose for more than 20 years.

```
Basic steps( sudo code) :

Select K points as the initial centroids
    Repeat
From K cluster by assigning all points to the closest centroid.
Recompute the centroid of each cluster
    Until the centroids don't change
```

The following are the limitations of the k-means algorithm:

- **Handling empty clusters**: An empty cluster can be obtained if no points are allocated to a cluster during the assignment step.

- **Outliers**: When outliers are present, the resulting cluster mean/centroid may not be representative as they otherwise would be, and thus the **Sum of Squared Error** (**SSE**) will be higher as well.

## How to do it...

1. Let's use a dataset readily available at

   `https://archive.ics.uci.edu/ml/machine-learning-databases/auto-mpg/auto-mpg.data`

   The format of the data is as follows:

   | Mpg | continuous |
   | --- | --- |
   | Cylinders | multi-valued discrete |
   | Displacement | continuous |
   | Horsepower | continuous |
   | Weight | continuous |
   | Acceleration | continuous |
   | model year | multi-valued discrete |
   | Origin | multi-valued discrete |
   | Car name | string (unique for each instance) |

   The data is as follows:

   | | | | | | | | | |
   | --- | --- | --- | --- | --- | --- | --- | --- | --- |
   | 18.0 | 8 | 307.0 | 130 | 3504 | 12.0 | 70 | 1 | "chevrolet chevelle malibu" |
   | 15.0 | 8 | 350.0 | 130.0 | 3693 | 11.5 | 70 | 1 | buick skylark |

2. Create a folder in the Hadoop HDFS location by executing the following command:

   ```
   Hadoop fs -mkdir chapter10/k-meancluster-input
   ```

    You can also clean up the file using the Linux sed command, say the file is at your current working directory.

   ```
   sed -ie "s/[[:space:]]\+/ /g" chap10-kmean.txt
   ```

3. Place this file in the respective Hadoop cluster:

```
Hadoop fs -put  chap10-kmean.txt chapter10/kmean-cluster-input
```

Now, we have to write Java code to parse the preceding `chap10-kmean.txt` file that will use the Hadoop/Hbase configuration to run the job or the invovation main class file; it can be run both as a job or using the invocation from the command line or calling it using another class:

```java
/**
 * @param
 */
import java.io.IOException;

import org.apache.hadoop.conf.Configuration;
import org.apache.hadoop.fs.Path;
import org.apache.hadoop.fs.FileSystem;

public class MahoutProcessData {
  static String inputPath = "chapter10/k-meancluster-input";
  static String inputSeq = "chap10-kmean.txt";

  public static void main(String args[]) {
    try {

      Configuration conf = new Configuration();
      conf.addResource(new Path("/usr/local/hadoop/conf/core-site.
xml"));// path for core site xml
      conf.addResource(new Path("/usr/local/hadoop/conf/hdfs-site.
xml"));// path for the hdfs site

// xml
      /*
       * the config objects which has the path for both the file
is passed to the new file system
       * object
       */
      FileSystem fso = FileSystem.get(conf);
      Path inputDir = new Path(inputPath);// Path for Input
directory is passed
      Path inputSeqDir = new Path(inputSeq);// Path for Input
sequence directory is passed
      if (fso.exists(inputSeqDir)) {
        System.out.println("Output already exists and no need to
create");
        fso.delete(inputSeqDir, true);// if the dir exist it this
will delete the directory.
```

```
            System.out.println("deleted output directory");
        }

        // This will encode the vectors using the //
RandomAccessSparseVector
        InputDriver.runJob(inputDir, inputSeqDir, "org.apache.
mahout.math.RandomAccessSparseVector",
            conf);

    } catch (ClassNotFoundException ene) {
      ene.printStackTrace();
    } catch (InterruptedException ie) {
      ie.printStackTrace();
    } catch (IOException io) {
      io.printStackTrace();
    }
  }
}
```

4. Use Apache InputDriver to invoke the runjob method.

```
import java.io.IOException;

import org.apache.mahout.clustering.conversion.InputMapper;
import org.apache.commons.cli2.CommandLine;
import org.apache.commons.cli2.Group;
import org.apache.commons.cli2.Option;
import org.apache.commons.cli2.OptionException;
import org.apache.commons.cli2.builder.ArgumentBuilder;
import org.apache.commons.cli2.builder.DefaultOptionBuilder;
import org.apache.commons.cli2.builder.GroupBuilder;
import org.apache.commons.cli2.commandline.Parser;
import org.apache.hadoop.conf.Configuration;
import org.apache.hadoop.fs.Path;
import org.apache.hadoop.io.Text;
import org.apache.hadoop.mapreduce.Job;
import org.apache.hadoop.mapreduce.lib.input.FileInputFormat;
import org.apache.hadoop.mapreduce.lib.output.FileOutputFormat;
import org.apache.hadoop.mapreduce.lib.output.
SequenceFileOutputFormat;
import org.apache.mahout.common.CommandLineUtil;
import org.apache.mahout.common.commandline.DefaultOptionCreator;
import org.apache.mahout.math.VectorWritable;
import org.slf4j.Logger;
```

```
import org.slf4j.LoggerFactory;

/**
 * This class converts text files containing space-delimited
floating point numbers into
 * Mahout sequence files of VectorWritable suitable for input to
the clustering jobs in
 * particular, and any Mahout job requiring this input in general.
 *
 */
public final class InputDriver {

  private static final Logger log = LoggerFactory.
getLogger(InputDriver.class);

  private InputDriver() {
  }

  public static void main(String[] args) throws IOException,
InterruptedException, ClassNotFoundException {
    DefaultOptionBuilder obuilder = new DefaultOptionBuilder();
    ArgumentBuilder abuilder = new ArgumentBuilder();
    GroupBuilder gbuilder = new GroupBuilder();

    Option inputOpt = DefaultOptionCreator.inputOption().
withRequired(false).create();
    Option outputOpt = DefaultOptionCreator.outputOption().
withRequired(false).create();
    Option vectorOpt = obuilder.withLongName("vector").
withRequired(false).withArgument(
      abuilder.withName("v").withMinimum(1).withMaximum(1).
create()).withDescription(
      "The vector implementation to use.").withShortName("v").
create();

    Option helpOpt = DefaultOptionCreator.helpOption();

    Group group = gbuilder.withName("Options").
withOption(inputOpt).withOption(outputOpt).withOption(
      vectorOpt).withOption(helpOpt).create();

    try {
      Parser parser = new Parser();
      parser.setGroup(group);
```

```
      CommandLine cmdLine = parser.parse(args);
      if (cmdLine.hasOption(helpOpt)) {
        CommandLineUtil.printHelp(group);
        return;
      }

      Path input = new Path(cmdLine.getValue(inputOpt,
  "testdata").toString());
      Path output = new Path(cmdLine.getValue(outputOpt,
  "output").toString());
      String vectorClassName = cmdLine.getValue(vectorOpt,
          "org.apache.mahout.math.RandomAccessSparseVector").
  toString();
      //runJob(input, output, vectorClassName);
    } catch (OptionException e) {
      InputDriver.log.error("Exception parsing command line: ",
  e);
      CommandLineUtil.printHelp(group);
    }
  }


  public static void runJob(Path input, Path output, String
  vectorClassName,Configuration config)
    throws IOException, InterruptedException,
  ClassNotFoundException {
    Configuration conf = config;
    conf.set("vector.implementation.class.name", vectorClassName);
    Job job = new Job(conf, "Input Driver running over input: " +
  input);

    job.setOutputKeyClass(Text.class);
    job.setOutputValueClass(VectorWritable.class);
    job.setOutputFormatClass(SequenceFileOutputFormat.class);
    job.setMapperClass(InputMapper.class);
    job.setNumReduceTasks(0);
    job.setJarByClass(InputDriver.class);

    FileInputFormat.addInputPath(job, input);
    FileOutputFormat.setOutputPath(job, output);

    job.waitForCompletion(true);
  }

}
```

5. This is the class for Clustering:

```java
import java.io.BufferedReader;
import java.io.InputStreamReader;
import java.io.IOException;
import java.util.Arrays;

import org.apache.hadoop.conf.Configuration;
import org.apache.hadoop.fs.FileSystem;
import org.apache.hadoop.fs.Path;
import org.apache.hadoop.io.LongWritable;
import org.apache.hadoop.io.SequenceFile;
import org.apache.hadoop.io.Text;
import org.apache.mahout.clustering.kmeans.KMeansDriver;
import org.apache.mahout.clustering.kmeans.Kluster;
import org.apache.mahout.common.distance.EuclideanDistanceMeasure;
import org.apache.mahout.math.RandomAccessSparseVector;
import org.apache.mahout.math.SequentialAccessSparseVector;
import org.apache.mahout.math.Vector;
import org.apache.mahout.math.VectorWritable;

public class MahoutClusterExample implements MahoutClusterIntrface
{

  public static void main(String args[]) throws IOException {

    Configuration conf = new Configuration();
    conf.addResource(new Path(coreSiteXML));// See Interface file
    conf.addResource(new Path(hdfsSiteXML));// See Interface file
    FileSystem fileSystem = FileSystem.get(conf);
    Path inFileDir = new Path(inpFile); // See Interface file
    Path outFileDir = new Path(outFile);// See Interface file
    if (!fileSystem.exists(inFileDir)) {
      System.out.println("Input file not found");
      return;
    }
    if (!fileSystem.isFile(inFileDir)) {
      System.out.println("Input should be a file");
    }
    if (fileSystem.exists(outFileDir)) {
      System.out.println("Output already exists");
      fileSystem.delete(outFileDir, true);
      System.out.println("deleted output directory");
    }
```

```
        BufferedReader bufferedReader = null;
        int counter = 0;
        int number_of_col = 0;
        try {
          bufferedReader = new BufferedReader(new
InputStreamReader(fileSystem.open(inFileDir)));
          String line = bufferedReader.readLine();
          @SuppressWarnings("deprecation")
          SequenceFile.Writer writer =
              new SequenceFile.Writer(fileSystem, conf, outFileDir,
LongWritable.class,
                    VectorWritable.class);

        while (line != null) {
          String[] columnDetail = line.split(" ", -1);
          double[] d = new double[columnDetail.length];
          number_of_col = columnDetail.length;
          for (int i = 0; i < columnDetail.length; i++) {
            try {
              d[i] = Double.parseDouble(columnDetail[i]);

            } catch (Exception e) {
              d[i] = 0;
            }
          }
          Vector vec = new RandomAccessSparseVector(columnDetail.
length);
          vec.assign(d);
          VectorWritable writable = new VectorWritable();
          writable.set(vec);
          writer.append(new LongWritable(counter++), writable);
          line = bufferedReader.readLine();
          System.out.println("Number of lines written=" + counter);
        }
      } catch (IOException e) {
        e.printStackTrace();
      } finally {
        bufferedReader.close();
      }

      Path outputPath = new Path(clustringOut);// See interface file

      if (fileSystem.exists(outputPath)) {
```

```
         System.out.println("Output already exists");
         fileSystem.delete(outputPath, true);
         System.out.println("deleted output directory");
      }
      Path cluster_init_path = new Path(clustringInital);// See
Interface file
      @SuppressWarnings("deprecation")
      SequenceFile.Writer writerClusterInitial =
          new SequenceFile.Writer(fileSystem, conf, cluster_init_
path, Text.class, Kluster.class);
      for (int i = 0; i < 2; i++) {
         double[] array = new double[number_of_col];
         Arrays.fill(array, i + 1);
         Vector vec = new SequentialAccessSparseVector(number_of_
col);
         vec.assign(array);
         Kluster cluster = new Kluster(vec, i, new
EuclideanDistanceMeasure());
         writerClusterInitial.append(new Text(cluster.
getIdentifier()), cluster);
      }
      writerClusterInitial.close();

      Path kmeans_output = new Path("clustering_output");

      if (fileSystem.exists(kmeans_output)) {
        System.out.println("Output already exists");
        fileSystem.delete(kmeans_output, true);
        System.out.println("deleted output directory");
      }
      try {
        KMeansDriver.run(conf, outFileDir, cluster_init_path,
kmeans_output, 0.001, 10, true, 0,
          false);

        System.out.println("Kmeans completed");
      } catch (ClassNotFoundException e) {
        // TODO Auto-generated catch block
        e.printStackTrace();
      } catch (InterruptedException e) {
        // TODO Auto-generated catch block
        e.printStackTrace();
      } catch (IndexOutOfBoundsException e) {
```

```
        System.out.println("IndexOutOfBoundsException while runnig
    Kmeans");
        e.printStackTrace();

    }
  }


}
```

6.  Step is the Interface class

```
public interface MahoutClusterIntrface {
/**
This interface contains the path of
core-site.xml
hdfs-site.xml
input file location of k-meancluster
output file location
cluster initial
**/

  public static final String coreSiteXML = "/usr/local/hadoop/
conf/core-site.xml";
  public static final String hdfsSiteXML ="/usr/local/hadoop/conf/
hdfs-site.xml";
  public static final String inpFile = "chapter10/k-meancluster-
input/chap10-kmean.txt";
  public static final String outFile = "clustering_seq/";
  public static final String clustringOut ="clustering_output";
  public static final String clustringInital ="clustering_initial/
part-00000";

}
```

## How it works...

K-means is a simple three-step process:

1.  The first step is to start with an n-dimension vector pointing to n-dimension space.

2.  Now we have to represent the centroid of the cluster as the input.

3.  We iterate the loop until the cluster vectors are moved until a minimum threshold or a number of iterations have been done.

In the preceding class, it's represented as the following:

1. We ran the `MahoutClusterExample.java` file, which is run from the command prompt.

   Make sure that JAVA_HOME is set for the current JDK, or EXPORT JAVA_HOME=' /usr/lib/jvm/jdk1.8.0_05', or where you have your Java setup.

2. In the input file, we defined the location of the seed file where we have kept the data that needs to be parsed.

3. Then, we provided the location of the output file where the data needs to be available, post parsing.

4. `BufferReader` reads the file line by line and splits the data based on " ".

5. Then this data is iterated using `RandomAccessSparseVector`.

6. This data is then passed as `ClusterOutput`, and then passed to `SequentalAccessSparseVector`.

7. This creates an array object and is passed to `EuclideanDistanceMeasure`.

8. This cluster object is passed to the `SequenceFile` Writer.

9. Once the file has been created, the `kmeans_output` path is passed as a parameter to the `KMeanDriver` run method, which runs and generates the output in the output directory.

## There's More...

http://mahout.apache.org/users/clustering/k-means-clustering.html

For command-line options:

http://mahout.apache.org/users/clustering/k-means-commandline.html

# Full text indexing using Hbase

Text messages (e-mail, chat, and so on) have become the most widespread method of communication, so there is much value to be extracted by making all text searchable and readily available for further analysis. This common scenario is applicable to different use cases where you have large volumes (ongoing) of content updates that need to be pushed into live search indexes and content should be instantly (near real-time) searchable.

Some common use cases that involve text analysis are customer satisfaction, customer sentiment analysis of the people texting, interest of the customer on which targeted advertising can be done, and others.

Every company or business domain can extract tremendous value based on its own business needs if they can understand the text communication in various forms.

Thus, it becomes important to collect, share, search, and do deep mining on the datasets that all of us are transacting everyday.

These texts can be of a very structured format or totally unstructured, but all are meaningful if we are able to apply intelligence to them and transform them in a meaningful way.

## Getting ready

Before we start, we need the following so that we don't get the right version of jars so that we don't get the compatibility mode:

- HBase 0.94.x
- Solr 4.x in cloud mode
- ZooKeeper 3.x (required by the two preceding packages)

## How to do it...

1. Make a Git clone by executing the following command:

   ```
   git clone https://github.com/NGDATA/hbase-indexer.git
   ```

2. Once you get the entire folder, you can check to see whether all the related folders and libraries are present:

```
drwxr-xr-x+  4 r0choud  HOMEOFFICE\Domain Users    136 Nov 29 16:05 hbase-indexer-server
drwxr-xr-x+  5 r0choud  HOMEOFFICE\Domain Users    170 Nov 29 16:05 hbase-indexer-mr
drwxr-xr-x+  5 r0choud  HOMEOFFICE\Domain Users    170 Nov 29 16:05 hbase-indexer-morphlines
drwxr-xr-x+  4 r0choud  HOMEOFFICE\Domain Users    136 Nov 29 16:05 hbase-indexer-model
drwxr-xr-x+  4 r0choud  HOMEOFFICE\Domain Users    136 Nov 29 16:05 hbase-indexer-engine
drwxr-xr-x+  4 r0choud  HOMEOFFICE\Domain Users    136 Nov 29 16:05 hbase-indexer-dist
drwxr-xr-x+  7 r0choud  HOMEOFFICE\Domain Users    238 Nov 29 16:05 hbase-indexer-demo
drwxr-xr-x+  4 r0choud  HOMEOFFICE\Domain Users    136 Nov 29 16:05 hbase-indexer-common
drwxr-xr-x+  4 r0choud  HOMEOFFICE\Domain Users    136 Nov 29 16:05 hbase-indexer-cli
drwxr-xr-x+  3 r0choud  HOMEOFFICE\Domain Users    102 Nov 29 16:05 hbase-indexer-all
drwxr-xr-x+  5 r0choud  HOMEOFFICE\Domain Users    170 Nov 29 16:05 conf
drwxr-xr-x+  4 r0choud  HOMEOFFICE\Domain Users    136 Nov 29 16:05 bin
-rw-r--r--+  1 r0choud  HOMEOFFICE\Domain Users    823 Nov 29 16:05 README.md
-rw-r--r--+  1 r0choud  HOMEOFFICE\Domain Users  11357 Nov 29 16:05 LICENSE.txt
-rw-r--r--+  1 r0choud  HOMEOFFICE\Domain Users  33248 Nov 29 16:05 pom.xml
drwxr-xr-x+ 12 r0choud  HOMEOFFICE\Domain Users    408 Nov 29 16:05 hbase-sep
```

3. Copy the `hbase-sep` JAR file from the lib directory by executing the following command and copy it to the `hbase/lib` folder:

   ```
   /opt/HbaseB/hbase-0.98.5-hadoop2/lib
   ```

4. Once this step is done, we have to restart the cluster and the Hbase region servers.

5. Now, let's create a table, messages, or you can alternatively create a table, e-mail messages or raw messages; it's up to you to design it based on your application's needs:

```
create 'message', {NAME => 'email', BLOOMFILTER => 'ROW', VERSIONS
=> '1', IN_MEMORY => 'false', KEEP_DELETED_CELLS => 'false', DATA_
BLOCK_ENCODING => 'NONE',COMPRESSION => 'NONE', MIN_VERSIONS =>
'0', BLOCKCACHE => 'true', BLOCKSIZE => '65536', REPLICATION_SCOPE
=> '0'}
```

6. Once you run this command, a table with the specified parameters will be created.

7. Run the list command on the Hbase shell command prompt and you will see the following tables:

```
hbase(main):010:0> list

TABLE

01

City_Table

MyClickStream

SYSTEM.CATALOG

SYSTEM.SEQUENCE

SYSTEM.STATS

customer

hivehbasek

message     → this is the table we created just now

mywebproject:myclickstream

mywebproject:mywebsiteuser

wordcount

12 row(s) in 0.0360 seconds
```

8. Now start the `hbase-indexer server`:

```
./hbase-indexer server
```

9. Before you do this, create `hbase-solrIntegration.xml`, which will index all the data coming to the column family `'email'`:

```
<?xml version="1.0"?>
<indexer table="message">
<field name="email" value="email:*" type="string"/>
</indexer>
```

We have kept the table name the same. In the XML file, the e-mail field will take a string object as a datatype.

10. Now, we have to pass this `hbase-solrIntegration.xml` to the indexer server using the following command:

```
./hbase-indexer add-indexer -n sampleindex -c hbase-
solrIntegration.xml -cp solr.collection=core0
```

**core0–**: depends upon the core you are using in your solr cluster.

Make sure that the solr server is up and running.

11. Let's try to add a couple of records to the Hbase table, message, which we created earlier:

```
Hbase> put 'message', 'row0000001:','email:value','Email -
messaging system and its meaning'
```

12. Now you can search this record in real time.

13. Alternatively, you can delete the record and it will be deleted in real time.

From the Hbase shell, execute the following command:

```
Deleteall 'message' , 'row1'.
```

Once the delete is executed, near real time, the data in solr will also be deleted.

## How it works...

1. The library in `hbase-sep*` contains the integration that allows the indexer to communicate between solr and Hbase directly.

2. When we create a table as message, the table is just created without any mapping to solr.

3. Then, we created an XML file (`hbase-solrIntegration.xml`) that is passed as a parameter while starting the hbase-indexer process.

4. This file uses the grammar that the solr cloud system understands; the core used is 0. In this case, we are not using a cluster solr environment.

5. This allows the mapping from the Hbase table (message) to the message table and field as e-mail in solr.

6. Once the data is updated in Hbase, the listener in Hbase pushes the data immediately to the solr schema.

7. This allows the indexer to index the data in the way it's designed in `hbase-solrIntegration.xml`.

8. It is a similar case for when we have to execute a `delete` command.

## There's more...

http://blog.cloudera.com/blog/2013/09/email-indexing-using-cloudera-search/

https://lessc0de.github.io/connecting_hbase_to_elasticsearch.html

# 10
# Optimizing Hbase
# for Cloud

In this chapter, we will consider setting up Hbase on Amazon cloud, benefits of using cloud, components that we can use to monitor the cloud setup and various other details as follows:

- Configuring HBase for cloud
- Launching a cluster on Amazon EMR
- Connecting to HBase using the command line
- Backing up and restoring HBase
- Terminating an HBase cluster
- Accessing HBase data with hive
- Viewing the HBase user interface
- Viewing HBase log files
- Monitoring HBase with CloudWatch
- Monitoring HBase with Ganglia

## Introduction

Hadoop/Hbase was designed to crunch a huge amount of data in a batch mode and provide meaningful results to this data. However, as the technology evolved over the years, the original architecture was fine tuned to move from the world of big-iron to the choice of cloud infrastructure:

1. It provides optimum pricing for the provisioning of new hardware, storage, and monitoring the infrastructure.

2. One-click setup of additional nodes and storage.

3. Elastic load-balancing to different clusters within the Hbase ecosystem.

4. Ability to resize the cluster on-demand.

5. Share capacity with different time-zones, for example, doing batch jobs in different data centers to and real-time analytics near to the customer.

6. Easy integration with other Cloud-based services.

7. HBase on Amazon EMR provides the ability to back up your HBase data directly to **Amazon Simple Storage Service** (**Amazon S3**). You can also restore from a previously created backup when launching an HBase cluster.

# Configuring Hbase for the Cloud

Before we start, let's take a quick look at the supported versions and the prerequisites you need to move ahead.

The list of supported versions is as below:

| Hbase Version | AMI Versions | AWS CLI configuration parameters | Hbase Version details |
|---|---|---|---|
| 0.94.18 | 3.1.0 and later | --ami-version 3.1<br><br>--ami-version 3.2<br><br>--ami-version 3.3<br><br>--applications Name=Hbase | Bug fixes |
| 0.94 | 3.0-3.0.4 | --ami-version 3.0<br>--applications Name=Hbase | |
| 0.92 | 2.2 and later | --ami-version 2.2 or later<br>--applications Name=HBase | |

Now let's look at the prerequisites:

▶ **At least two instances (Optional)**: The cluster's master node runs the HBase master server and Zookeeper, and slave nodes run the HBase region servers.

For optimum performance and production systems, HBase clusters should run on at least two EC2 instances, but you can run HBase on a single node for evaluation purposes.

▶ **Long-running clusters**: HBase only runs on long-running clusters. By default, the CLI and Amazon EMR console create long-running clusters.

▶ **An Amazon EC2 key pair set (Recommended)**: To use the **Secure Shell** (**SSH**) network protocol to connect with the master node and run HBase shell commands, you must use an Amazon EC2 key pair when you create the cluster.

▶ **The correct AMI and Hadoop versions**: HBase clusters are currently supported only on Hadoop 20.205 or later.

▶ **The AWS CLI**: This is needed to interact with Hbase using the command-line options.

▶ **Use of Ganglia tool**: For monitoring, it's advisable to use the Ganglia tool; this provides all information related to performance and can be installed as a client lib when we create the cluster.

▶ **The logs for Hbase**: They are available on the master node; it's a standard practice in a production environment to copy these logs to the Amazon S3 cluster.

## How to do it...

1. Open a browser and copy the following URL: (`https://console.aws.amazon.com/elasticmapreduce/`); if you don't have an Amazon AWS account, then you have to create it.

2. Then choose Create cluster as shown in the following:

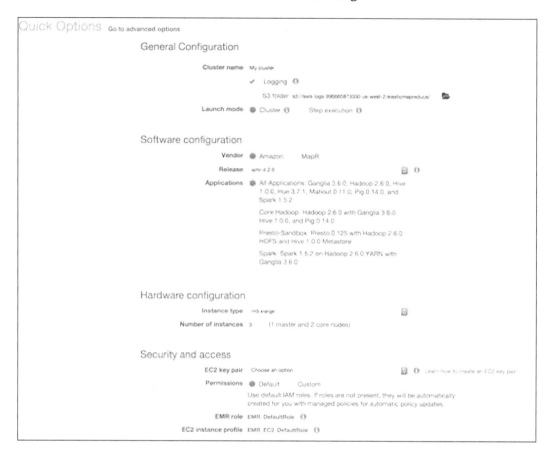

3. Provide the cluster name; you must select Launch mode as cluster

4. Let's proceed to the software configuration section. There are two options: Amazon template or MapR template. We are going to use Amazon template. It will load the default applications, which includes Hbase.

5. Security is key when you are using `ssh` to the login to the cluster. Let's create a security key, by selecting NETWORK & SECURITY on the left section of the panel (as shown in the following). We have created as `Hbase03`:

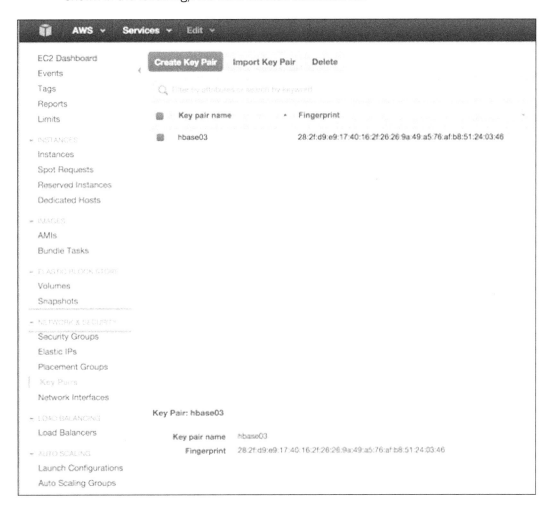

6. Once you create this security key, it will ask for a download of a `.pem` file , which is known as `hbase03.pem`.

7. Copy this file to the  user location and change the access to:

   ```
   chmod 400 <hbase03.pem>
   ```

   This will ensure the write level of access is there on the file and is not accessible two-way.

8. Now select this pair from the drop-down box in the EC2 Key pair; this will allow you to register the instance to the key while provisioning the instance.

   You can do this later too, but I had some challenges in doing this so it is always better to provision the instance with the property

9. Now, you are ready to provision the EMR cluster. Go ahead and provision the cluster.

   It will take around 10 to 20 mins to have a cluster fully accessible and in a running condition.

10. Verify it by observing the console:

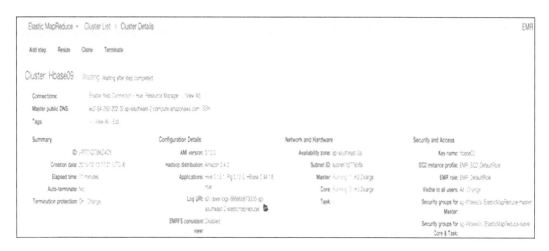

## How it works...

When you select the cluster name, it maps to your associate account internally and keeps the mapping the cluster is alive (or net destroyed).

When you select an installation using the setting it loads all the respective JAR files, which allows it to perform in a fully distributed environment. You can select the EMR or MapR stable release, which allows us to load the compatible library, and hence focus on the solution rather than troubleshooting integration issues within the Hadoop/Hbase farms.

Internally, all the slaves connects to the master, and hence, we considered an extra-large VM.

# Connecting to an Hbase cluster using the command line

## How to do it...

1. You can alternatively SSH to the node and see the details as follows:

2. Once you have connected to the cluster, you can perform all the tasks which you can perform on local clusters.

The preceding screenshot gives the details of the components we selected while installing the cluster.

3. Let's connect to the Hbase shell to make sure all the components are connecting internally and we are able to create a sample table.

## How it works...

The communication between your machine and the Hbase cluster works by passing a key every time a command is executed; this allows the communication to be private.

The shell becomes the remote shell that connects to the Hbase master via a private connection. All the base shell commands such as put, create, and scan get all the known Hbase commands.

# Backing up and restoring Hbase

Amazon Elastic MapReduce provides multiple ways to back up and restore Hbase data to S3 cloud. It also allows us to do an incremental backup; during the backup process Hbase continues to execute the write commands, helping us to keep working while the backup process continues.

> There is a risk of having an inconsistency in the data. If consistence is of prime importance, then the write needs to be stopped during the initial backup process, synchronized across nodes. This can be achieved by passing the-consistent parameter when requesting a backup.

When you back up HBase data, you should specify a different backup directory for each cluster.

An easy way to do this is to use the cluster identifier as part of the path specified for the backup directory.

For example, s3://mybucket/backups/j-3AEXXXXXX16F2. This ensures that any future incremental backups reference the correct HBase cluster.

## How to do it...

When you are ready to delete old backup files that are no longer needed, we recommend that you first do a full backup of your HBase data. This ensures that all data is preserved and provides a baseline for future incremental backups. Once the full backup is done, you can navigate to the backup location and manually delete the old backup files:

1. While creating a cluster, add an additional step scheduling regular backups, as shown in the following.

2. You have to specify the location of the backup to which a backup file with the data will be kept, based on the backup frequency selected. For highly valuable data, you can have a backup on an hourly basis. For less sensitive data, it can be planned daily:

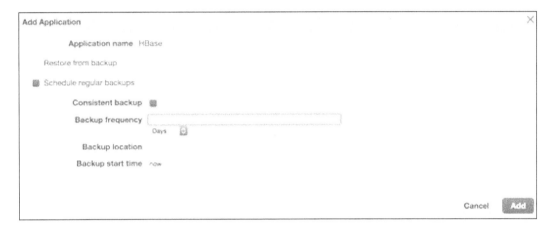

3. It's a good practice to back up to a separate location in Amazon S3 to ensure that incremental backups are calculated correctly.

4. It's important to specify the exact time from when the backup will be started, the time zone specified is UTC for our cluster.

5. We can proceed with creating the cluster as planned; it will create a backup of the data to the location specified.

6. You have to provide the exact location of the backup file and restore it.

7. The version that is backed up needs to be specified and saved, which will allow the data to be restored.

## How it works...

During the backup process, Hbase continues to execute write commands; this ensures the cluster remains available throughout the backup process.

Internally, the operation is done in parallel, thus there is a chance of it being inconsistent.

If the use case requires consistency, then we have to pause the write to Hbase. This can be achieved by passing the consistent parameter while requesting a backup.

This internally queues the writes and executes them as soon as the synchronization complete.

# Terminating an HBase cluster

Before terminating the cluster, it is advisable to make sure that a backup of the data is done, and the nodes are not writing to the master so that there is consistence in the data.

## How to do it...

The termination step is very simple—simply go the cluster list, select the cluster, and click on the Terminate button. This will start the logical termination and eventually the resources will be released to other applications running is the same cluster (at the hardware level):

# Accessing HBase data with hive

The Hive architecture is by design scalable and can easily scale for hundreds or millions of users; clubbing it with Hbase makes the right integration choice. It also make Hbase interoperate with Hive; a simple Hbase table can be accessed from Hive as if it was a Hive table itself.

A single hive query can perform joins, unions, and Cartesian joins by aggregating a combination of Hbase and Hive tables.

Similarly, the inserts can also be applied between Hbase and native Hive tables.

In a nutshell, we can solve the following usecase:

> ▸ Incremental refresh problems by keeping a near real-time replica of MySql data in Hbase

> ▸ We can pick and chose when to use Hbase and when to use native Hive tables as hive tables are much faster to read and write.

## How to do it ...

Connecting Hive to Hbase:

1. I am assuming your EMR cluster is still running and you are able to connect using putty or directly `ssh` to the cluster.

2. Write hive in the command shell and you will be connected to the hive shell. You are now inside the hive shell and ready to take commands.

3. Now we have to point the Hbase client from the hive cluster to the Hbase cluster that contains our data:

```
Set hbase.zookeeper.quorum=<your public-DNS-Name>
```

4. Once this connection is made, the data store on the Hbase cluster can be accessed. For this, you have to create an external table to interface between the Hbase and Hive endpoints. Say we refreshed it as `IntegrationTouchPointInputTable`.

```
CREATE EXTERNAL TABLE IntegrationTouchPointInputTable(key
int, value string) STORED BY 'org.apache.hadoop.hive.hbase.
HBaseStorageHandler'WITH SERDEPROPERTIES ("hbase.columns.
mapping" = "cf1:val")TBLPROPERTIES("hbase.table.name" = "
IntegrationTouchPointInputTable");
```

5. Once created, you can check it by running the following command on the hive shell:

```
Select count(*) from IntegrationTouchPointInputTable ;
```

The two `SERDEPROPERTIES` that control the mapping of HBase columns to Hive are as follows:

**`hbase.columns.mapping`**

`hbase.table.default.storage.type` can have a value of either string (the default) or binary; this option is only available as of Hive 0.9 and the string behavior is the only one available in earlier versions

The column mapping support currently available is somewhat cumbersome and restrictive— for each Hive column, the table creator must specify a corresponding entry in the comma-delimited `hbase.columns.mapping` string (so for a Hive table with n columns, the string should have n entries); whitespace should not be used in between entries since these will be interpreted as part of the column name, which is almost certainly not what you want. A mapping entry must be either :key or of the form column `family-name:[column-name]` `[#(binary|string)` (the type specification delimited by # was added in Hive 0.9.0; earlier versions interpreted everything as strings).

If no type specification is given, the value from `hbase.table.default.storage.type` will be used. Any prefixes of the valid values are valid too (that is, #b instead of #binary)

If you specify a column as binary the bytes in the corresponding HBase cells are expected to be of the form that HBase's Bytes class yields.

There must be exactly one key mapping (this can be mapped either to a string or struct column–see Simple Composite Keys and Complex Composite Keys).

> Before HIVE-1228 in Hive 0.6, key mapping was not supported, and the first Hive column implicitly mapped to the key; as of Hive 0.6, it is now strongly recommended that you always specify the key explicitly; we will drop support for implicit key mapping in future).

If no column name is given, then the Hive column will map to all columns in the corresponding HBase column family, and the Hive MAP datatype must be used to allow access to these (possibly sparse) columns.

There is currently no way to access the HBase timestamp attribute, and queries always access data with the latest timestamp.

Since HBase does not associate data-type information with columns, the serde converts everything to a string representation before storing it in HBase; there is currently no way to plug in a custom serde per column.

It is not necessary to reference every HBase column family, but those that are not mapped will be inaccessible via the Hive table; it's possible to map multiple Hive tables to the same HBase table.

# Viewing the Hbase user interface

To view the Hbase UI master, some configuration needs to be done so that the access is via proxy, and if fully secure to your cluster only.

## How to do it ...

There are two ways to connect to the cluster, as follows:

Using SSH and via Browser:

As we are more browser-centric here, we will be connecting using Firefox and Chrome.

1. On Mac OS X, choose `Applications>Utilities>Terminal` and open a Terminal:

   Replace `hbase03.pem`, replace `8157` with an unused , local port number, and replace `ec2-54-252-202-32.ap-southeast-2.compute.amazonaws.com` with the master public DNS name of your cluster.

2. Now you can use the following command:

   ```
   ssh -i ~/hbase03.pem -N -D 8157 hadoop@ ec2-54-252-202-32.ap-southeast-2.compute.amazonaws.com
   ```

> D is used for dynamic port forwarding, which allows you to specify a local port used to forward data to all remote ports on the master node's local webserver. Dynamic port forwarding also creates a local SOCKS proxy listening on the specified in the command.

3. This allows a tunnel between the two endpoints on your system and your cluster. Keep the terminal window open till the time you are using the web interface.

   Alternatively, use FireProxy to do the same operation. To do this, download the FoxyProxy from `http://getfoxyproxy.org/downloads.html`.

4. Create a `foxyproxy-setting.xml` file in your text editor:

   ```
   <?xml version="1.0" encoding="UTF-8"?>
   <foxyproxy>
       <proxies>
           <proxy name="emr-socks-proxy" id="2322596116"
   notes="" fromSubscription="false" enabled="true"
   mode="manual" selectedTabIndex="2" lastresort="false"
   animatedIcons="true" includeInCycle="true" color="#0055E5"
   proxyDNS="true" noInternalIPs="false" autoconfMode="pac"
   clearCacheBeforeUse="false" disableCache="false"
   ```

```
        clearCookiesBeforeUse="false" rejectCookies="false">
            <matches>
                <match enabled="true" name="*ec2*.amazonaws.com*"
        pattern="*ec2*.amazonaws.com*" isRegEx="false" isBlackList="false"
        isMultiLine="false" caseSensitive="false" fromSubscription="false"
        />
                <match enabled="true" name="*ec2*.compute*"
        pattern="*ec2*.compute*" isRegEx="false" isBlackList="false"
        isMultiLine="false" caseSensitive="false" fromSubscription="false"
        />
                <match enabled="true" name="10.*"
        pattern="http://10.*" isRegEx="false" isBlackList="false"
        isMultiLine="false" caseSensitive="false" fromSubscription="false"
        />
                <match enabled="true" name="*10*.amazonaws.com*"
        pattern="*10*.amazonaws.com*" isRegEx="false" isBlackList="false"
        isMultiLine="false" caseSensitive="false" fromSubscription="false"
        />
                <match enabled="true" name="*10*.
        compute*" pattern="*10*.compute*" isRegEx="false"
        isBlackList="false" isMultiLine="false" caseSensitive="false"
        fromSubscription="false"/>
                <match enabled="true" name="*.compute.
        internal*" pattern="*.compute.internal*" isRegEx="false"
        isBlackList="false" isMultiLine="false" caseSensitive="false"
        fromSubscription="false"/>
                <match enabled="true" name="*.ec2.
        internal* " pattern="*.ec2.internal*" isRegEx="false"
        isBlackList="false" isMultiLine="false" caseSensitive="false"
        fromSubscription="false"/>
            </matches>
                <manualconf host="localhost" port="8157" socksversion="5"
        isSocks="true" username="" password="" domain="" />
            </proxy>
        </proxies>
</foxyproxy>
```

This file includes the following settings:

Port 8157 is the local port number used to establish the SSH tunnel with the master node. This must match the port number you used in PuTTY or terminal.

The `*ec2*.amazonaws.com*` and `*10*.amazonaws.com*` patterns match the public DNS name of clusters in US regions.

The `*ec2*.compute*` and `*10*.compute*` patterns match the public DNS name of clusters in all other regions.

The `10.*` pattern provides access to the `JobTracker` log files in Hadoop 1.x. Alter this filter if it conflicts with your network access plan.

5. Choose **Firefox | Add-ons**.

6. On the **Add-ons** tab, to the right of **FoxyProxy Standard**, choose **Options**.

7. In the FoxyProxy Standard dialog, navigate to **File | Import Settings**.

8. Browse to the location of `foxyproxy-settings.xml`, select the file, and choose **Open**.

9. Choose **Yes** when prompted to overwrite the existing settings and then choose **Yes** to restart Firefox.

10. When Firefox restarts, on the **Add-ons** tab, to the right of FoxyProxy Standard, choose **Options**.

11. In the FoxyProxy Standard dialog, for **Select Mode**, choose **Use proxies** based on their pre-defined patterns and priorities.

12. Choose close:

| Name of Interface | URL |
|---|---|
| Hadoop ResourceManager | `http://master-public-dns-name:9026/` |
| Hadoop HDFS NameNode | `http://master-public-dns-name:9101/` |
| Ganglia Metrics Reports | `http://master-public-dns-name/ganglia/` |
| HBase Interface | `http://master-public-dns-name:60010/`<br>`master-status` |
| Hue Web Application | `http://master-public-dns-name:8888/` |
| Impala Statestore | `http://master-public-dns-name:25000` |

Viewing HBase log files:

For viewing Hbase logs, you can go to the following location in the AWS cluster:

`mnt/var/log`

`[hadoop@ip-172-31-26-174 log] $`

This will contain different log files, you can look for the files that are of your users by using the following command:

`ls -l | sort -k 3 t`

This produces a list of file sorted with `user_id` and group, as follows:

```
drwxr-xr-x+ 2 hadoop hadoop 12288 Dec 21 00:03 hadoop-state-pusher
drwxr-xr-x+ 2 hadoop hadoop 12288 Dec 21 00:03 metrics-server
drwxr-xr-x+ 3 hadoop hadoop 12288 Dec 21 00:08 hadoop
drwxrwxr-x+ 3 hadoop hadoop    16 Dec 21 00:18 tmp
drwxr-xr-x+ 2 hadoop hadoop 20480 Dec 21 00:03 instance-controller
drwxr-xr-x+ 2 hadoop hadoop 40960 Dec 21 00:18 instance-state
drwxr-xr-x+ 2 hadoop hadoop  4096 Dec 14 04:08 hbase
drwxrwxr-x+ 4 hadoop hadoop    42 Dec 14 04:08 bootstrap-actions
drwxr-xr-x+ 4 hadoop hadoop    87 Dec 21 00:00 apps
drwxrwxr-x+ 2 ln     sys       6 Jul  6 23:46 cups
```

You can also go to the `hadoop` folder located at:

**/mnt/var/log/hadoop**

This allows you to see the logs as follows. You can tail these logs and see on the runtime what's going on in the cluster:

```
-rw-rw-r--+ 1 hadoop hadoop 406119 Dec 20 21:59 hadoop-hadoop-namenode-ip-172-31-26-174.log.2015-12-20-21
-rw-rw-r--+ 1 hadoop hadoop   2920 Dec 20 21:59 mapred-hadoop-historyserver-ip-172-31-26-174.log.2015-12-20-21
-rw-rw-r--+ 1 hadoop hadoop 408193 Dec 20 22:59 hadoop-hadoop-namenode-ip-172-31-26-174.log.2015-12-20-22
-rw-rw-r--+ 1 hadoop hadoop   2920 Dec 20 22:59 mapred-hadoop-historyserver-ip-172-31-26-174.log.2015-12-20-22
-rw-rw-r--+ 1 hadoop hadoop 406124 Dec 20 23:59 hadoop-hadoop-namenode-ip-172-31-26-174.log.2015-12-20-23
-rw-rw-r--+ 1 hadoop hadoop   2920 Dec 20 23:59 mapred-hadoop-historyserver-ip-172-31-26-174.log.2015-12-20-23
-rw-rw-r--+ 1 hadoop hadoop    211 Dec 21 00:00 yarn-hadoop-resourcemanager-ip-172-31-26-174.log
-rw-rw-r--+ 1 hadoop hadoop   2549 Dec 21 00:47 mapred-hadoop-historyserver-ip-172-31-26-174.log
-rw-rw-r--+ 1 hadoop hadoop 331186 Dec 21 00:49 hadoop-hadoop-namenode-ip-172-31-26-174.log
```

Alternatively, you can also monitor it on a web console in the AWS console:

# Monitoring HBase with CloudWatch

Cloud watch provides and extensive way of monitoring the Hbase/Hadoop nodes in various ways as listed here:

- ▸ Cluster status
- ▸ Node status
- ▸ I/O
- ▸ Hbase

Let's discuss Cluster status—it provides the following areas to look at:

Is Idle, Container allocated—container reserved, container pending, apps completed.

Apps failed, apps killed, apps pending, apps running, apps submitted. We will go over one area for explanation.

By double-clicking, a child window is popped up (overlay), which provides details as follows. You can explicitly get the detail by customizing the graph based on hours, days, or mins ago; the graph pulls the data accordingly.

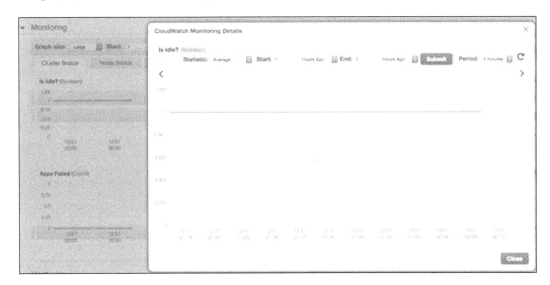

Node status provides details of the following:

▸ **Core Nodes running /pending**: As we have two nodes the graph is marked at 2

▸ **Live data nodes**: The data node is fully live hence we see the 100 percentage

▸ **Map Reduce total nodes**: The total MR node us 2 hence its showing 2

▸ **MR Active nodes**: The total active MR nodes are 2 hence its showing 2

- ▸ **MR lost nodes**: There is no lost node hence its showing 0

- ▸ **MR unhealthy nodes**: There are no unhealthy nodes hence its showing 0

- ▸ **MR Decommissioned nodes**: There is no node that was decommissioned hence it's 0

- ▸ **MR Rebooted nodes**: There is no node rebooted hence its showing 0

I/O details: This contains the details of read and write operations happening on the different disk, which is serving different a purpose as follows:

- ▸ S3 Bytes Read/Write

- ▸ HDFS utilization in bytes Read/Write

- ▸ Missing blocks

- ▸ Total load

- ▸ Memory Total in MB

- ▸ Memory reserved/available/allocated in MB

- ▸ Pending deletion block

- ▸ Under replication blocks

- ▸ DFS pending replication blocks

- ▸ Capacity remaining

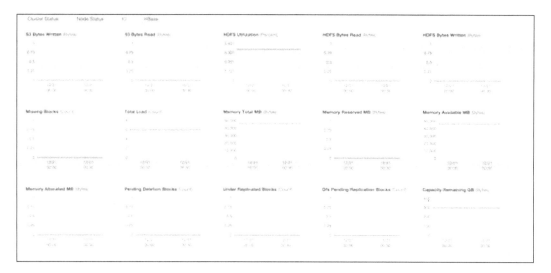

Hbase covers mainly three types of matric:

▸ **HbaseBackup failed**: This provides information of the last backup failed; it's set to 0 by default and updated to 1 if the previous backup attempt failed.

This matric is only reported for the Hbase cluster:

▸ **HBaseMostRecentBackupDuration**: The duration it took while taking a previous backup. This is reported even if the last backup has failed. If the backup is going on, it reports the time remaining since the backup started.

This is also only available for Hbase clusters.

▸ **HBaseTimeSinceLastSuccessfulBackup**: Time elapsed since the last successful Hbase backup started on your cluster.

This is also only available for Hbase clusters.

# Monitoring Hbase with Ganglia

The Ganglia open source project is a scalable distributed system designed to monitor clusters and grids while minimizing the impact on their performance. When you enable Ganglia on your cluster, you can generate reports and view the performance of the cluster as a whole, as well as inspect the performance of individual node instances.

For more information about the Ganglia open source project, go to `http://ganglia.info/`. For more information about using Ganglia with Amazon EMR clusters, see the Monitor Performance with Ganglia recipe.

You configure Ganglia for HBase using the `configure-hbase-for-ganglia` bootstrap action. This bootstrap action configures HBase to publish metrics to Ganglia.

 You must configure HBase and Ganglia when you launch the cluster; Ganglia reporting cannot be added to a running cluster. Once the cluster is launched with Ganglia reporting configured, you can access Ganglia graphs and reports using the graphical interface running on the master node. Ganglia also stores log files on the server at `/mnt/var/log/ganglia/rrds`. If you configured your cluster to persist log files to an Amazon S3 bucket, the Ganglia log files will be persisted there as well.

▶ **To view HBase metrics in the Ganglia web interface**: You can view the Ganglia metrics by opening a browser window with `http://master-public-dns-name/ganglia/`, where `master-public-dns-name` is the public DNS address of the master server in the HBase cluster.

For information on how to locate the public DNS name of a master node, see To retrieve the public DNS name of the master node using the Amazon EMR console.

▶ **To view Ganglia log files on the master node**: If the cluster is still running, you can access the log files by using SSH to connect to the master node and navigating to the `/mnt/var/log/ganglia/rrds` directory.

For information about how to use SSH to connect to the master node, see the Connect to the Master Node Using SSH recipe.

 It's assumed that the preceding configuration for the web interface is configured properly and working.

The following are the details which will be accessible for the cluster:

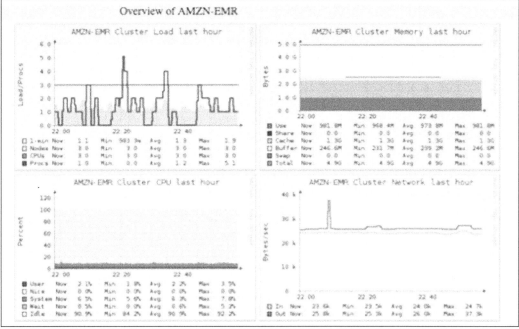

## How it works...

Amazon EMR is a set of services that perform task in a cohesive and distributed way using the core or customized Hadoop/Hbase framework to run on the cloud infrastructure.

When it launches a Hadoop cluster, it take advantage of the elastic and scalable Amazon EC2 architecture. It also uses the concept of nodes and steps.

- ▸ **Nodes**: In the landscape of Amazon EMR, there are three roles a server can play in a large cluster.
    - ❑ **Master node**: Its main task is to manage the distribution of the Map Reduce executable and subset row data to the core and instance groups. It also tracks the status of each task performed and monitors the health of the instances grouped together.

There can be once mater node in the cluster.
    - ❑ **Core Nodes**: It runs the task and stores data using the HDFS; this is equivalent to a Hadoop slave node.
    - ❑ **Task Nodes**: This runs the tasks; it maps to a Hadoop slave node.

▶ **Steps**: These are processed in the order in which they are listed in the cluster. Steps are run following this sequence: all steps have their state set to *PENDING*. The first step is run and the step's state is set to *RUNNING*. When the step is completed, the step's state changes to *COMPLETED*. The next step in the queue is run, and the step's state is set to *RUNNING*. After each step completes, the step's state is set to *COMPLETED,* and the next step in the queue is run. Steps are run until there are no more steps. The processing flow returns to the cluster. If a step fails, the step state is FAILED and all remaining steps with a *PENDING* state are marked as *CANCELLED*. No further steps are run and processing returns to the cluster. Data is normally communicated from one step to the next using files stored on the cluster's **Hadoop Distributed File System** (**HDFS**). Data stored on HDFS exists only as long as the cluster is running. When the cluster is shut down, all data is deleted. The final step in a cluster typically stores the processing results in an Amazon S3 bucket.

## There is more ...

There are various optimizations that AWS cloud infrastructure provides for different workloads:

▶ `Hbase.regionserver.handler.count`: The `handler.count` is the thread the region server will keep open to accommodate the request coming in for the tables. It is recommended to define this parameter based on the payload for each request. If the payload is small then the count needs to be high and when the payload is big then the count needs to be low, it's also essential to know the count of CPUs or VCPUs on the region servers; we need to configure these. The default size is 10, which is low with a high number of concurrent clients:

```
--bootstrap-action s3://elasticmapreduce/bootstrap-actions/
configure-hbase,Args=["-s","hbase.regionserver.handler.count=32"]
```

 This can be setup in a non cloud environment `hbase-site.xml`:

```
<property>
<name>hbase.regionserver.handler.count</name>
<value>32</value>
</property>
```

▶ `hbase.hregion.max.filesize`: The default size is 256 MB, which will work okay when there is not a large amount of data; this parameter controls the maximum `Hstore` file size the default size creates Hbase cluster to split frequently when there is a heavy load of data to the cluster. By increasing the size to 1 GB (1073741824 KB) and makes the region bigger, we can reduce the split.

```
--bootstrap-action s3://elasticmapreduce/bootstrap-
actions/configure-hbase,Args=["-s","hbase.hregion.max.
filesize=1073741824"]
```

This can be set up in a non-cloud environment via `hbase-site.xml`:

```
<property>
<name>hbase.hregion.max.filesize</name>
<value> 1073741824 </value>
</property>
```

It will increase the time to load-balance regions from one server to another.

▸ `hbase.hregion.memstore.flush.size`: When the data is loaded to the memstore, the limit of the memstore is checked; once the max limit is reached in bytes, the data is flushed to the disk. The idea is to keep the write data in-memory if there is a sudden spike of data and not start writing to the disk. This gives a better performance when there are spikes during write operations. The default value is set to 64 MB; this is checked by a thread that runs every `hbase.server.thread.wakefrequency`:

```
--bootstrap-action s3://elasticmapreduce/bootstrap-actions/
configure-hbase,Args=["-s","hbase.hregion.memstore.flush.
size=134217728"]
```

 This can be set up in a non-cloud environment via `hbase-site.xml`:

```
<property>
<name>hbase.hregion.memstore.flush.size</name>
<value>134217728</value>
</property>
```

▸ `zookeeper.session.timeout`: It's very important to locate any server crash quickly so that the master can recover from the crash. The default timeout is three min, which is very high. Before we do this change, we must check the GC cycles and make sure there are no long pauses in the GC; if it happens, the Zookeeper session timeout will take the region server out of the traffic and

```
--bootstrap-action s3://elasticmapreduce/bootstrap-actions/
configure-hbase,Args=["-s","zookeeper.session.timeout=60000"]
```

Now, we have moved it to one min.

This can be set up in a non-cloud environment via `hbas-site.xml`:

```
<property>
<name>zookeeper.session.timeout</name>
<value>180000</value>
<description>ZooKeeper session timeout. HBase passes
this to the zk quorum as suggested maximum time
for a session (This setting becomes zookeeper's
'maxSessionTimeout'). See http://hadoop.apache.org/
zookeeper/docs/current/zookeeperProgrammers.html#ch_
zkSessions "The client sends a requested timeout, the
server responds with the timeout that it can give the
client. " In milliseconds.
</description>
</property>
```

Refer to the following website for more information on Amazon EMR:
`http://docs.aws.amazon.com/ElasticMapReduce/latest/DeveloperGuide/emr-what-is-emr.html`.

# 11

# Case Study

In this chapter, we are going to cover the following recipes:

- Hbase can work as a primary data aggregation and ingestion engine
- Hbase can traverse petabytes with ease

## Introduction

This chapter gives a holistic picture of how we can integrate the different distributed components and create a project or make meaningful work out of it. There are different ways to bridge Solr and Hbase to make it work as a single integrated unit like.

- Batch-indexing Hbase tables using MapReduce jobs
- Lily Hbase indexer services
- Registering a Lily Hbase Indexer configuration with the Lily Hbase Indexer Services.

 For this book we will consider Lily Hbase solr platform and work with the examples.

Lily simplifies the integration touch points between Hbase, Solr, Hadoop and other distributed Hadoop frameworks.

Some features included in the Lily framework are:

- Ease of use through a high-level schema supporting rich and mixed, structured and unstructured, data sets

- Developer-friendly, powerful, and expressive REST and Java API

- Flexible, configurable indexing system supporting real-time indexing into Solr

- Under the hood, Lily operates a high-preferment yet robust queuing mechanism, Lily SEP, which allows for the additional integration of Apache HBase with external processes.

# Configuring Lily Platform

Before we start, let's take a quick look at the supported versions and prerequisites you'll need to move ahead.

- **NOTE:**
- Only Linux and different flavors of Unix are supported currently.

The list of supported versions are as follows:

| JDK/Java | 1.6 version onwards | java –version should show<br><br>java version "1.8.0_31"<br><br>Java(TM) SE Runtime Environment (build 1.8.0_31-b13)<br><br>Java HotSpot(TM) 64-Bit Server VM (build 25.31-b07, mixed mode) | Remarks<br><br>Check whether JAVA_HOME is set or not.<br><br>Using echo $JAVA_HOME should point to the Java lib in your machine. |
|---|---|---|---|

## How to do it...

1. Open a terminal window and run the following command:
   ```
   wget  http://lilyproject.org/release/2.4/lily-2.4.tar.gz
   ```
   This will copy the latest lily tar file.

2. Run the following command:
   ```
   tar zxvf lily-2.4.tar.gz
   ```

This will create a folder containing all the files and libraries that will be used as we go.

```
total 856128
-rw-r--r--+   1 r0choud   HOMEOFFICE\Domain Users  193818849 Jul 17  2013 lily-2.4.tar.gz
drwxr-xr-x+  24 r0choud   HOMEOFFICE\Domain Users        816 Dec  8  2014 pig-0.12.1
drwxr-xr-x+   7 r0choud   HOMEOFFICE\Domain Users        238 Dec  8  2014 gis-tools-for-hadoop
drwxr-xr-x+  21 r0choud   HOMEOFFICE\Domain Users        714 Dec  8  2014 sqoop-1.4.5.bin__hadoop-1.0.0
drwxrwxr-x+  14 r0choud   HOMEOFFICE\Domain Users        476 Dec  8  2014 hive-0.12.0
drwxrwxr-x+  13 r0choud   HOMEOFFICE\Domain Users        442 Dec  8  2014 apache-flume-1.5.0.1-bin
-rw-r--r--+   1 r0choud   HOMEOFFICE\Domain Users    1050940 Dec  8  2014 sqoop-1.4.5.tar.gz
-rw-r--r--+   1 r0choud   HOMEOFFICE\Domain Users   25319586 Dec  8  2014 apache-flume-1.5.0.1-bin.tar.gz
drwxr-xr-x+  18 r0choud   HOMEOFFICE\Domain Users        612 Dec  8  2014 sqoop-1.4.5
-rw-r--r--+   1 r0choud   HOMEOFFICE\Domain Users    1248273 Dec  8  2014 gangli
drwxr-xr-x+  16 r0choud   HOMEOFFICE\Domain Users        544 Dec  8  2014 mahou
-rw-r--r--+   1 r0choud   HOMEOFFICE\Domain Users    2855110 Dec  8  2014 gangl
drwxr-xr-x+  17 r0choud   HOMEOFFICE\Domain Users        578 Dec  8  2014 hadoo
drwxr-xr-x+  36 r0choud   HOMEOFFICE\Domain Users       1224 Dec  8  2014 spark
-rw-r--r--+   1 r0choud   HOMEOFFICE\Domain Users   81288181 Dec  8  2014 hive-
-rw-r--r--+   1 r0choud   HOMEOFFICE\Domain Users   54246778 Dec  8  2014 apach
drwxr-xr-x+  44 r0choud   HOMEOFFICE\Domain Users       1496 Dec  8  2014 ganglia-3
drwxr-xr-x+  25 r0choud   HOMEOFFICE\Domain Users        850 Dec  8  2014 zookeeper-
drwxrwxr-x+  12 r0choud   HOMEOFFICE\Domain Users        408 Dec  8  2014 apache-hi          3.1-bin
-rw-r--r--+   1 r0choud   HOMEOFFICE\Domain Users    6456084 Dec  8  2014 sqoop-1.4          __hadoop-1.0.0.tar.gz
drwxr-xr-x+  21 r0choud   HOMEOFFICE\Domain Users        714 Dec  8  2014 ambari-1.
-rw-r-----@   1 r0choud   HOMEOFFICE\Domain Users   71958249 Mar  2  2015 phoenix-4          -bin.tar.gz
drwxrwxr-x+  13 r0choud   HOMEOFFICE\Domain Users        442 Mar 22  2015 hbase-0.9          -hadoop2
-rw-r--r--@   1 r0choud   HOMEOFFICE\Domain Users       9293 Sep 20 23:24 seeds_dat     t.txt
-rw-r--r--+   1 r0choud   HOMEOFFICE\Domain Users      30286 Sep 20 23:27 chap10-km    n.txte
-rw-r--r--+   1 r0choud   HOMEOFFICE\Domain Users      30286 Sep 20 23:29 chap10-km   an.txt
drwxr-xr-x+   4 r0choud   HOMEOFFICE\Domain Users        136 Nov 22 16:59 HbaseElastic
drwxr-xr-x+  20 r0choud   HOMEOFFICE\Domain Users        680 Jan 23 16:40 hbase-indexer
drwxr-xr-x+  14 r0choud   HOMEOFFICE\Domain Users        476 Jan 23 16:53 lily-2.4
  _SRR3QT7EET-M-HbaseR_r0choud$
```

> A folder lily-2.4 is Created

Now let's go to the folder where your lily-2.4 directory is created.

1. Lily requires JDK1.7 onwards version and you need to have this JDK in your path, I am assuming here that your JDK path is set.

2. Run the following command:

```
sudo bin/launch-test-lily
```

This will start the following on the localhost:

| Components | Status | How to check |
|---|---|---|
| HDFS | `-------------------------`<br><br>`HDFS is running`<br><br><br>`HDFS web ui: http://localhost:57537`<br><br><br>`-------------------------` | You can point to the browser and invoke it; you will see the HDFS screen |

| Components | Status | How to check |
|---|---|---|
| Hbase, Zookeeper | HBase is running<br><br>HBase master web ui: http://localhost:60010<br><br>To connect to this HBase, use the following properties:<br><br>hbase.zookeeper.quorum=localhost<br><br>hbase.zookeeper.property.clientPort=2181<br><br>In Java code, create the HBase configuration like this:<br><br>Configuration conf = HBaseConfiguration.create();<br><br>conf.set("hbase.zookeeper.quorum", "localhost");<br><br>conf.set("hbase.zookeeper.property.clientPort", "2181"); | This shows the Hbase master is running on port 60010.<br><br>You can connect to the localhost using the Hbase client Via ZooKeeper.<br><br>This also shows ZooKeeper running on port 2181 |
| MapReduce | MapReduce is running<br><br>JobTracker web ui: http://localhost:57604<br><br>Configuration conf = new Configuration();<br><br>conf.set("mapred.job.tracker", "localhost:9001");<br><br>Job job = new Job(conf); | MapReduce is running; you can track jobs by opening the URL in a browser. |

| Components | Status | How to check |
|---|---|---|
| Solr | Solr is running<br><br>Use this as the Solr URL when creating an index:<br><br>http://localhost:8983/solr<br><br>Web GUI available at:<br><br>http://localhost:8983/solr/admin/<br><br>Index is not auto-committed, you can commit it using:<br><br>curl http://localhost:8983/solr/update -H 'Content-type:text/xml' --data-binary '<commit/>' | Solr's search engine is running and listing on port 8983<br><br>There are two URLs; one is used while indexing and one is via all the administration activities can be performed. |
| Lily | Lily is running<br><br>Using the configuration from: /var/folders/zz/zyxvpxvq6csfxvn_n0000000000000/T/lily-launcher-7436ed7e-ace7-4e14-a0d5-34bee1bdbb60/lilyconf<br><br>You can connect a LilyClient to it using zookeeper connect string "localhost:2181"<br><br>REST interface available at: http://localhost:12060/<br><br>From Java, use:<br><br>LilyClient lilyClient = new LilyClient("localhost:2181", 20000); | This indicates the lily system is up and responding to the request, in JSON format. |

This means the system is ready for the sample data to be loaded.

1. We will use the existing sample example provided by the lily package. But we will explain each and every step in detail.

2. Before we start indexing, we need to know the details of the file and what it means to which system and why:

```
Books_samle_solr_schema.xml
Book_sample_indexerconf.xml
Books_sample.json


Lets discuss  "Books_samle_solr_schema.xml".
<?xml version="1.0" encoding="UTF-8" ?>
<!--
/*
 * Copyright 2013 NGDATA nv
 *
 * Licensed under the Apache License, Version 2.0 (the "License");
 * you may not use this file except in compliance with the
License.
 * You may obtain a copy of the License at
 *
 *        http://www.apache.org/licenses/LICENSE-2.0
 *
 * Unless required by applicable law or agreed to in writing,
software
 * distributed under the License is distributed on an "AS IS"
BASIS,
 * WITHOUT WARRANTIES OR CONDITIONS OF ANY KIND, either express or
implied.
 * See the License for the specific language governing permissions
and
 * limitations under the License.
 */
-->
<schema name="example" version="1.5">

  <types>
    <fieldType name="string" class="solr.StrField"
sortMissingLast="true" omitNorms="true"/>

    <fieldType name="text" class="solr.TextField"
positionIncrementGap="100">
      <analyzer type="index">
```

```
        <tokenizer


class="solr.WhitespaceTokenizerFactory"/>
        <filter class="solr.WordDelimiterFilterFactory"
generateWordParts="1" generateNumberParts="1" catenateWords="1"
                catenateNumbers="1" catenateAll="0"
splitOnCaseChange="1"/>
        <filter class="solr.LowerCaseFilterFactory"/>
        <filter class="solr.SnowballPorterFilterFactory"
language="English" protected="protwords.txt"/>
      </analyzer>
      <analyzer type="query">
        <tokenizer class="solr.WhitespaceTokenizerFactory"/>
        <filter class="solr.WordDelimiterFilterFactory"
generateWordParts="1" generateNumberParts="1" catenateWords="0"
                catenateNumbers="0" catenateAll="0"
splitOnCaseChange="1"/>
        <filter class="solr.LowerCaseFilterFactory"/>
        <filter class="solr.SnowballPorterFilterFactory"
language="English" protected="protwords.txt"/>
      </analyzer>
    </fieldType>

    <fieldType name="long" class="solr.TrieLongField"
precisionStep="0" positionIncrementGap="0"/>
 </types>



 <fields>
   <!-- The _version_ field is required when using the Solr update
log or SolrCloud (cfr. SOLR-3432) -->
   <field name="_version_" type="long" indexed="true"
stored="true"/>

   <!-- Fields which are required by Lily -->
   <field name="lily.key" type="string" indexed="true"
stored="true" required="true"/>
   <field name="lily.id" type="string" indexed="true"
stored="true" required="true"/>
   <field name="lily.table" type="string" indexed="true"
stored="true" required="true"/>
   <field name="lily.vtagId" type="string" indexed="true"
stored="true"/>
```

```
        <field name="lily.vtag" type="string" indexed="true"
    stored="true"/>
        <field name="lily.version" type="long" indexed="true"
    stored="true"/>

        <!-- Your own fields -->
        <field name="title" type="text" indexed="true" stored="true"
    required="false"/>
        <field name="authors" type="text" indexed="true" stored="true"
    required="false" multiValued="true"/>
     </fields>

     <!-- Field to use to determine and enforce document uniqueness.
          For Lily, this should always be lily.key -->
     <uniqueKey>lily.key</uniqueKey>

    </schema>
```

3. Now let's visit the sample json file:

```
    {
      namespaces: {
        /* Declaration of namespace prefixes. */
        "org.lilyproject.bookssample": "b"
    /* to identify the schema of booksample uniquely */
      },
      fieldTypes: [
        {
          /* The 'b' refers to the namespace declared above, the
    dollar sign
             separates the namespace prefix from the name. */
          name: "b$title", /* namespace +tile of the book */
          valueType: "STRING", /* data type String*/
          scope: "versioned"
        },
        {
          name: "b$pages", ", /* namespace +pages of the book */
          valueType: "INTEGER",/* data type Integer */
          scope: "versioned" /* yes it needs to have a version number
    */
        },
        {
          name: "b$language",
          valueType: "STRING",
```

```
          scope: "versioned"
      },
      {
        name: "b$authors",
        valueType: "LIST<LINK>",
        scope: "versioned"
      },
      {
        name: "b$name",
        valueType: "STRING",
        scope: "versioned"
      },
      {
        name: "b$bio",
        valueType: "STRING",
        scope: "versioned"
      }
    ],
    recordTypes: [
      {
        name: "b$Book",
        fields: [
          {name: "b$title", mandatory: true },
          {name: "b$pages", mandatory: false },
          {name: "b$language", mandatory: false },
          {name: "b$authors", mandatory: false }
        ]
      },
      {
        name: "b$Author",
        fields: [
          {name: "b$name", mandatory: true },
          {name: "b$bio", mandatory: false }
        ]
      }
    ],
    records: [
      {
        type: "b$Author",
        id: "USER.mary_shelley",
        fields: {
```

4. `"b$name"`: "Mary Shelley", /* value of name which will be added once indexing is done */

5. `"b$bio"`: "Mary Shelley (30 August 1797 – 1 February 1851) was a British novelist, short story writer, dramatist, essayist, biographer, and travel writer, best known for her Gothic novel Frankenstein: or, The Modern Prometheus (1818). She also edited and promoted the works of her husband, the Romantic poet and philosopher Percy Bysshe Shelley." /* value of bio */

```
          }
        },
        {
          type: "b$Book",
          fields: {
            "b$title": "Frankenstein", /* title of the book */
            "b$pages": 288, /* pages of the book */
            "b$language": "English", /* language used */
            "b$authors": ["USER.mary_shelley"]
          }
        }
     ]
   }
```

Last time we checked, the Lily server was running and the command prompt should display the following:

```
----------------------------------------------------
Lily is running

Using configuration from: /var/folders/zz/zyxvpxvq6csfxvn_n00000000000000/T/lily-launcher-23ed3b3d-3810-4f55-9b56-7f9e2162a891/lilyconf
You can connect a LilyClient to it using zookeeper connect string "localhost:2181"

REST interface available at: http://localhost:12060/

From Java, use:
LilyClient lilyClient = new LilyClient("localhost:2181", 20000);
```

 Note: This will store data into a temp directory and the directory will be lost each time we restart test-lilly.

6. The next step is to create a field and record type.

**Record:**

- A record is the core entity managed by the Lily repository. All data you store in Lily is in the form of records.

- A record is the unit of atomic modification in Lily, thus the granularity of a read, update or delete operation.

- A record contains a set of fields. A field is a pair—{field type id, value}.

- Besides a pointer to its record type, a record has no built-in properties (like "last modified", "owner", ...), so there is no unwanted overhead from these.

- Records can have versions, so that older data stays available, but versioning is optional.

**Field**:

- Fields can reside in three scopes: the non-versioned scope, the versioned scope, and the versioned-mutable scope. We respectively speak of non-versioned fields, versioned fields and versioned-mutable fields.

- Fields that belong to the non-versioned scope are, as the name implies, not versioned. If a record has only fields in the non-versioned scope, the record will have no versions. If the record does have versions while it also has non-versioned fields, then you can consider the non-versioned fields as fields whose value counts for any version (= cross-version fields). For such records, if you modify only a non-versioned field, no new version will be created.

- Fields that belong to the versioned scope are (obviously) versioned: each time a record is updated with new values for such fields, a new version will be created in the record (the fields are not versioned individually). Fields in the versioned scope are immutable after creation: you cannot modify their value in existing versions.

- Fields that belong to the versioned-mutable scope are somewhat special: these fields are part of versions like versioned fields, but they stay mutable (modifiable) in existing versions. They are ideal for metadata about a version, such as the version's review status, a version comment, and the like.

- Typically, you will either choose to use versioning or not to use it, and most fields will fall in to one of these scopes. It can still be useful to have non-versioned fields when using versioning, for example, for a field that determines access permissions for the record, as you will want this to affect all versions.

- Versions currently can not be deleted.

Now let's run the command and see what happens:

```
SB830T7FFT-M:lily-2.4 r0choud$ sudo bin/lily-import -s samples/books/books_sample.json
```

The -S option specifies that we want to only upload the schema at this point.

1. The next step is to define the index.

For this, we will run the following command:

```
^CL-SB830T7FFT-M:lily-2.4 r0choud$ bin/lily-add-index --name books \
>                 --indexer-config samples/books/books_sample_indexerconf.xml \
>                 --solr-mode classic \
>                 --solr-shards shard1:http://localhost:8983/solr

ZooKeeper connection string not specified, using default: localhost
```

2. This will modify the configuration of indexes stored in Zookeeper. In response to this, the lily server will put everything necessary to keep the index up-to-date.

3. Now we will load the records in the schema that we created earlier.

4. Now using the import lily tool, we will import the json record set which we created.

```
L-SB830T7FFT-M:lily-2.4 r0choud$ sudo bin/lily-import samples/books/books_sample.json
Password:

ZooKeeper connection string not specified, using default: localhost

[INFO ][20:24:29,880][main     ] org.lilyproject.client.LilyClient - Current Lily servers = [l-sb830t7fft-m:12020]
[WARN ][20:24:31,010][main     ] org.apache.hadoop.conf.Configuration - fs.default.name is deprecated. Instead, use fs.defaultFS
2016-01-24 20:24:31.055 java[50144:1460037] Unable to load realm mapping info from SCDynamicStore
```

5. This will upload the records we created by running (`http://localhost:8983/solr/#/core0/query`).

6. Now we can see the XML results.

7. To get Json in the solr console, you can chang the wt field to json as shown in the following.

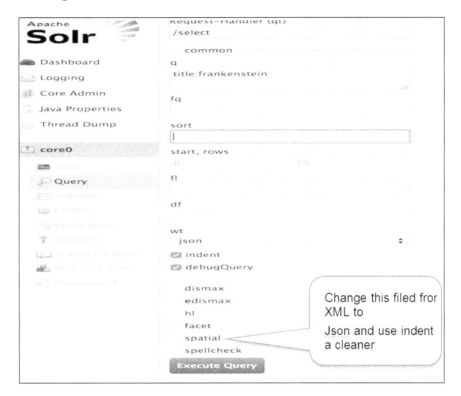

8. You can Query the Solr index using the following URL and work:

`http://localhost:12060/repository/record/USER.mary_shelley`

## There's more...

In this section, we will talk about the internals of the Lily system so that we are able to template the bigger picture and the internal system behavior.

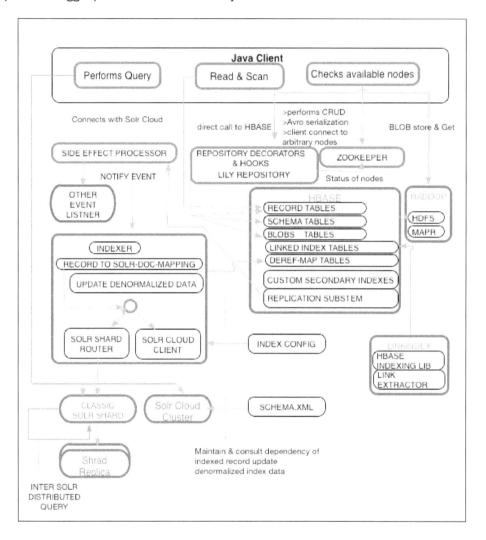

Lily uses Hbase to store data in a binary format and provides a mechanism by which it can run read, write, and scan a very large dataset. The layer that morphs the Hbase layer is the repository. The repository provides CURD functionality. The client always connects to the repository using Avro (an efficient binary serialization system)-based protocol. The repository connects to Hbase using the Hbase Java client, which makes an RPC call based on an efficient binary serialization system.

The basic entity managed by **repository** is called a record. While the reading client can specify some fields as read-only, and while updating a record, a client only needs to communicate to the changed field.

Fields in a record can be blobs; these blobs are stored in Hbase and transferred internally to HDFS.

One record can have multiple version, which can be mapped to one row in Hbase. Hbase handles unit of atomicity this way.

**Side Effect Processors (SEP)**: It is based on the HBase replication mechanism. This has various interesting properties, such as: there will be an event if and only if the corresponding update happened. This is because HBase replication is based on processing the write-ahead log files of Hbase. There is no additional cost, storage or system involved: the HBase write-ahead files are written anyway.

**Indexer**: It keeps the Solr-indexer synced when a records are created, updated, or deleted. Indexer listens to the SEP events.

In a nutshell, Indexer maps lily records to the Solr documents by intelligently segregating which records, and which files in the record, need to be indexed. It uses the tika library to perform content extraction.

**Denormalization**

Lily records can contain link fields. Link fields are links to other records. During indexing, you can include information from linked records within the index of the current record.

This is called denormalization. Information can be denormalized by following links multiple levels deep. Denormalization at index time is an alternative for SQL-join-like functionality at query time.

General join-queries are not available in Lucene, and are complicated to do with shared databases in general. Denormalization makes querying faster and easier, but complicates indexing.

Denormalization assumes you know beforehand (= when indexing) what sort of queries you will want to do on linked content.

A consequence of denormalization is that, when a record is updated, the index entries of other records might also become invalid when they contain information from the updated record.

The Lily Indexer will automatically update such index entries. For this, it maintains special tables that store the dependencies of indexed records, which allows us to quickly and accurately find out which records need reindexing in response to repository changes.

**Solr**

Lily supports both SolrCloud and classic (non-cloud) Solr. For classic Solr, Lily is able to do the distributed indexing (the routing towards the shards), something which is taken care of automatically when using SolrCloud.

**ZooKeeper**

ZooKeeper provides the coordination of distributed applications, like distributed synchronization, leader election, and configuration. ZooKeeper is used by Lily, HBase, and SolrCloud, and in the entire Hadoop landscape.

# Integrating elastic search with Hbase

In this case study, we will concentrate on how we can take advantage of using a lighting-fast open source search engine called elastic search to cater to the analytic world.

Elastic search brings many advantages in terms of speed and flexibility and has weak constituency; combining it with the Apache Phoenix engine as an integration bridge that connects to Hbase as a primary source of data makes for a robust proposition.

# Configuring

The prerequisites for this are as follows:

| JDK/Java | Version 1.6 onwards | java –version should show<br>Java version "1.8.0_31"<br>Java(TM) SE Runtime Environment (build 1.8.0_31-b13)<br>Java HotSpot(TM) 64-Bit Server VM (build 25.31-b07, mixed mode) | Remarks<br>Check whether JAVA_HOME is set or not.<br>Using echo $JAVA_HOME<br>should point to the Java lib in your machine. |
|---|---|---|---|
| Apache Phoenix | Phoenix-3.1.0 | phoenix-3.1.0-bin.tar.gz | |
| Hbase | Hbase 0.94.22 | hbase-0.94.22.tar.gz | |
| Elastic search | Elasticsearch-1.3.2 | elasticsearch-1.3.2.zip | |

## How to do it...

1. Check the version of JDK you are using by just typing java –version; it should show java version "1.7.0_X" or greater:

```
L-SB830T7FFT-M:hbase-0.94.22 r0choud$ java -version
java version "1.8.0_31"
Java(TM) SE Runtime Environment (build 1.8.0_31-b13)
Java HotSpot(TM) 64-Bit Server VM (build 25.31-b07, mixed mode)
L-SB830T7FFT-M:hbase-0.94.22 r0choud$ []
```

2. The second step is to download Hbase. If you are using the existing version as described in the previous chapter, then you have to use the compatible version of all the distributed components, such as Phoenix, drivers and elastic search:

```
mkdir hbaseElasticSearch
```

```
cd hbaseElasticSearch
```

```
wget http://archive.apache.org/dist/hbase/hbase-0.94.22/
hbase-0.94.22.tar.gz
```

```
make sure you have read write rights for the user your are using.
```

```
tar xvzf hbase-0.94.22.tar.gz
```

```
now
```

```
cd hbase-0.94.22
```

```
now you are in the folders as below.
```

```
L-SB830T7FFT-M:hbase-0.94.22 r0choud$ pwd
/Users/r0choud/opt/opt/HbaseB/hbaseElasticSearch/hbase-0.94.22
L-SB830T7FFT-M:hbase-0.94.22 r0choud$ █
```

It's time to set the path so that HBASE_HOME is pointed to this directory:

```
export HBASE_HOME=' /Users/r0choud/opt/opt/HbaseB/
hbaseElasticSearch/hbase-0.94.22'
```

```
Note: You can alternatively change the path in ~/.bashrc or
~/.profile to be consistent for all the shells.
```

3.  Now let's download Phoenix, now `cd ../../`, which will take you out from the Hbase directory to your directory where you want to download the other tars:

    ```
    wget http://www.motorlogy.com/apache/phoenix/phoenix-3.1.0/bin/
    phoenix-3.1.0-bin.tar.gz
    ```

    ```
    this will download the tar to the /User/opt/hbaseElasticSearch
    ```

    ```
    tar xvzf phoenix-3.1.0-bin.tar.gz
    ```

    ```
    this will untar to a directory phoenix-3.1.0-bin
    ```

    ```
    cd phoenix-3.1.0-bin
    ```

    ```
    now set the path by
    ```

    ```
    export PHOENIX_HOME='/Users/r0choud/opt/opt/HbaseB/
    hbaseElasticSearch/phoenix-3.1.0-bin'
    ```

This will set the path as follows, you can test is using.

```
L-SB830T7FFT-M:hbase-0.94.22 r0choud$ echo $PHOENIX_HOME
/Users/r0choud/opt/opt/HbaseB/hbaseElasticSearch/phoenix-3.1.0-bin
```

Now use `cd../`, which will take you back to the hbaseElasticSearch directory.

At this point, we have phoenix and hbase untar directories with the respective libraries. Now we need to make sure both are integrated and work as single unit.

We have to copy the phoenix-core-3.1.0.jar file to `$HBASE_HOME/lib`.

```
cp $PHOENIX_HOME/common/phoenix-core-3.1.0.jar $HBASE_HOME/lib/
```

Now, you are all set to start hbase, which will connect with Phoenix and provide you with an interface, which can be used for SQLs:

1.  Now, we can start Hbase in standalone mode.

    ```
    $HBASE_HOME/bin/start-hbase.sh
    ```

    Check the logs for exceptions.

2. Now, point the browser to `localhost:60010/master-status`. You will see the following screen:

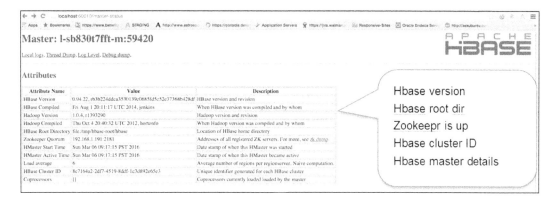

3. Let's move to PHOENIX_HOME:

   `cd $PHOENIX_HOME and run the following command`

   `$PHOENIX_HOME/hadoop1/bin/sqlline.py 192.168.1.191(your IP or hostname)`

This will allow you to connect it to the Phoenix and intern Hbase.

```
L-SB830T7FFT-M:logs r0choud$ $PHOENIX_HOME/hadoop1/bin/sqlline.py 192.168.1.191
Setting property: [isolation, TRANSACTION_READ_COMMITTED]
issuing: !connect jdbc:phoenix:192.168.1.191 none none org.apache.phoenix.jdbc.PhoenixDriver
Connecting to jdbc:phoenix:192.168.1.191
Connected to: Phoenix (version 3.1)
Driver: org.apache.phoenix.jdbc.PhoenixDriver (version 3.1)
Autocommit status: true
Transaction isolation: TRANSACTION_READ_COMMITTED
Building list of tables and columns for tab-completion (set fastconnect to true to skip)...
59/59 (100%) Done
Done
sqlline version 1.1.2
```

You will see a prompt similar to the following with your hostname or IP:

`jdbc:phoenix:192.168.1.191>`

Let's create a table:

```
CREATE TABLE URL_HITS (url_pk bigint not null,u.url_name varchar(250),u.
click_name varchar(250) CONSTRAINT pk PRIMARY KEY (url_pk));
```

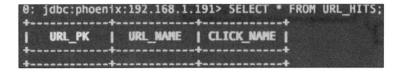

Now, let's create a `data.csv` file, which will load this table.

The data file will contain the following:

```
1000001,https://www.google.com,922
1000002,https://www.gmail.com,321
1000003,https://www.facebook.com,120
1000004,https://www.amazon.com,10
1000005,https://www.cnn.com,110
1000006,https://www.bbc.com,10
1000007,https://www.twitter.com,200
1000008,https://www.yahoo.com,221
1000009,https://www.target.com,2
10000010,https://www.apache.com,47
10000011,https://www.target.com,2
10000012,https://www.msnbc.com,14
10000013,https://www.foxnews.com,15
10000015,https://www.mail.yahoo.com,16
```

Now, lets run the following command.

```
L-SB830T7FFT-M:hadoop1 r0choud$ bin/psql.py -t URL_HITS localhost /Users/
r0choud/opt/opt/HbaseB/lily-2.4/samples/books/data.csv
```

This will result in loading all 14 rows.

```
L-SB830T7FFT-M:hadoop1 r0choud$ bin/psql.py -t URL_HITS localhost /Users/r0choud/opt/opt/HbaseB/lily-2.4/samples/books/data.csv
csv columns from database.
CSV Upsert complete. 14 rows upserted
Time: 0.023 sec(s)
```

Now run the `SELECT * from URL_HITS` command.

```
0: jdbc:phoenix:192.168.1.191> SELECT * FROM URL_HITS;
+-----------+----------------------------+-------------+
|  URL_PK   |   URL_NAME    | CLICK_NAME  |
+-----------+----------------------------+-------------+
|  1000001  | https://www.google.com | 922        |
|  1000002  | https://www.gmail.com | 321         |
|  1000003  | https://www.facebook.com | 120       |
|  1000004  | https://www.amazon.com | 10         |
|  1000005  | https://www.cnn.com | 110          |
|  1000006  | https://www.bbc.com | 10           |
|  1000007  | https://www.twitter.com | 200        |
|  1000008  | https://www.yahoo.com | 221         |
|  1000009  | https://www.target.com | 2          |
|  10000010 | https://www.apache.com | 47         |
|  10000011 | https://www.target.com | 2          |
|  10000012 | https://www.msnbc.com | 14          |
|  10000013 | https://www.foxnews.com | 15         |
|  10000015 | https://www.mail.yahoo.com | 16      |
+-----------+----------------------------+-------------+
14 rows selected (0.072 seconds)
```

To make sure that the table is there in Hbase, you can see the table in the Hbase master, as follows:

This completes the integration between Hbase and Apache Phoenix.

We can download Elastic search by running the `wget` command:

```
wget http://download.elasticsearch.org/elasticsearch/elasticsearch/
elasticsearch-1.3.2.zip

unzip elsaticsearch-1.3.2.zip

then cd elsaticsearch-1.3.2

export ESL_HOME= '/Users/r0choud/opt/opt/HbaseB/hbaseElasticSearch/
elasticsearch-1.3.2'
```

We have to get the JDBC connector to make sure elastic search connects to PHOENIX at one end and to elastic search at the other end.

```
$ELS_HOME/bin/plugin --install jdbc --url http://xbib.org/repository/org/
xbib/elasticsearch/importer/elasticsearch-jdbc/2.2.0.0/elasticsearch-
jdbc-2.2.0.0-dist.zip
```

Now run the following command:

```
nohup $ELS_HOME/bin/elasticsearch &
```

This will start the elastic search process on the `9200` port.

You can run a `curl` command to see the output from the search engine.

```
L-SB830T7FFT-M:elasticsearch-1.3.2 r0choud$ curl -X GET http://localhost:9200/
{
  "status" : 200,
  "name" : "Rawhide Kid",
  "version" : {
    "number" : "1.3.2",
    "build_hash" : "dee175dbe2f254f3f26992f5d7591939aaefd12f",
    "build_timestamp" : "2014-08-13T14:29:30Z",
    "build_snapshot" : false,
    "lucene_version" : "4.9"
  },
  "tagline" : "You Know, for Search"
```

Now you can curl with `-XPUT` to put the data into elastic search:

```
curl -XPUT 'localhost:9200/_river/phoenix_jdbc_river/_meta' -d {"type":"j
dbc","jdbc":{"url":"jdbc:phoenix:192.168.1.191","":"","":"","sql":"select
* from URL_HITS"}}'
```

This command pushes the select statement to the index and executes it when invoked as a search parameter using the following query:

```
curl 'localhost:9200/jdbc/_search?pretty&'
```

You will get the following response:

```
L-SB830T7FFT-M:hbaseElasticSearch r0choud$ curl localhost:9200/jdbc/_search?pretty
{
  "took" : 2,
  "timed_out" : false,
  "_shards" : {
    "total" : 5,
    "successful" : 5,
    "failed" : 0
  },
  "hits" : {
    "total" : 12,
    "max_score" : 1.0,
    "hits" : [ {
      "_index" : "jdbc",
      "_type" : "jdbc",
      "_id" : "YSYHrxpBRfyFhqnswRM_pw",
      "_score" : 1.0,
      "_source":{ "URL_PK" : "10002","URL_NAME":"https://www.cnn.com","CLICK_NAME":"110"}
    }, {
      "_index" : "jdbc",
      "_type" : "jdbc",
      "_id" : "qjeaji-BQS-x3yeDCvQvVA",
      "_score" : 1.0,
      "_source":{ "URL_PK" : "10002","URL_NAME":"https://www.yahoo.com","CLICK_NAME":"221"}
    }, {
      "_index" : "jdbc",
      "_type" : "jdbc",
      "_id" : "kBJLCcQ6Rr6Kx8Ty4cEf-w",
      "_score" : 1.0,
      "_source":{ "URL_PK" : "10002","URL_NAME":"https://www.foxnews.com","CLICK_NAME":"15"}
    }, {
      "_index" : "jdbc",
      "_type" : "jdbc",
      "_id" : "qMXe3yaQQ4yLEdOyxnxu_w",
      "_score" : 1.0,
      "_source":{ "URL_PK" : "10002","URL_NAME":"https://www.amazon.com","CLICK_NAME":"10"}
    }, {
      "_index" : "jdbc",
      "_type" : "jdbc",
      "_id" : "ql3SLGvYRdGpPNl0t2so8Q",
      "_score" : 1.0,
      "_source":{ "URL_PK" : "10002","URL_NAME":"https://www.target.com","CLICK_NAME":"2"}
    }, {
      "_index" : "jdbc",
      "_type" : "jdbc",
      "_id" : "WCxnUOjbQx-YBTMayT3FYA",
      "_score" : 1.0,
      "_source":{ "URL_PK" : "10002","URL_NAME":"https://www.mail.yahoo..com","CLICK_NAME":"16"}
    }, {
      "_index" : "jdbc",
      "_type" : "jdbc",
      "_id" : "S1RW_aBoS06pLNdrvm-vFg",
      "_score" : 1.0,
      "_source":{ "URL_PK" : "10002","URL_NAME":"https://www.bbc.com","CLICK_NAME":"10"}
    }, {
      "_index" : "jdbc",
      "_type" : "jdbc",
      "_id" : "BmDJ6urRQK6OmEuMgDs6ww",
      "_score" : 1.0,
      "_source":{ "URL_PK" : "10001","URL_NAME":"https://www.google.com","CLICK_NAME":"922"}
    }, {
      "_index" : "jdbc",
      "_type" : "jdbc",
      "_id" : "C3CQAjw8SMaKz8_G336Txg",
      "_score" : 1.0,
      "_source":{ "URL_PK" : "10002","URL_NAME":"https://www.gmail.com","CLICK_NAME":"321"}
    }, {
      "_index" : "jdbc",
      "_type" : "jdbc",
      "_id" : "sClNpRw3RoebWgfAnpMAIg",
      "_score" : 1.0,
      "_source":{ "URL_PK" : "10002","URL_NAME":"https://www.facebook.com","CLICK_NAME":"120"}
    } ]
  }
}
```

## There's more...

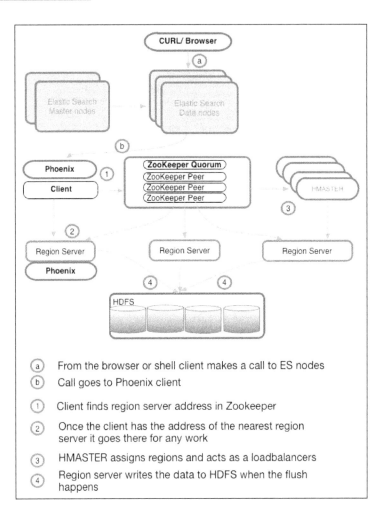

<table>
<tr><td>(a)</td><td>From the browser or shell client makes a call to ES nodes</td></tr>
<tr><td>(b)</td><td>Call goes to Phoenix client</td></tr>
<tr><td>(1)</td><td>Client finds region server address in Zookeeper</td></tr>
<tr><td>(2)</td><td>Once the client has the address of the nearest region server it goes there for any work</td></tr>
<tr><td>(3)</td><td>HMASTER assigns regions and acts as a loadbalancers</td></tr>
<tr><td>(4)</td><td>Region server writes the data to HDFS when the flush happens</td></tr>
</table>

- https://phoenix.apache.org/bulk_dataload.html

- https://www.elastic.co/guide/en/elasticsearch/plugins/2.2/intro.html

- https://phoenix.apache.org/language/#delete

- https://www.elastic.co/guide/en/logstash/current/plugins-inputs-jdbc.html

- https://www.elastic.co/guide/en/elasticsearch/plugins/2.2/index.html

# Index

## A

**ACID (Atomicity, Consistency, Isolation, Durability)  128-130**
**Amazon EMR**
about  297
core nodes  297
master node  297
nodes  297
task node  297
URL  300
**Apache Avro**
about  184
references  195
using  184-195
**Apache HBase**
Hive, using  75-77
**Apache Thrift**
about  180
URL  181
using  181-184
**Apache Yarn  18**
**Auto Scaling**
Auto Splitting  86
Force Splitting  87
Pre-Splitting  86
Region  84
with AWS  97-103
with built-in fault tolerance  84-97

## B

**Big Data Extensions**
prerequisites  105
scalability, benefits  104
scaling  104-109
**bloom filters  129**

**BucketCache  124**
**bulk load process**
reference link  67
**BulkLoad Tool  58**
**Bulk utilities**
considerations  71
data, loading  70-74

## C

**Cloud**
HBase, configuring  278-282
prerequisites, for HBase configuration  279
**CloudWatch**
HBase, monitoring  292-295
**clusters**
administering  36-48
managing  48-56
with Log dump  46
with Metrics dump  47
**column mapping**
reference link  77
**column metadata  150**
**column qualifier  144**
**columns family  144**
**combiner  207**
**command line**
used, for connecting HBase cluster  283, 284
**component configuration**
compaction  234
major compaction  116, 234
minor compaction  116, 234
modifying, for performance optimization  234-236
region splitter  234
**compression  130**

**Concurrent Mark Sweep (CMS)**
 versus Garbage First (G1) 231
**ConcurrentSkipListMap 116**
**coprocessors**
 about 94
 System Coprocessors 94
 Table Coprocessors 94
**CounterProtos 201**
**cyclic replication**
 about 138
 deploying 136

# D

**data**
 extracting, from Oracle 58-67
 loading, with Bulk utilities 70-74
 loading, with Oracle Big data connector 67-70
**data block encoding types**
 Fast Diff 135
 Prefix Tree 135
**data compression 81**
**Data Definition Languages (DDL) 95**
**data delete 113, 114**
**data model**
 about 145-148
 alternative query path 158
 column families, in table 158
 column families, storing 156
 column metadata 150
 column qualifier 144, 145
 columns family 144
 columns, versus column family 158
 considerations 149-153
 constrains 158
 data, in column family 158
 deleted cells, backup 157
 delete operations 148, 149
 hashing 160
 joins 150
 logical view 142
 namespace 143, 144
 random key 160
 row key, design 154
 salting 159
 secondary indexes 158

 supported data types 155
 tables 143
 timestamps 149, 150
 Time to Live (TTL) 156
 versioning 150
 versions 156
**data science 239**
**date read 113**
**delete operations**
 reference link 149
**denormalization 315**
**Dynamic Resource Scheduler (DRS) 108**

# E

**Elasticsearch**
 integrating, with HBase 316-323
 prerequisites 316
**Extract transform Load (ETL) system 66**

# F

**file system**
 cluster, starting 28, 29
 cluster, validating 29-33
 HBase, setting up 26-28
 using 21-25, 34-36
**flat-wide table layout**
 versus tall-narrow table layout 160
**FT (Fault tolerant) 106**
**full text indexing**
 with HBase 271-274

# G

**Ganglia**
 gmetad 48
 gmond 48
 gweb 49
 HBase, monitoring 295-300
 reference link 56
 setting up 49
 URL 49, 295
 using 56
**Garbage First (G1)**
 versus Concurrent Mark sweep (CMS) 231

# H

**Hadoop Distributed File System (HDFS)**
about  1, 21, **298**
benefits  21
used, for performance optimization  237
**HA (High Availability)  106**
**HBase**
backing up  284-286
configuring  2-21
configuring, for Cloud  278-282
data accessing, with Hive  286-288
deploying  2-21
Elasticsearch, integrating with  316-323
machine learning  239-259
MapReduce, implementing  211-214
MapReduce jobs, creating in  207-210
monitoring, with CloudWatch  292-295
monitoring, with Ganglia  295-300
restoring  284-286
used, for full text indexing  271-274
**HBase-61**
URL  116
**HBase cluster**
connecting, command line used  283, 284
terminating  286
**HBase REST**
with Java client  165-175
**Hive**
about  214
HBase data, accessing  286-288
URL  75
using, with Apache HBase  75-77

# I

**ImportTsv tool  58**
**infrastructure/operating systems**
balanced workload  223
compute intensive  223
expansion, planning  225
I/O intensive  223
memory, sizing  224
network, using  224
operating system, selecting  226
processors, selecting  224

selecting, for performance
optimization  222-230
server, selecting  224

# J

**Java client**
HBase REST, using  165-175
**Java virtual machine (JVM)**
for performance optimization  230-233
references  233
**JBOD  4**
**joins  150**

# K

**K-means  261**

# L

**large scale data, processing**
Block cache  20
Bucket cache  21
HFile  19
HFile V2  20
HMaster  19
HTable  19
LruBlockCache  20
MemStore  20
Multilevel caching  21
SlabCache  20
**Lily**
configuring  302-316
denormalization  315
features  302
fields  311
indexer  315
record  311
Side Effect Processors (SEP)  315
**logical view  142**
**log-structured merge-tree**
about  112, 113
references  114
**LZ4 compressor**
about  134
URL  134
using  134

**LZO compression**
about  132
URL  132, 133
using  132, 133

# M

**machine learning**
with HBase  239-259
**Mahout**
and HBase, used for real-time
data analysis  260-271
**major compaction  116**
**MapFile  115**
**mapper  206**
**MapReduce**
implementing, with HBase  211-213
references  215, 220
usage, considerations  215
using, on multiple tables  215-220
**MapReduce, components**
combiner  207
mapper  206
output format  207
partitioner  207
record reader  206
shuffle  207
sort  207
**MapReduce jobs**
creating, in HBase  207-210
**MapReduce jobs, classes**
CellCounter  207
CellCreator  207
CopyTable  208
Export  208
GroupingTableMapper  208
HFileOutputFormat2  208
HRegionPartitioner<KEY,VALUE>  208
IdentityTableMapper  208
IdentityTableReducer  208
Import  208
ImportTsv  208
KeyValueSortReducer  208
LoadIncrementalHFiles  208
Mapper class  209
MultiTableInputFormat  208
MultiTableInputFormatBase  208

MultiTableOutputFormat  208
PutCombiner<K>  208
PutSortReducer  208
RowCounter  208
SimpleTotalOrderPartitioner<VALUE>  208
TableInputFormat  208
TableInputFormatBase  208
TableMapper<KEYOUT,VALUEOUT>  208
TableMapReduceUtil  208
TableOutputCommitter  208
TableOutputFormat<KEY>  208
TableRecordReader  209
TableRecordReaderImpl  209
TableReducer<KEYIN,VALUEIN,KEYOUT>  209
TableSnapshotInputFormat  209
TableSplit  209
TextSortReducer  209
TsvImporterMapper  209
TsvImporterTextMapper  209
WALInputFormat  209
WALPlayer  209
**master-master replication**
about  137
deploying  136
**master-slave replication  137**
**master-slave setup**
DataNode  18
HBase Master  18
JobTracker  18
Journal Node  18
MapReduce  18
NameNode  17
ResourceManager (RM)  18
**matric, HBase**
HbaseBackup failed  295
HBaseMostRecentBackupDuration  295
HBaseTimeSinceLastSuccessfulBackup  295
**memory management**
BlockCache  124
BucketCache  125
DoubleBlockCache  124
LruBlockCache  126
MemStore  124
multilevel caching  124
Off-heap  124
SlabCache  125
**memstore  150**

minor compaction  116
multiversion concurrency
        control (MVCC)  128-130, 150

# N

namespace  143
Network Time Protocol (NTP)  105

# O

observers
  about  94
  MasterObserver interface  95
  RegionObserver interface  94
  WalObserver interface  95
Oracle
  data, extracting  58-67
Oracle Big data connector
  data, loading  67-70
  URL  67
  usage  70
output format  207

# P

parallelism  81, 82
partitioner  207
performance optimization  221, 222
Pig
  about  214
  reference link  202
  using  201-204
Protocol buffer
  about  196
  advantages  196
  references  201
  using  196-201
Put API  57

# R

RAID  4
read path  115-117
real-time data analysis
  with HBase and Mahout  260-271
record reader  206

region server
  setting up  10
replication
  about  135
  benefits  135
  cyclic replication  138
  disabling, at peer level  139
  implementation  135-137
  master-master replication  137
  master-slave replication  137

# S

Safemode  22
scheduler  228
schema design
  about  153
  considerations  153-164
  references  164
seek
  versus transfer  112
Shell
  using  201-204
shell commands
  alter  203
  Count  203
  Create  203
  Describe  203
  disable  203
  Disable_all  203
  Drop  203
  Drop_all  203
  Enable_peer  204
  flush  203
  Get  203
  Hlog_roll  204
  ls_disable  203
  List  203
  List_peers  204
  major_compaction  203
  move  203
  Scan  203
  Show_filters  203
  split  203
  status  203
  Truncate  203

version 203
whoami 203
zk_dump 204
**shuffle 207**
**Side Effect Processors (SEP) 315**
**snappy**
about 131
URL 131
using 131
**snapshot process**
about 30
snapshot, configuring 31
snapshot, deleting 31
snapshot, listing 32
**snapshots, parameters**
Hbsae Snapshots 33
Offline Snapshots 33
Online Snapshots 33
Snapshots 33
WebInterface 33
**Solr 316**
**sort 207**
**Sqoop**
about 77
references 82
using 77-81
**storage 114**

# T

**tables 143**

**tall-narrow table layout**
versus flat-wide table layout 160
**timestamps 149**
**tombstoning marker 115**
**transfer**
versus seek 112

# U

**user interface (UI)**
viewing 289-292

# V

**versioning 150**

# W

**wget command 322**
**write-ahead log (WAL) 58, 122**
**write path 118-127**

# X

**XFS filesystem 228**

# Z

**ZFS filesystem 228**
**ZooKeeper**
about 316
setting up 10

www.ingramcontent.com/pod-product-compliance
Lightning Source LLC
LaVergne TN
LVHW081332050326
832903LV00024B/1128